Praxis Elementary Education Content Knowledge for Teaching 7811

How to *Think Like a Test Maker*™ and pass the Praxis 7811 CKT using effective test prep, relevant practice questions, and proven strategies.

KATHLEEN JASPER

Kathleen Jasper LLC
Estero, FL 33928
http://www.kathleenjasper.com | info@KathleenJasper.com

Praxis Elementary Education Content Knowledge for Teaching 7811: *How to Think Like a Test Maker*™ and pass the Praxis 7811 CKT using effective test prep, relevant practice questions, and proven strategies.

Printed in the United States of America
ISBN: 9798397240963

I'm Kathleen Jasper, and for the last 8 years, I've been helping prospective teachers and school leaders pass their certification exams and get the positions they want in education. To date, I've helped over 80,000 educators on their certification journeys.

I've had many positions in public education. I started off as a substitute teacher and went through the certification process you are going through right now. I was hired as a high school reading and biology teacher, and a couple of years later had the opportunity to work in curriculum at the district office. Finally, I became a high school assistant principal.

I left public education to start my own company, Kathleen Jasper LLC, and now I write study guides, conduct online courses, create content, and more to help you pass your exams and land your desired position.

I am thrilled you're here. Thank you for taking the time to review my content and purchase my products. It means the world to me to help educators all over the country.

Would you mind leaving a review?

Did you purchase this book on Amazon? If so, I would be thrilled if you would leave an unbiased review at your convenience. Did you purchase this book from kathleenjasper.com? If so, you can leave a review on Facebook, Google, or directly on our website on the product page. Thank you so much.

Check out my other products.

I have built several comprehensive, self-paced online courses for many teacher certification exams. I also have other books, webinars, and more. Go to https://kathleenjasper.com/ and use offer code **EE7811** for 10% off any of my products.

If you have any questions, don't hesitate to reach out to info@kathleenjasper.com. It will be my pleasure to help. Good luck with your exam.

~Kathleen Jasper, Ed.D.

Follow me on social media.

 @kathleenjasperEdD @kathleen_jasper

 KathleenJasperEdD @kj_kathleenjasper @kathleenjasper

This page intentionally left blank.

Table of Contents

About the Test. 7

7812 – Reading and Language Arts. 9

About the Reading and Language Arts CKT – 7812 11

I. Foundational Skills 13

Practice Questions 33

II. Language. 37

Practice Questions 51

III. Constructing Meaning 59

Practice Questions 77

Language Arts and Reading 7812 - Practice Test. 81

Answer Explanations 99

7813 – Mathematics. 107

About the Mathematics CKT – 7813 109

I. Counting and Operations with Whole Numbers. 111

Practice Questions 125

II. Place Value and Decimals. 129

Practice Questions 133

III. Fractions, Operations with Fractions, and Ratios. 137

Practice Questions 147

IV. Early Equations and Expressions, Measurement, and Geometry. 153

Practice Questions 179

Mathematics 7813 - Practice Test. 183

Answer Explanations 193

7814 – Science 203

About the Science CKT – 7814.. 205

I. Earth and Space Sciences 207

Practice Questions.. 219

II. Life Sciences.. 225

Practice Questions.. 235

III. Physical Sciences 239

Practice Questions.. 247

IV. Engineering, Technology, and the Application of Science 251

Practice Problems... 255

Science 7814 - Practice Test 259

Answer Explanations 269

7815 – Social Studies 275

About the Social Studies CKT - 7815....................................... 277

I. History.. 279

Practice Questions.. 293

II. Government and Citizenship 297

Practice Questions.. 303

III. Human and Physical Geography... 307

Practice Questions.. 317

IV. Economics 321

Practice Questions.. 327

V. Educational Practices for Teaching Social Studies 331

Practice Questions.. 337

Social Studies 7815 - Practice Test...................................... 341

Answer Explanations 355

Data Driven Decisions Using Assessments 363

Practice Questions.. 371

Good Words List 375

Bibliography 379

About the Test

The Praxis Elementary Content Knowledge for Teaching 7811 exam is designed to assess standards-based knowledge, skills, and competencies of elementary education teachers. The tests consist of four subtests: language arts and reading, mathematics, science, and social studies.

This exam will not only assess your content knowledge for these subjects, but it will also assess your ability to apply this to methods of teaching. Many of the questions are scenario-based, meaning you will have to evaluation a classroom situation within the content area and then choose the best approach.

Test at a Glance	
Test Name	Elementary Education Assessment
Test Code	7811
Time	4 hours, 45 minutes
Format	The test consists of a variety of selected-response and numeric-entry questions, where you select one or more answer choices and other types of questions. An on-screen, four-function calculator is provided. The reading and Language arts section may include questions with an audio component.
Test Delivery	Computer delivered

Subtests	Subject Test Length (minutes)	Approximate # of Questions
7812 – Reading and Language Arts	90	63
7813 – Mathematics	85	52
7814 – Science	60	47
7815 – Social Studies	50	60

This page intentionally left blank.

7812 Reading and Language Arts

Praxis 7812 | 9

This page intentionally left blank.

About the Reading and Language Arts CKT – 7812

The Praxis 7812 Reading and Language Arts Content Knowledge for Teaching (CKT) test is designed to assess the knowledge and skills of aspiring educators in the field of language arts and reading instruction. This test evaluates candidates' understanding of various aspects of language, including phonology, morphology, syntax, semantics, and pragmatics, as well as their ability to apply this knowledge in reading instruction.

Test takers are expected to demonstrate proficiency in analyzing and interpreting different types of texts, including fiction, non-fiction, poetry, and drama. The exam also covers topics such as reading comprehension strategies, vocabulary development, literacy instruction for diverse learners, and assessment techniques.

Successful performance on the Praxis 7812 test indicates a strong foundation in language arts and reading instruction, essential for effective teaching in this domain.

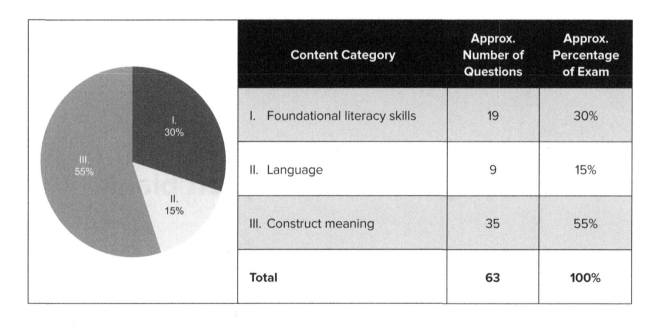

Content Category	Approx. Number of Questions	Approx. Percentage of Exam
I. Foundational literacy skills	19	30%
II. Language	9	15%
III. Construct meaning	35	55%
Total	63	100%

This page intentionally left blank.

I. Foundational Skills

The following topics are aligned with the test specifications of the Praxis 7812. It is important that you examine these closely because these are the skills assessed on the exam.

A. Print concepts

B. Alphabetic Principle

C. Phonological Awareness

D. Phonics and Word Recognition

E. Fluency

A. Print Concepts

The very beginning stages of word recognition include print awareness. When students have print awareness, they understand that written words communicate a message. They also understand that words are separated by spaces, text is written in a particular direction, and sentences have distinguishing features, such as capitalization and punctuation.

Understanding the difference between print and pictures

Print awareness refers to a child's understanding of the nature and uses of print. Children develop print awareness when they can recognize words as distinct elements of oral and written communication. Both skills are acquired in the child's natural environment.

Environmental print is the print of everyday life. It is the name given to the print that appears on signs, labels, and logos. Street signs, candy wrappers, labels on peanut butter and cereal boxes are other examples of environmental print.

Print concepts involve understanding the difference between letters, words, punctuation, and directionality. Print concepts foster reading comprehension and vocabulary growth. Print concepts include:

- **Directionality** – reading from left to right and top to bottom
- **Layout** – front and back of books
- **Differentiation** – words vs. pictures and letters vs. words

Teachers must nurture students' desire to interact with books. In the early stages, students will pretend to read or pretend to write, which are very important aspects of print awareness. Students will also point to words as they read, indicating they are tracking print, an essential skill in beginning reading.

Strategies to promote print awareness and tracking print:

- Hang labels on key objects in the classroom—door, sink, library, blocks.
- Use posters that include captions and pictures.
- Display an oversized book to show directionality and print.
- Point out the title, headings, beginning, middle, and end of a book or passage before reading.

5 early signs of print awareness:

1. The child holds a book correctly. If you hand a book that is upside down to the child, the child will turn it right side up.

2. The child understands that books are read from left to right, top to bottom, and front to back.

3. The child pretends to write by scribbling. This means the child understands that pictures and writing are distinct from one another.

4. The child points to a story and asks you to read it, understanding that the words on the page have meaning.

5. The child picks up a familiar book and reads it aloud. The child is using a memory of the story and is not actually reading the book.

Understand the connection between spoken and written language.

Oral language consists of six major areas: phonology, vocabulary, morphology, grammar, pragmatics, and discourse.

1. **Phonology** encompasses the organization of sounds in language.

2. **Vocabulary** (semantics) encompasses both expressive (speaking) and receptive (listening) vocabulary.

3. **Morphology** is the study of the smallest units of meaning in words. An example of morphology is breaking up compound words and analyzing their meanings.

4. **Grammar** (syntax) is the structure of language and words.

5. **Pragmatics** focuses on the social cues or norms in language. This is often referred to as situations in language.

6. **Discourse** focuses on speaking and listening skills in language. Discourse means dialogue.

Readers at the beginning (emergent) stage are learning to read and understand words by decoding the reading process as they engage with the text. Emergent literacy involves the skills, knowledge, and attitudes that are developmental precursors to conventional forms of reading and writing. Emergent literacy skills begin developing in early infancy and early childhood through participation with adults in meaningful activities involving speaking and reading.

B. Alphabetic Principle

The alphabetic principle is the idea that letters and letter patterns represent the sounds of spoken language. Learning that there are predictable relationships between sounds and letters allows children to apply these relationships to both familiar and unfamiliar words and to begin to read with fluency.

To promote the alphabetic principle, teachers should:

- Teach letter-sound relationships explicitly and in isolation.

- Provide opportunities for children to practice letter-sound relationships in daily lessons.

- Provide practice opportunities that include new sound-letter relationships, as well as cumulatively reviewing previously taught relationships.

- Use writing or print to represent what students say during class, so students understand that speech can be represented in print.

▼ **Pre-Alphabetic Phase**
Students read words by memorizing visual features or guessing words from context.

▼ **Partial-Alphabetic Phase**
Students recognize some letters and can use them to remember words by sight.

▼ **Full-Alphabetic Phase**
Readers possess extensive working knowledge of the graphophonemic system, and they can use this knowledge to analyze the connections between graphemes and phonemes in words. They can decode unfamiliar words and store sight words in memory.

▼ **Consolidated-Alphabetic Phase**
Students consolidate their knowledge of grapheme-phoneme blends into larger units that recur in different words.

The following example question is how this might look on the exam.

Example Problem

A teacher is using picture cards to help students recognize words. Students see the picture below and say, "Sun!" What phase of word recognition are the students in?

A. Pre-alphabetic

B. Partial-alphabetic

C. Full-alphabetic

D. Consolidated-alphabetic

Correct Answer: A

The students are only seeing a picture. Therefore, they are in the pre-alphabetic stage. Partial, full, and consolidated phases all require the use of letter recognition. In this case, there is only a picture.

C. Phonological Awareness

Phonological awareness is an overarching skill that includes identifying and manipulating units of oral language, including parts of words, syllables, onsets, and rimes.

Children who have phonological awareness can:

- Identify and make oral rhymes.
- Clap the number of syllables in a word.
- Recognize words with the same initial sounds as in *monkey* and *mother*.
- Recognize the sound of spoken language.
- Blend sounds together (*bl, tr, sk*).
- Divide and manipulate words.

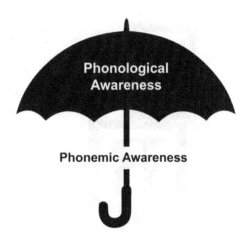

Phonemic awareness is understanding the individual sounds (or phonemes) in words. For example, students who have phonemic awareness can separate the sounds in the word *cat* into three distinct phonemes: /k/, /æ/, and /t/.

Phonics is understanding the relationship between sounds and the spelling patterns (graphemes) representing those sounds. For example, when a student sees the letter *c* is followed by an *e, i,* or *y*, the student knows the *c* makes an /s/ sound, as in the words *cycle*, *circle*, and *receive*.

Quick Tip

Think of phonological awareness as the umbrella encompassing many skills students need for literacy: syllabication, onsets, rimes, spelling, etc. Phonemic awareness is a more nuanced skill that requires students to identify individual sounds in words.

The role of phonological and phonemic awareness in reading development

Phonological and phonemic awareness is critical in reading development because these skills help students develop the foundational skills needed for word recognition, spelling, syllabication, fluency, and reading compression.

Reading and spelling require a level of metalinguistic speech that is not natural or easily acquired. Therefore, teachers must focus on phonemic and phonological awareness explicitly. Phonological awareness is critical for learning to read any alphabetic writing system.

Example Question

Why is it important for teachers to focus on students' phonological awareness during emergent reading development?

    A. Memorizing sight words is necessary to read quickly and efficiently.

    B. Spelling correctly leads to success in other subjects like social studies and science.

    C. Understanding how the smallest units in words function is necessary for spelling and reading development.

    D. Being able to read fluently allows students to achieve on standardized reading exams.

Correct Answer: C

Phonological awareness is essential in developing spelling and word recognition. The foundational skills in phonological awareness are necessary for students to acquire the phonics skills (spelling) necessary for reading.

The difference between phonemic awareness and phonics skills

The terms phonemic awareness and phonics can be confusing to new teachers. Both skills fall under phonological awareness, and both skills are emergent reading skills. However, there are significant differences between the two skills.

Phonemic Awareness includes the skills that encompass using sounds in words. When you think phonemic awareness, think of sounds only. For example, if students are recognizing individual sounds in words or blending sounds in words without having to see the word, it is phonemic awareness.

Phonics is understanding letter-sound correspondence or phoneme-grapheme correspondence. Students must see the letters or words to engage in phonics. For example, in the word *receive*, students know the *c* makes an /s/ sound because the *c* is followed by an *e*, *i*, or *y*. That is a basic example of letter-sound correspondence.

Phonemic Awareness	Phonics
Focus on phonemes or the smallest units of sounds	Focus on graphemes or letters and their corresponding sounds
Spoken language	Written language/print
Mostly auditory	Both visual and auditory
Manipulating sounds in words	Reading and writing letters according to sounds, spelling, patterns, and phonological structure

Strategies for teaching phonological awareness

Students can break words down into smaller pieces by focusing on letter-sound relationships. For example, words can be broken down by:

- inflected forms (*-s, -es, -ed, -ing, -ly*)
- contractions
- possessives
- compound words
- syllables
- base words
- root words
- prefixes
- suffixes beginning with consonants
- end consonants
- medial consonants
- consonant blends (*bl, gr, sp*)
- consonant digraphs (*sh, th, ch*)
- short vowels
- long vowels
- vowel pairs (*oo, ew, oi, oy*)

Blending – putting all the sounds in the words together, as in /p/-/a/-/t/ - /pat/. Later we will discuss consonant blending and vowel blending.

Onsets – beginning consonant or consonant cluster.

Rimes – vowel and consonants that follow the onset consonant cluster. Some common rimes are: *-ack, -an, -aw, -ick, -ing, -op, -unk, -ain, -ank, -ay, -ide, -ink, -or, -ock, -ight, -ame, -eat, -ine*.

Rhyming – the repetition of sounds in different words. Students listen to the sounds within words and identify word parts. For example, the /at/ sound in the word *mat* is the same /at/ sound in the words *cat, rat, sat,* and *splat*.

Segmentation – breaking a word apart. This can be done by breaking compound words into two parts, segmenting by onset and rime, segmenting by syllables, or breaking the word into individual phonemes.

Examples of Segmenting		
Compound words	baseball	*base ball*
Onset and rime	dad	*/d/ -/ad/*
Syllables	behind	*/be-hind/*
Individual phonemes	cat	*/c/ /a/ /t/*

Isolation – to separate word parts or to isolate a single sound in the word. For example, if the teacher says, "Say just the first sound in bat," the students reply with /b/.

Deletion – omitting a sound in a word. For example, using the word *mice*, a teacher may ask students to delete the initial */m/* sound, resulting in the word *ice*. This skill is usually practiced orally.

Substitution – when students replace one sound with another in a word. For example, substitute the first sound in the word *cat* with an /s/ sound. Students will say *sat*.

Blending - the ability to string together the sounds that each letter stands for in a word. For example, when students see the word *black*, they blend the */bl/*, the */a/* sound, and the ending */k/* sound. Sometimes blending exercises focus just on the consonant blend, like the */br/* sound in the word *brick*.

Example Question

Which of the following strategies would be most helpful for students who are working on onset and rime skills?

    A. Count the number of sounds in the word *back*.

    B. Identify the beginning sound in the word *back*.

    C. Substitute the /b/ sound in back with a /t/ sound.

    D. Segment the word *back* into two sounds /b/ and /ack/.

Correct Answer: D

Answer D is an example of onset and rime. The /b/ is the onset and /ack/ is the rime. All the other answer choices focus on phonemic awareness.

While phonemic awareness, a subskill of phonological awareness, is a foundational skill, there are levels within phonemic awareness that students move through as they begin to acquire this skill. This is called the phonemic awareness continuum.

Phonemic Awareness Continuum

There are six main levels of phonemic awareness. You will see questions on the exam where you are asked to match a scenario to the correct level of phonemic awareness.

1. **Phoneme isolation** is when students hear and separate out individual sounds in words. For example, the student can isolate the /b/ sound in the word *bat*.

2. **Blending** is when students can combine sounds in a word. For example, the three sounds in cat—/c/ /a/ /t/—make up the word *cat*.

3. **Segmenting** is when students can divide the word into individual sounds. This also includes being able to count or identify how many sounds are in a word. For example, in the word *mat*, there are three sounds—/m/ /a/ /t/.

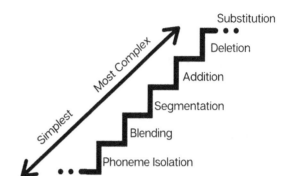

The following steps involve ***manipulation*** or changing the words. These skills are considered complex phonemic awareness skills.

4. **Addition** is when students can manipulate a word by adding a sound that is not originally in the word. For example, start with the word *pay* and add an /l/ sound after the /p/ sound, and the word becomes *play*.

5. **Deletion** is when students manipulate the word by deleting sounds to make a new word. For example, start with the word *play* and delete the /l/ sound and the word becomes *pay*. Remember, it is not the spelling we are concerned with in these activities. It is just the sounds.

Quick Tip

Students learn the beginning and ending sounds in consonants before they identify medial, or middle, sounds in words. For example, in the word *sun*, students will identify the /s/ and /n/ sound before they recognize the /u/ sound.

6. **Substitution** is the highest level of phonemic awareness because students not only have to identify the sounds and locate them in the word, but they also must switch them with other sounds. For example, start with the word *moth* and switch the /o/ sound with an /a/ sound and the word becomes *math*.

Example Question

Asking students to listen to the word *can* and add a /t/ sound is most appropriate for students who have a:

    A. Beginning level of phonemic awareness

    B. Beginning level of phonics skills

    C. Relatively high level of phonemic awareness

    D. Relatively high level of phonics

Correct Answer: C

Remember, manipulation of words is part of the complex stage of phonemic awareness. Therefore, the students must have a relatively high level of phonemic awareness to engage in this activity. Because the scenario is talking about sounds in words, the question is focused on phonemic awareness, not phonics. Therefore, we can eliminate answers B and D.

Test Tip

Remembering that **deletion** and **substitution** are at the top of the phonemic awareness continuum will help you identify correct answer choices on the test.

Phonological Awareness Continuum

Students also acquire phonological awareness on a continuum. Like the phonemic awareness continuum, the phonological awareness continuum's highest levels include manipulating words. Notice that the phonological awareness continuum uses the skills students acquired in the phonemic awareness continuum.

1. **Rhyme** is when students can match ending sounds of words as in *bat, hat, cat.*

2. **Alliteration** is when students can identify and produce words with the same initial sound as in *sat, see, silly.*

3. **Sentence segmentation** is when students can segment sentences into words as in *He | went | to | the | beach.*

4. **Syllable segmentation** is when students can blend and segment syllables of spoken words as in *hap-py, de-light, sum-mer.*

5. **Onset and rime blending and segmenting** is when students can blend or segment the (onset) initial consonant or consonant cluster and the (rime) vowel and consonant sounds following the rime as in *tr- -ack, b- -at, sl- -eep.*

6. **Phoneme manipulation** is when students can manipulate sounds in words. This is the most complex skill on the continuum and includes several skills:

   - Blend phonemes (*br, bl, pl, sn*)

   - Segment individual phonemes (/b/ /a/ /t/)

   - Add and delete individual phonemes (*bat* becomes *at*)

   - Substitute phonemes to create new words (*bat* becomes *sat, cat, or back*)

Phoneme Blending & Manipulation
CV, CVC, CVCC, CCVCC words.

Onset/Rime Blending & Segmentation
/r/ /ope/   /st/ /op/   /pl/ /ay/

Syllable Segmentation
care-ful, be-lieve

Sentence Segmentation
She |runs |fast.

Alliteration
(*six, squiggly, snakes*)

Rhyme
(*top, mop, pop*)

Most Complex

Simplest

Evidence-based strategies to promote phonological and phonemic awareness.

According to the National Institute of Child Health and Human Development, explicit instruction in phonemic and phonological awareness involves systematically teaching children to manipulate phonemes with letters, focusing the instruction on one or two types of phoneme manipulations rather than multiple types, and teaching children in small groups.

Explicit instruction in phonemic awareness and phonological awareness has strong results in spelling and reading development.

Quick Tip

The **explicit approach** to phonemic and phonological awareness is the one adopted by most states, districts, and schools because research supports that the explicit approach is most effective.

Implicit instruction in phonemic awareness is sometimes called the *whole language approach*. This is when students are not taught sounds in isolation. Instead, they hear the words and see the words in their entirety.

Phonological Skills

Phonological processing is when students use phonemes to process spoken and written language. Phonological processing includes *phonological awareness*, *phonological working memory*, and *phonological retrieval.*

It is very important that teachers develop the following skills in all students, including those students who struggle and those who are English learners (ELs). Teachers can do this by differentiating instruction and helping ELs develop phonemic awareness in their first language, so they can develop these skills in their second language.

Phonological Awareness

Phonological awareness is the awareness of the sound structure of a language and the ability to consciously analyze and manipulate this structure via a range of tasks, such as speech sound segmentation and blending at the word, onset-rime, syllable, and phonemic levels.

Phonological Working Memory

Phonological working memory involves storing phoneme information in temporary, short-term memory. This phonemic information is then readily available for manipulation during phonological awareness tasks. For example, when students use substitution, they are also using their phonological working memory because they are accessing stored phoneme information to substitute sounds in words.

Phonological Retrieval

Phonological retrieval is the ability to recall the phonemes associated with specific graphemes (letters), which can be assessed by rapid naming tasks (e.g., rapid naming of letters and numbers). This ability to recall the speech sounds in one's language is also integral to phonological awareness.

All components of phonological processing are important for speech production as well as the development of the spoken and written language skills necessary for reading.

Example Question

An English learner is struggling to identify certain sounds in words. What would be the best approach to help the student develop phonemic awareness?

A. Determine if the student has phonemic awareness in the first language.

B. Have the student work with an English learner who is fluent in English.

C. Require the student to use English only when speaking.

D. Use pictures to help the student identify different words.

Correct Answer: A

The question is asking about phonemic awareness, which is skills focused on sounds only. Nurturing students' first language so the students can master the skills in their second language is very important for English learners.

D. Phonics and Word Recognition

Phoneme-grapheme correspondence, also called letter-sound correspondence, is the essence of phonics and word recognition. Recall in the previous section, we focused mainly on phonemic awareness, which is associated with the sounds in words. With phonics, students must understand that a written symbol or letter represents a sound. For example, the letter c is a symbol in the English language that when followed by an *a, u,* or *o* usually makes a /k/ sound. However, when that same symbol—the letter c—is followed by *an e, i,* or *y*, it makes an /s/ sound. See the following examples.

- The letter **c** in the words *cat, cut, cot,* and *cable* makes a /k/ sound.
- The letter **c** in the words *cell, cycle, receive,* and *city* makes an /s/ sound.

This is one example of letter-sound or phoneme-grapheme correspondence.

Explicit phonics instruction is a method of teaching students how to connect the graphemes (letters) with phonemes (sounds) and how to use this letter-sound relationship to read and spell words.

Systematic phonics instruction is using a logical and specific scope and sequence that is developmentally appropriate to teach students the major letters and sounds. This includes short and long vowels, blends, and consonant digraphs (*oi, ea, sh, th, etc.*). This plan is carefully thought out, strategic, and designed before activities and lessons are developed.

Recursive phonics instruction involves lessons built on those previously taught, and students will have to draw and recall from previous lessons. Lessons move from simple to complex and include clear, concise student objectives. Students have to use their prior knowledge to learn complex skills.

As students begin to read words, they also begin to decode words based on letter-sound relationships or phonics. Students will use the general rules of phonics to decode or sound out words as they read. In the beginning stages of decoding, students use the basic rules of phonics.

Decoding, encoding, fluency, and reading comprehension are interrelated. A student must have these skills to be a proficient reader. Typically, students follow this order when acquiring these skills:

1st. **Decoding** – sounding out words while reading. The student uses phonics generalizations, letter sound correspondence, and phonological awareness.

2nd. **Encoding** – the process of hearing a word and spelling it based on sounds and phonics. Encoding is usually assessed with a spelling test.

3rd. **Fluency** –moving through the text accurately without having to stop to decode.

4th. **Comprehension** – reading fluently and understanding the text by forming pictures in the brain, predicting, and asking questions.

Students also use generalizations of phonics to decode words. Not all English words follow these generalizations. However, it is important that student understand grapheme types to generalize in phonics to read words.

Grapheme Types

The following table includes examples of how teachers and students can use letter sound correspondence, spelling conventions, and graphemes to teach literacy. This information was adapted from the Common Core State Standards for English Language Arts and Literacy - Appendix A.

Grapheme Type	Definition	Examples
Single letters	A single consonant letter can be represented by a phoneme.	b, d, f, g, h, j, k, l, m, n, p, r, s, t, v, w, y, z
Doublets	A doublet uses two of the same letters to spell a consonant phoneme.	ff, ll, ss, zz
Digraphs	Digraphs are two-letter (di-) combinations that create one phoneme.	th, sh, ch, wh, ph, ng (sing), gh (cough), ck
Trigraphs	Trigraphs are three-letter (tri-) combinations that create one phoneme.	-tch -dge
Diphthong	Diphthongs are sounds formed by the combination of two vowels in a single syllable, in which the sound begins as one vowel and moves toward another. They can appear in the initial, middle, or final position in a word.	aisle coin loud
Consonant blends	Consonant blends include two or three graphemes, and the consonant sounds are separate and identifiable.	s-c-r (scrape) c-l (clean) l-k (milk)
Silent letter combinations	Silent letter combinations use two letters: one represents the phoneme and the other is silent.	kn (knock) wr (wrestle) gn (gnarl)
Combination *qu*	These two letters always go together and make a /kw/ sound.	**qu**ickly
Single letters	A single vowel letter that stands for a vowel sound.	(short vowels) cat, hit, gem, pot, sub (long vowels) me, no, mute
Vowel teams	Vowel teams are combinations of two, three, or four letters that stand for a vowel sound.	(short vowels) head, hook (long vowels) boat, rain, weigh (diphthongs) soil, bout
Schwa sound	A schwa is a vowel sound in an unstressed syllable, where a vowel does not make its long or short vowel sound. It is often called the "lazy" sound in a word. The symbol for this is ə.	a: balloon e: problem i: family o: bottom u: support y: analysis
/zh/ sound	This sound often occurs after the letter G, but not always. For example, after the letter S, the consonant that most commonly forms the /ʒ/ sound is "soft G." This sound, however, cannot be represented by any one letter and instead can be formed by s, si, g, and ge.	vision – vi/zh/un garage – gara/zh/ measure – mea/zh/ur decision – deci/zh/un visual – vi/zh/ual

Example Problem

Which of the following pairs of words represents a consonant digraph where the consonant sound cannot be represented by one letter?

    A. *make* and *cry*

    B. *ceiling* and *save*

    C. *garage* and *character*

    D. *head* and *hook*

Correct Answer: C

In the word *garage*, the /zh/ sound at the end of the word cannot be represented by one consonant. In the word *character*, the /k/ sound at the beginning of the word cannot be represented by one consonant.

Consonant-Vowel Patterns

Other strategies for helping students decode words involve following common consonant-vowel patterns (CVC, CVCC, CVCe, CVVC patterns).

Pattern	Description	Example
CVC	consonant-vowel-consonant	bat, cat, tap
CVCe	consonant-vowel-consonant-silent e	make, take, bake
CCVC	consonant-consonant-vowel-consonant	trap, chop, grit
CVCC	consonant-vowel-consonant-consonant	tack, hunt, fast

Test Tip

Be sure you understand inflectional morphemes. Foundational skills include understanding inflectional endings (*-s, -es, -ed, -ing*). This is part of morphology.

- *-s* or *-es* makes the word plural
- *-ed* makes the word past tense
- *-ing* implies the action is happening right now

Teaching Syllable Patterns

In addition to teaching systematic consonant vowel patterns, effective teachers also use systematic instruction when teaching syllable patterns.

The following table shows the common syllable structures in the English language.

Syllable Type	Description	Example
Closed	A syllable with a single vowel followed by one or more consonants. The vowel is closed in by a consonant. The vowel sound is usually short.	cat bat clock letter
Open	A syllable that ends with a single vowel. The vowel is not closed in by a consonant. The vowel is usually long. The letter *y* acts like a vowel.	go no fly he
Vowel-Consonant-Silent e	A syllable with a single vowel followed by a consonant then the vowel e. The first vowel sound is long, and the final e is silent. Can be referred to as the sneaky silent e.	bike skate kite poke
Vowel Teams (Diphthong)	A syllable that has two consecutive vowels. Vowel teams can be divided into two types: ‒ Long vowel teams: Two vowels that make one long vowel sound. ‒ Variant vowel teams: Two vowels that make neither a long nor a short vowel sound but rather a variant. Letters *w* and *y* act as vowels.	Long vowel teams: eat, seat, say, see Variant vowel teams: stew, paw, book Exceptions: bread (makes a short vowel sound)
R-controlled	A syllable with one or two vowels followed by the letter *r*. The vowel is not long or short. The *r* influences or controls the vowel sound.	car far her fur sir
Consonant le (-al, -el) Final syllable	A syllable that has a consonant followed by the letters *le*, *al*, or *el*. This is often one syllable. This is the only syllable type without the vowel sound.	ta<u>ble</u> sta<u>ble</u> lo<u>cal</u>

Common activities to teach syllables

- **Syllable clapping** – Students clap and say the syllable at the same time. For example, in the word *apple*, students clap once for *-ap* and then again for *-ple*. The word *evenly* has three claps: *-e, -ven, -ly.*
- **Syllable lists** – create a list of prefixes, suffixes, roots, *ly, le*, and others.
- **Multisyllabic word manipulation** – Write different syllables on note cards. Jumble the cards and have students put them in the correct order so the word makes sense.
- **Syllable scoop** – students scoop under each syllable of multisyllable words.

Using structural analysis to teach complex multisyllable words

Structural analysis is breaking up words into different parts. For example, in the compound word *sidewalk*, students would break the word into two parts: side and walk.

Using structural analysis, students can also break words up by their prefixes, suffixes, and roots. For example, In the word *predictable*, the students can break the words into pre/ dict/ able.

Morphology

Morphology is the study of word parts and their meanings. Morphemes are the smallest units of meaning in a word. For example, in the word *unbelievable*, there are three morphemes—*un (not), believe (trust), able (capable)*. The following list provides categories and examples of using morphology to develop decoding skills.

- **Compound words.** Two words put together.

  Example: *mailman, sidewalk*

- **Root words.** A root word is the basic part of the word. It stands alone in meaning often comes from Latin languages.

  Example: In the word *unbelievable* the root word is *believe*. In the word *complex*, the root word is *plex*.

- **Affixes.** These are additional elements placed at the beginning or end of a root, stem, or word, or in the body of a word, to modify its meaning.

  Example: The word *unbelievable* contains affixes in the form of a prefix (*un*) and a suffix (*able*).

- **Prefixes.** These are additions to the beginning of root words that help to form a new word with another meaning from that of the root word. Prefixes are at the beginning of a word. Prefixes are considered affixes.

  Example: Prefixes that indicate not: *un-* (unknown), *dis-* (disregard), *im-*(impossible), *in-* (inaccurate), *mis-* (misunderstand), and *ir-* (irrational).

- **Suffixes.** These are additions to the end of root words that form a new word with another meaning from that of the root word. Suffixes are considered affixes. They change the part of speech (past tense, present tense) or verb tense of a word. They also indicate whether the word is plural or singular.

  Example: *-ed, -ing,* and plural *-s* are all suffixes

Etymology is the study of the origins of words and how they have changed over time. If students are analyzing root words and their meaning, they are using etymology.

For example, if students are discussing how the word *complexity* comes from the Latin word *complexus* "surrounding, encompassing," they are using etymology.

Think About It

When students use morphemes to decode words, they are usually using prefixes, suffixes, and roots. They will also break apart compound words. This is also referred to as structural analysis because students are breaking down the morphemic structure of the word to figure out its meaning. In addition, you may see the term *affixes* on the test. Affixes are additions to roots; prefixes and suffixes are affixes.

Free Morphemes. These morphemes can stand alone because they mean something in and of themselves. For example, in the word *closely*, the morpheme *close* is a free morpheme. It can stand alone.

Bound Morphemes. These morphemes only have meaning when they are connected to another morpheme. In the word *closely,* the morpheme *ly* cannot stand on its own and only has meaning when it is attached to another morpheme.

Students use multilettered groups in word structure to:

- Automatically recognize and pronounce long words.

- Use word parts to indicate meaning—for example, the prefix un- in *unhappy*, the suffix *-ly* in *friendly*, and the root word *sign* in *signal* and *signature*.

- Use syllables as units of pronunciation, such as the syllables *dis*, *trib*, and *ute* in *distribute*.

- Use strategy for analyzing long words, which is sometimes more efficient than other word identification strategies.

To sum this up, readers can use morphology to chunk words, separate words, and organize words so readers can develop fluency and comprehension.

High Frequency or Sight words. Words that show up in text very frequently. Students should memorize these words because it helps them save their cognitive endurance for more difficult reading tasks.

Quick Tip

Remember, the spelling of a suffix can vary depending on its root word. For example, the suffixes *able* and *ible* both mean capable.

- Use the –*able* ending if the root word is not changed like in *comfort – comfortable*.

- Use the –*ible* ending when you can't hear the whole root word like in *invisible*.

Quick Tip

A chunk is a group of letters that represents meaning and sound (the **re** in *regroup* the **un** and **able** in *unbelievable*).

Test Tip

One of the only times memorization is a good practice is when increasing students' automaticity. This is done through memorizing high-frequency words.

- want
- what
- why
- walk
- talk
- not
- saw
- say

- said
- see
- there
- those
- been
- because
- ever
- every

- by
- are
- would
- should
- water
- called
- over
- only

Increasing Phonics Skills

Teachers can provide students with opportunities to build and extend their phonics skills in a variety of ways. The most important way is to expose students to a variety of literary and informational text. The more print students are exposed to, the more words they learn and the more comfortable they become with their phonics skills.

Teachers can also use:

- **Decodable texts** – carefully sequenced to progressively incorporate words that are consistent with the letter–sound relationships that have been taught to the new reader.

- **Authentic and shared reading tasks** – an interactive reading experience where the teacher guides students as they read text. The teacher explicitly models the skills of proficient readers, including reading with fluency and expression.

- **Oral reading** – When students read aloud in class, to a partner, in cooperative groups, or with a teacher.

- **Whisper reading** – Instead of reading out loud or silently, students read in a whisper voice. This allows students to make mistakes without feeling embarrassed. It also helps students with decoding and fluency.

- **Word walls** - A word wall is a literacy tool composed of an organized collection of words which are displayed in large visible letters on a wall, bulletin board, or other display surface in a classroom. These will be discussed further in the vocabulary section of the study guide.

- **Interactive writing** – when students and teacher share the process of writing. The teacher begins by writing a word or a piece of a word, and the student continues.

Cueing Systems

As students begin to read, they use different methods to figure out words. Cueing systems allow students to use their background knowledge (schema) and apply that to understanding words. There are several types of cues students use when they read.

Semantic Cues

Semantic cues refer to the meaning in language that assists in comprehending texts, including words, speech, signs, symbols, and other meaning-bearing forms. Semantic cues involve the learners' prior knowledge of language. Gradually, students independently relate new information to what is known and personally meaningful.

Semantic cues are especially helpful for homographs—words that are spelled the same but have different meaning.

- For example: Thinking about leaving her friends made Jane blue.

The word *blue* in context is not the color but rather the feeling of sadness. Semantic cues help the student understand this.

Syntactic Cues

Syntactic cues involve the structure of the word as in the rules and patterns of language (grammar) and punctuation. As students read, they use structural cues.

Example: Joey *sat* in class yesterday.

In this case, the student is sure to say *sat* not *sit* because the word *yesterday* indicates there needs to be a past tense verb—*sat*.

Graphophonic Cues

Graphophonic cues involve the letter-sound or sound-symbol relationships of language. Readers identifying unknown words by relating speech sounds to letters or letter patterns are using graphophonic cues. This process is often called decoding.

Example: The student knows that the word *make* has a long /a/ sound because an *e* follows the *k*. This is a CVCe word.

Example Problem

A teacher is helping students use language structure and grammar to figure out difficult words in grade-level text. The students are using what cueing system?

A. Semantic

B. Syntactic

C. Graphophonic

D. Phonological

Correct Answer: B

The students are using language structure and grammar, which is syntactic. Semantic is meaning, graphophonic is sound-letter relationships, and phonological is not a cueing system.

Test Tip

Remember, a reader's oral vocabulary knowledge helps them derive meaning as they are decoding words. Vocabulary knowledge supports the semantic cueing system.

E. Fluency

Fluency is defined as the ability to read at an appropriate rate with accuracy and proper expression. Fluency is a necessary skill for reading comprehension. For students to understand text, they must first read through the text with fluency. When students have fluency, they can focus on meaning in text rather than focusing on decoding words.

Comprehension is the essence of reading. Comprehension is when students begin to form images in their minds as they read. They can predict what might happen next in a story because they understand what is currently happening in the story. Students who are in the comprehension stage of reading do not need to decode (sound out) words. They read fluently with prosody, automaticity, and accuracy.

Teachers perform fluency checks or fluency reads to measure students' reading progress. While the student reads, the teacher follows along. As the student reads, the teacher checks for automaticity, which is reading effortlessly. The teacher also checks students' accuracy and rate.

- **Prosody** – timing, phrasing, emphasis, and intonation that readers use to help convey aspects of meaning and to make their speech lively. Prosody includes stopping at periods, pausing at commas, reading with inflection, and reading with expression.

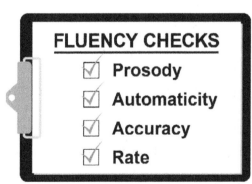

- **Automaticity** – effortless word recognition that comes with repeated reading practice. When students are reading at > 95 percent accuracy, they have automaticity.

- **Accuracy** – the number of words a student reads correctly. Typically, accuracy is measured by having students read aloud during a fluency read (also called a running record). The student reads, and the teacher marks any words the student miscues.

- **Rate** – the speed at which students read words correctly. Rate is typically expressed in correct words per minute (wpm).

Fluency at various stages of reading development

Like the other foundational skills discussed in this study guide, fluency has definitive stages students move through as they acquire the skill. The following are the general stages of fluency.

Stages of Fluency

1. Accurate, automatic letter naming
2. Word reading
3. Reading connected text
4. Reading complex academic texts

It is important to identify and understand the interrelationship among decoding skills (phonics and word analysis), fluency, and reading comprehension.

- Fluency is the bridge between decoding and comprehension.
- Prosody is the bridge between fluency and comprehension.

Test Tip

Prosody, or reading with expression, helps students comprehend text. Speed reading through the text without expression can hinder comprehension. Teachers can help students with their prosody by modeling good prosody during read-alouds.

Fluency supports cognitive endurance. When students have cognitive endurance, they can read through large sections of text and build meaning from that text. Students are not wasting cognitive energy on decoding words. Instead, they are reading fluently, using their cognitive energy toward comprehension and critical thinking.

Fluency is important because it allows students to use cognitive energy on building comprehension of text rather than using cognitive energy on sounding out words. All of the following strategies are effective for English language learners (ELLs) as well.

Example Problem

A teacher encourages second-grade English language learners to take a decodable passage home and read it two times each night for five nights. The primary purpose of this strategy would be to increase:

   A. Comprehension

   B. Phonics

   C. Automaticity

   D. Metacognition

Correct Answer: C

This is a repeated reading exercise. Repeated reading helps to increase automaticity and fluency.

Evidence-based practices for developing fluency

Fluency is important because it allows students to use cognitive energy on building comprehension of text rather than using cognitive energy on sounding out words. The following instructional methods work to develop fluency and are effective strategies to increase automaticity, accuracy, prosody, and rate.

Choral Reading. Reading aloud in unison with a whole class or group of students. Choral reading helps build students' fluency, self-confidence, and motivation. Choral reading can be done a variety of ways.

- **Unison** – The whole class reads together in unison.
- **Refrain** – One student reads the narrative part of the text; the rest of the class reads the refrain.
- **Antiphon** – The class is divided in two groups; one group reads one part, and the other group reads the other part.

Repeated Reading. Reading passages again and again, aiming to read more words correctly per minute each time. This helps to increase automaticity.

Running Records. Following along as a student reads and marking when the student makes a mistake or miscues. At the end, the teacher counts how many correct words per minute (wpm) the student read.

Miscue Analysis. Looking over the running record, analyzing why the student miscued, and employing strategies to help the student with miscues.

Conferencing. Conferencing individually with students to go over fluency goals and strategies is very effective. Teachers and students can look over fluency data and decide how to move forward to build better fluency.

Data folders. Often, students will keep their fluency data in a data folder. It is effective to chart progress over time so students can see their growth. Data should be kept confidential and only discussed between the teacher, student, and parents.

The following table outlines reading strategies helpful in building students' fluency and comprehension skills.

Fluency Strategy	Definition	Example	Helps with...
Basal reading	Leveled reading books	Dick and Jane series	Automaticity
Running records	Assessing student's fluency by determining the student's rate or how many words per minute (wpm) a student reads correctly.	Following along as a student reads and marking when he or she makes a mistake or miscues. At the end, the teacher counts how many words per minute (wpm) the student read correctly.	Automaticity, accuracy, rate, prosody
Miscue analysis	Looking over the running record, analyzing why the student miscued, and employing strategies to help the student with miscues.	After a fluency read, the teacher and student analyze the mistakes the student made and come up with strategies to fix those mistakes.	Accuracy
Repeated reading	Reading text that is at the student's independent reading level over and over again to help with fluency.	The teacher has a student read a passage and then re-read the passage several times over the course of a week to build automaticity and reading confidence.	Automaticity, rate, accuracy, prosody
Readers' theater	A strategy for developing reading fluency. It engages students by having students read parts of a script.	Students are reading a story; each student is one of the characters in the book. Students read aloud through the text.	Prosody
Choral reading	Reading aloud in unison through a piece of text.	The teacher uses choral reading with ELL students to help them with fluency and confidence.	Accuracy, prosody
Silent sustained reading	Students read silently on their own.	The teacher dedicates 15 minutes every day to having students read their novels on their own.	Automaticity, accuracy, rate, prosody

This page intentionally left blank.

1. Students are learning to identify individual sounds in words. Which foundational skill are they working on?

    A. Phonemic awareness

    B. Phonics

    C. Morphology

    D. Sight reading

2. A teacher has students replace the beginning sound in *play* with the /st/ sound, making the word *stay*. What type of activity are the students working on?

    A. Phoneme manipulation

    B. Onset and rime

    C. Morphology

    D. Etymology

3. Emma breaks down the word *unhappiness* into its meaningful parts, "un-," "happy," and "-ness." Which foundational skill is she using?

    A. Phonemic awareness

    B. Phonics

    C. Morphology

    D. Sight word recognition

4. A teacher asks students to create a new word by changing the onset of the original word. Which student response indicates the student understands this concept?

    A. I will change the word *bat* to *bit*.

    B. I will change the word *track* to *black*.

    C. I will change the word *play* to *plan*.

    D. I will change the word *bot* to *bit*.

5. The teacher is helping students understand closed syllables. She writes the word "rabbit" on the board and asks the students to identify the closed syllable(s) in the word. Which of the following responses is correct?

    A. There are no closed syllables in the word rabbit.

    B. There is one open and one closed syllable in the word rabbit – ra/bbit

    C. There are two open syllables and one closed syllable in the word rabbit – ra/ b /it.

    D. Both syllables are closed – rab/bit

6. A second-grade teacher is assessing students' reading fluency. He asks each student to read a passage aloud. He notices that one student struggles to read larger words and often stops to sound them out. Which aspect of fluency is the student likely struggling with?

    A. Phonemic awareness

    B. Automaticity

    C. Prosody

    D. Comprehension

7. A second-grade teacher is conducting a lesson on CVCe words. She presents a series of word cards to her students and asks them to identify the CVCe word. Which word is a CVCe word?

    A. Cat

    B. Clap

    C. Stick

    D. Bake

8. As a student is reading, she stops to figure out a word. To help prompt the student, the teacher encourages her to look at the pictures next to the paragraph to see if that helps. Which cueing system is the teacher using?

    A. Syntactic

    B. Morphological

    C. Semantic

    D. Graphophonic

9. Mr. Thompson, a third-grade teacher, is introducing diphthongs to his students. He writes several words on the board and asks the students to identify the word that contains a diphthong. Which word contains a diphthong?

    A. Sit

    B. Keep

    C. Dog

    D. Coin

10. Which **TWO** of the following words contain a bound morpheme?

    ☐ A. Closely

    ☐ B. Accurate

    ☐ C. Believe

    ☐ D. Unprotected

    ☐ E. Severe

Number	Answer	Explanation
1.	A	Phonemic awareness refers to the ability to identify and manipulate individual sounds (phonemes) in spoken words.
2.	A	The students are engaging in a substitution activity with phonemes in words. Therefore, they are engaging in phoneme manipulation.
3.	C	Morphology focuses on understanding the structure and meaning of words, including prefixes, suffixes, and root words.
4.	B	The onset of a word is the first consonant sound or consonant cluster. The student in answer B is correctly changing the onset of the word *track*, with is /tr/ to *black*, which is /bl/.
5.	D	The proper way to break the word rabbit up by its syllables is rab/bit. In this case, both syllables are closed because both end with a short vowel followed by a consonant.
6.	B	When students struggle to read and must sound out words, they are lacking in automaticity skills. Ways to help these students would be to engage in repeated reading.
7.	D	CVCe words have a long vowel sound followed by a consonant and silent e. The only word that does this is in the answer D.
8.	C	Pictures help students identify meaning. The semantic cueing system focuses on meaning.
9.	D	A diphthong is a combination of two vowel sounds within a single syllable. In the given options, the word "coin" contains a diphthong. The combination of the vowel sounds "o" and "i" creates a diphthong sound /ɔɪ/. In contrast, the other options "sit," "keep," and "dog" do not have diphthongs; they consist of single vowel sounds.
10.	A & D	The morphemes *ly, un,* and *ed* are considered bound morphemes because they do not have meaning unless they are connected to a word. The words *believe* and *accurate* are words that can stand on their own and have meaning. The word *severe* is unrelated to the task.

This page intentionally left blank.

II. Language

The following topics are aligned with the test specifications of the Praxis 7812. It is important that you examine these closely because these are the skills assessed on the exam.

A. Conventions of Standard Academic English

B. Vocabulary - Understanding a variety of words

C. Forms of Language

A. Conventions of Standard Academic English

For this exam, you will need to understand the basic rules of English grammar. While you will not be asked a lot of grammar-specific questions, there will be questions that assess your ability to determine the error and a strategy to fix the student's error.

Parts of Speech

Part of Speech	Description	Example
Noun	person, place, or thing.	car, boat, pilot, rock
Pronoun	replaces a noun	it, he, she, him/her, they, them
Verb	action words	run, walk, shop, talk
Adjective	describes nouns	pretty, exciting, small, big
Adverb	modifies verbs or adjectives	slowly, quickly, well, pleasantly
Preposition	word placed before a noun or pronoun to form a phrase modifying another word	by, over, under, with, for
Conjunction	words that join clauses or phrases	for, and, nor, but, or, yet, so (FANBOYS)
Interjection	words that express emotion	Oh! Wow! Yikes!

Verbs

Verbs are words used to describe **actions** or states, and they form the main part of the predicate of the sentence. Some common examples of verbs include *to be, to think, to take, to come, to see, to have, to do, to go,* and *to make.* Verbs can be regular or irregular, and depending on their status, they will be conjugated differently. For example, to show past tense of a regular verb, we add the *-ed* ending (e.g., *called*). However, not all verbs follow those rules. For example, to show the past-tense verb *to spend* is *spent.*

Standard verb forms

There are five main forms of verbs: simple or base form, third-person singular present (also called *s* form), past tense form, *-ing* form, and past participle form. Typically, verb form is assessed on the exam with questions that test your ability to spot and correct errors in incorrect form use.

Verb form	Definition	Example
Simple or base form	The simple form of the verb is the main verb in the present tense.	I **dance** at the wedding. The boys **walk** to school. I **buy** clothes at my favorite store.
Third person singular present (s form)	Most verbs in English form the third-person singular by adding -s or -es to the simple or base form of the verb. These actions are in the present tense.	She **dances** after school. The boy **walks** to school. The child **watches** TV.
Past tense form	This is the basic past tense of the verb. For regular verbs, add -ed to the root form of the verb (or just -d if the root form already ends in an e). However, some past tense verbs are irregular and do not have -ed attached to the end.	She **danced** in yesterday's competition. The kids **watched** the ballgame last night. The contest **was** held in the auditorium. The workers **built** the house quickly.
-ing form	A verb ending in -ing is either a present participle or a gerund. These two forms look identical. The difference is in their functions in a sentence.	**Present participle:** • He is **painting** in class. • She was **dancing** in the street. • I see the kids **playing** in the yard. **Gerund** – When the verb is the subject and functions as a noun. • **Painting** is a fun activity. • **Eating** dirt is a bad idea. • **Walking** to school is easier than driving.
Past participle form	The past participle is also used with *had* or *have* to form the past perfect tense.	I **have driven** that route before. She **had tried** to call him before the party. I **have completed** my homework.

Pronoun antecedent agreement

Pronoun antecedent agreement simply means that the pronoun used in the sentence agrees with the antecedent in the sentence.

First, let's distinguish between a pronoun and an antecedent by looking at the sentence below.

My **teacher** was excited to learn that three of **her** students were accepted to Ivy League colleges.

Antecedent   Pronoun

In the case above, the pronoun, **her**, matches the antecedent, **teacher**.

However, things get complicated when the test makers present the pronouns *they*, *them*, or *their* in a sentence.

Incorrect:

When a student comes to see me, <u>they</u> usually want to discuss extra credit.

↑
Plural pronoun

The sentence above is incorrect because the plural pronoun, *they*, does not agree with the singular noun in the subject, *student*.

Correct:

When <u>students</u> come to see me, <u>they</u> usually want to discuss extra credit.

Example question

Choose the option that corrects an error in the underlined portion(s). If no error exists, choose "No change is necessary."

The board of directors had <u>their</u> <u>meeting and</u> decided to postpone the event until after the <u>holidays</u>.
                    A   B   C

    A. its

    B. meeting, and

    C. Holidays

    D. No change is necessary.

Correct answer: A

In this case, there is a sneaky prepositional phrase and a collective noun to navigate. *The board* is a collective noun and therefore singular. To have pronoun antecedent agreement, the pronoun *its* is appropriate for the singular board. The phrase *of directors* is a prepositional phrase and can be taken out. Then the sentence would read: *The board had its meeting*.

In answer choice B, there is no need for the comma + conjunction because the *and* is only separating a dependent and independent clause, so the conjunction *and* by itself is correct. Finally, the term *holidays* is not a proper noun and does not need to be capitalized.

Example question

Choose the option that corrects an error in the underlined portion(s). If no error exists, choose "No change is necessary."

<u>A student should only go to their locker</u> before school, during lunch, or after school.

    A. Students should only go their locker

    B. A student should go to their lockers

    C. Students should only go to their lockers

    D. No change is necessary.

Correct answer: C

The way the sentence is written, the subject is singular (a student), and the pronoun is plural (their). Therefore, the best thing to do is change the subject to plural (students). Also, because we have multiple students, there are multiple lockers. Therefore, *locker* should be changed to a plural noun as well. Otherwise, it reads as though there are multiple students using one locker.

Test Tip

Whenever you see any one of the pronouns *their*, *them*, or *they*, slow down and check the subject of the sentence. This is a classic grammar assessment trick, where the test makers check your ability to maintain pronoun antecedent agreement and pronoun number case. If your subject is singular, you should use a singular pronoun or change the subject to plural as in the examples that follow.

Pronoun references

Sometimes it is unclear to what antecedent the pronoun is referring. In that case, you will be tasked to identify that in a sentence.

Incorrect:

My sister brought her dog on the road trip and she chewed the seats.

There are two antecedents in this sentence, and therefore, it is not clear who the pronoun *she* is referring to. Is *she* referring to the sister or the dog?

Correct:

My sister brought her dog on the road trip and the dog chewed the seats.

In this sentence, it is clear that the dog, not the sister, chewed the seats.

Pronoun case forms (e.g., subjective, objective, possessive)

Just like verbs, pronouns have cases. Pronouns can be either subjective (occurring in the subject of the sentence), objective (occurring as the direct object in the predicate of the sentence), or possessive (showing ownership). The following are examples of each pronoun case.

Subject Pronouns	Examples
I	**She** went to the store to buy milk.
he	↑
she	**She** is the subject of the sentence and therefore a subjective pronoun.
they	**They** rode bikes to school.
we	↑
you	**They** is the subject of the sentence and therefore a subjective pronoun.
who	

Object Pronouns	Examples
me	Jane went to the store to buy **him** some clothes.
him	↑
her	The pronoun *him* is the direct object of the sentence and therefore the objective pronoun.
them	Sally came over to the house to see **me**.
us	↑
you	The pronoun *me* is the direct object of the sentence and therefore the objective pronoun.
whom	

Possessive Pronouns	Examples
my	She went to get **her** clothes from the house.
his	↑
her	The pronoun *her* is the possessive pronoun.
their	We realized it was **their** car in the parking lot.
our	↑
your	The pronoun *their* is the possessive pronoun.
whose	

Compound and complex sentences

Effective writers use a mix of compound and complex sentences to illustrate sentence variety, which adds vibrancy and interest to text. You will see questions on the exam about helping students increase their writing skills by using sentence variety.

Sentence Type	Explanation	Example
Simple sentence	Consists of one **independent** clause	I went to the store.
Compound sentence	Consists of **two independent** clauses. Ensure that there is a comma between two independent clauses in a compound sentence. The comma should be followed by a coordinating conjunction (**FANBOYS**)	I went to the store, and I bought milk.

Sentence Type	Explanation	Example
Complex sentence	Consists of an independent clause and a dependent clause. When the sentence starts with a dependent clause, a comma is needed after the clause.	When I went to the store, I bought milk.
Compound complex sentence	Consists of at least two independent clauses and at least one dependent clause.	When I went to the store, I bought milk, and I bought cheese.

Quick Tip

If students are having trouble punctuating complex and compound sentences, use mini activities where they use the punctuation in their writing. For example, the teacher can incorporate daily edits as a bell-ringer activity. This way, students are getting incremental practice every day by applying their skills.

Identifying independent and dependent clauses

The best approach to this part of the assessment is to understand the difference between independent clauses and dependent clauses.

- An **independent clause** contains a subject and a verb and expresses a complete thought. An independent clause can stand on its own as a sentence.
- A **dependent clause** contains a noun and a verb but does not express a complete thought. A dependent clause cannot be a sentence on its own.

Example:

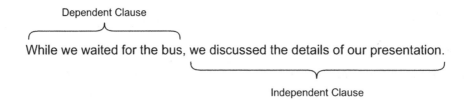

Dependent Clause

While we waited for the bus, we discussed the details of our presentation.

Independent Clause

Fragments

Dependent clauses, without the independent clause in a sentence, are fragments. Fragments are not sentences.

Correct:

Introductory Clause

Worrying she will fall and hurt herself, she often wears a helmet when she rides her bike.

A comma is used to separate a dependent clause from an independent clause in a sentence.

Independent Clause

Incorrect:

Conjunctions are used to combine parts of a sentence to make compound and complex sentences. The two types of conjunctions you will be asked about on the exam are coordinating conjunctions and subordinating conjunctions.

Coordinating Conjunctions

These are the seven words that combine two sentences (independent clauses that can stand alone as they state a complete thought) with the addition of a comma. These are the ONLY seven words used to combine two sentences using a comma.

The seven coordinating conjunctions (FANBOYS):

FOR	AND	NOR	BUT	OR	YET	SO

F	A	N	B	O	Y	S

- A coordinating conjunction alone can separate an independent clause and a dependent clause.
- A comma + a coordinating conjunction must be used when separating two independent clauses.

Example:

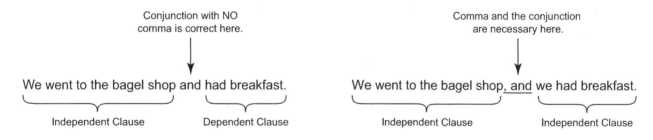

Subordinating conjunctions

These are all the other conjunctions used to combine clauses. These commonly include:

- Since
- Because
- Although
- While
- Due
- Though
- Whenever
- When
- If

Quick Tip

YES, you can start sentences with subordinating conjunctions.

- *While* I was watching TV, I did my homework.
- *Since* it was cold, I wore a jacket.
- *Whenever* I go to Canada, I stop in Vancouver.
- *Because* I was on the committee, I voted on the issue.

*When a subordinating conjunction starts a sentence, a comma will always follow.

Grammatically, there are two patterns for these subordinating conjunctions:

Pattern 1

Independent Clause + Subordinating Conjunction + Clause (independent, dependent, or prepositional)

Example:

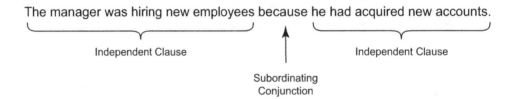

Pattern 2

Subordinating Conjunction + Clause (independent, dependent, or prepositional) + Comma + Independent Clause

Example:

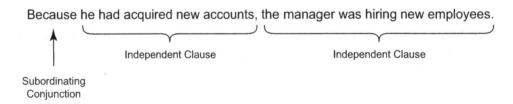

Standard punctuation – Semicolons

Semicolons join two independent clauses that are related. Semicolons are alternatives to a period or comma conjunction.

Examples:

I needed to go to the store; I was almost out of milk, egg, cheese, and bread.

He knew he would be punished for skipping school; he did it anyway.

In both examples above, there are two independent clauses joined by the semicolon. This is the only way to use a semicolon.

Standard punctuation – Colons

Colons are used to separate an independent clause and a list. Colons can also be used to separate an independent clause and an independent clause or dependent clause that elaborates, restates, explains, or defines.

Example:

I brought all the necessities to the campsite: tent, food, fishing pole, and tackle.

Notice that the clause *I brought all the necessities to the campsite* is a sentence—an independent clause. Therefore, the colon is used correctly.

Example:

We decided to focus on the most important thing: increasing student achievement.

The dependent clause, which is *increasing student achievement*, defines what the most important thing is.

Example:

I had lunch with the president of the university: Dr. Cunningham.

Here you have an independent clause followed by the name of the person mentioned in the first clause. Therefore, the colon is appropriate.

Standard punctuation – Apostrophe

There are two main reasons to use apostrophes:

1. To form a contraction such as do + not = don't. In this case, the apostrophe replaces or stands in for the letter that is taken out when the words are combined.

2. To show possession. When the noun is singular or plural but does not end in s, add 's to show possession. When the noun is singular or plural but does end in s, add the apostrophe after the s to show possession.

Example:

Please bring Lisa's book when you come to class tomorrow.

Lisa is a singular proper noun (there is only one Lisa here); therefore, the 's is appropriate.

Example:

We will be going to the women's soccer tournament on Wednesday.

Women is a plural noun that does NOT end in s; therefore, the 's is appropriate.

Example:

Please bring all the girls' books when you come to class tomorrow.

Girls is a plural noun that ends in s; therefore, the s' is appropriate.

Example:

We will be going to the ladies' luncheon on Friday.

Ladies is plural and ends in -s, and the ladies own the luncheon. Therefore, the s' is appropriate.

Example Question

Choose the option that corrects an error in the underlined portion(s). If no error exists, choose "No change is necessary."

I am not excited about <u>tomorrows</u> meeting.

A. tomorrow

B. tomorrow's

C. tomorrows'

D. No change is necessary.

Correct answer: B

In cases like this, the meeting belongs to tomorrow. Therefore, it should be tomorrow's meeting.

B. Vocabulary - Understanding a variety of words

When students begin to read, they acquire vocabulary skills. These skills progress in order: listening, speaking, reading, and writing.

Listening vocabulary. First students acquire listening vocabulary. Listening vocabulary refers to the words we need to know to understand what we hear. This is part of students' receptive vocabulary.

Speaking vocabulary. Next, students acquire speaking vocabulary. Speaking vocabulary consists of the words we use when we speak. This is part of students' expressive vocabulary.

Reading vocabulary. Next, students acquire reading vocabulary. Reading vocabulary refers to the words we need to know to understand what we read. This is part of students' receptive vocabulary.

Writing vocabulary. The last skill acquired is writing vocabulary. Writing vocabulary consists of the words we use in writing. This is part of students' expressive vocabulary.

Receptive Vocabulary vs. Expressive Vocabulary		
Receptive	Reading, Listening	Listening to a book on tape, reading an article
Expressive	Speaking, Writing	Engaging in role play, writing a poem

Listening comprehension. This skill relates to listening vocabulary. When students have listening comprehension, they can understand a story that is being read aloud. Students will often develop their listening comprehension before their reading comprehension.

Denotative vs. Connotative Meaning

Students must understand that word meaning can be expressed in different ways. During vocabulary instruction, teachers should incorporate the difference between denotative and connotative meaning.

Denotation – the formal definition of a word.

Connotation – an idea or feeling that a word invokes in addition to its literal or primary meaning.

When teaching students to select words to achieve the maximum desired effect, have them consider the following.

- **Meaning.** Students can choose words for either their denotative meaning, which is the definition found in a dictionary, or the connotative meaning, which are the emotions, circumstances, or descriptive variations the word evokes.

- **Specificity.** This helps students choose language that is concrete and directly related to the topic.
- **Audience.** Determining what audience students are writing for can help determine if the writing is meant to engage, amuse, entertain, inform, or incite.
- **Level of Diction.** The level of diction an author chooses directly relates to the intended audience. Diction is classified into four levels of language:
    1. **Formal** denotes serious discourse.
    2. **Informal** denotes relaxed but polite conversation.
    3. **Colloquial** denotes language in everyday usage.
    4. **Slang** denotes new, often highly informal words and phrases that evolve as a result of sociolinguistic constructs such as age, class, wealth status, ethnicity, nationality, and regional dialects.

Context Clues and Word Association

In reading and listening, a context clue is a form of information (such as a definition, synonym, antonym, or example) that appears near a word or phrase and offers direct or indirect suggestions about its meaning.

Strategy: Use context clues to identify difficult words

Synonym or restatement clues. These context clues restate the meaning of the word using a synonym. The sentence is essentially saying the same thing twice. For example, the sentence below contains a synonym or restatement clue.

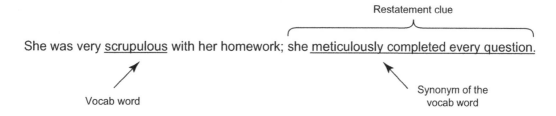

Antonym or contrast clues. These context clues state the opposite of the word in question. For example, the sentence below contains an antonym or contrast clue.

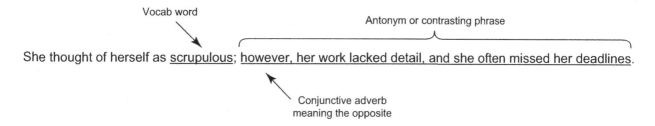

Inference clues. These context clues are subtle statements that drop hints to what the word means. For example, the sentence below uses inference.

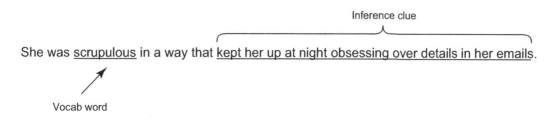

Test Tip

Some words will lack context clues in a passage. In that case, it is helpful to look the word up and find synonyms of the word and then substitute a synonym in for the unknown word. When the passage lacks context clues for difficult words, using a dictionary or thesaurus is appropriate.

Students must use non-contextual skills when acquiring vocabulary. This is usually done through direct, explicit vocabulary instruction. Direct instruction helps students learn difficult words, such as words that represent complex concepts that are not part of the students' everyday experiences. Direct instruction of vocabulary is aligned to morphology as discussed in the previous section.

Direct instruction includes:

- Providing students with instruction in specific words that are important to their content learning or understanding of a particular text

- Teaching students more general word-learning strategies that they can apply to a variety of words, such as analyzing parts of words (e.g., root words)

- Supporting students' oral vocabulary by providing opportunities for them to use new vocabulary in discourse, cooperative learning, and role play

Quick Tip

Learning vocabulary in context is also referred to as incidental vocabulary. Incidental vocabulary learning is the unintended learning of words that occurs during engagement in other activities. This is the real-world application of vocabulary and is regarded by some scholars as the most effective form of word learning.

An important thing to keep in mind when thinking about vocabulary instruction is to use activities that use new vocabulary in an authentic, real-world manner. While dictionaries are useful tools and glossaries provide support, they should not be the only mode of teaching vocabulary. The following table outlines dos and don'ts regarding vocabulary instruction.

Do	Don't
Have students use context to figure out difficult words.	Have students write words over and over again.
Use interactive word walls so students can engage with new vocabulary.	Have students copy definitions from the glossary.
Model think-aloud strategies for students to use when faced with difficult academic and domain specific words.	Assign extra vocabulary homework for those who struggle.

Domain Specific Vocabulary

Vocabulary differs from content area to content area. Words in science class are much different than the words used in English class. Those words are different than words used in general conversation.

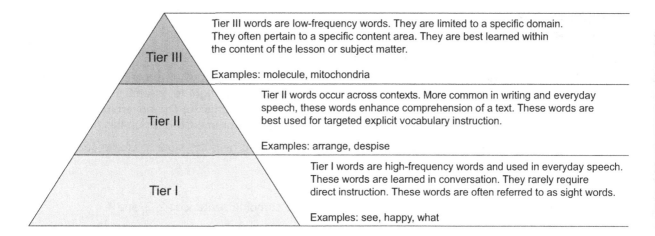

Teachers must prepare students to engage with conversational, general academic, and domain specific words.

It is important that you demonstrate knowledge of the importance of wide reading a variety of genres, cultures, perspectives, and levels of complexity) and frequent, extensive, and varied listening, speaking, and writing experiences in the development of academic language and vocabulary.

It is also important that teachers apply knowledge of strategies for promoting wide reading and for providing students with repeated, meaningful exposure to new words and language structures in their listening and reading and opportunities to use the new words and language structures in their speaking and writing.

This includes:

- Promoting an environment where students can experiment with new vocabulary in their reading and writing.

- Encourage students to use new vocabulary in their conversations with other students.

- Using high-level vocabulary when corresponding with students

C. Forms of Language

Writers use all different types of language to convey meaning in text. For example, in a narrative text, language is used to tell a personal story and how the narrator feels about it. In expository text, the writer uses technical language to explain concepts and situations. In persuasive or argumentative text, the writer uses strong language to appeal to the reader. Students must understand these differences to comprehend text and create their own writing appropriate for different audiences.

Example Question

If a writer wants to enhance characterization and show that the narrator is from a specific place in Louisiana, the writer can use:

A. Description

B. Dialect

C. Visuals

D. Preface

Correct Answer: B

The writer can use the regional dialect through dialogue in the writer to show the reader where the narrator is from. This is an important technique in literary text.

Example Question

The following sample is from a student's writing on the First Amendment of the Bill of Rights.

(1) The First Amendment protects some of our most important rights. (2) It protects religious liberty and free speech. (3) It protects a free press. (4) Also, it protects the right to assemble and petition the government. (5) Many people have to continue to fight for these rights. (6) The government sometimes tries to take them away. (7) Citizens can take their cases to the Supreme Court when this happens.

Which **TWO** of the following revisions can the teacher make to help the student create cohesion and readability of the text?

   ☐   A.   Eliminate sentence 7 because it is repetitive.

   ☐   B.   Use conjunctions and proper punctuation to combine sentences 2, 3, and 4.

   ☐   C.   Use a subordinating conjunction between sentences 5 and 6 to connect the two ideas.

   ☐   D.   Use more examples of what the amendment protects to further support the position.

   ☐   E.   Use more variation in how the piece refers to people and government.

Correct Answer: B & C

The first part of the writing is choppy and robotic. The teacher could encourage the student to use commas and conjunctions to connect the sentences, so they have continuity and readability.

Below is an example of using punctuation and a coordinating conjunction to combine the sentences.

It protects religious liberty, free speech, a free press, the right to assemble, and the right to petition the government.

The teacher can also suggest the student use the subordinating conjunction *because* to connect sentences 5 and 6.

Many people have to continue to fight for these rights <u>because</u> the government sometimes tries to take them away.

None of the other choices are relevant to the writing. Only choices B and C would make the writing more effective for its purpose.

Test Tip

The best choice for questions about improving writing often include combining sentences using proper punctuation and conjunctions. This helps writing to have better readability and movement.

Language Practice Questions

1. A fifth-grade teacher wants to reinforce how to use complex sentences in compositional writing. Which of the following would be most effective in reinforcing these skills so students can apply them to increase sentence variety in their writing?

    A. Diagram complex sentences and evaluate how dependent and independent clauses contribute to sentence variety.

    B. Look up complex words in the dictionary and use them appropriately to make the writing more complex and varied.

    C. Complete grammar worksheets and practice sentence skills so the skills become automatic.

    D. Work in cooperative groups to identify complex sentences in the text.

Use the following piece of student writing to answer questions 2-4.

(1) It is unfair that we must attend school five days a week and 180 days per year. (2) It does not make sense. (3) If we're being honest we can learn what we need to in just three days per week. (4) The amount of math we learn can be reduced to just a few lessons. (5) The amount of English we learn can be significantly cut.

2. Which of the following suggestions should the teacher make to help this student improve this piece of writing?

    A. Add two more sentences to make the paragraph have seven sentences instead of five.

    B. Add an introductory sentence to the beginning of the paragraph.

    C. Use conjunctions to make sentences 2 and 3 and sentences 4 and 5 complex sentences.

    D. Add commas before the conjunctions in each sentence.

3. Which error did the student make in the paragraph?

    A. A comma is needed in sentence 1 before the word *and*.

    B. A comma is needed in sentence 3 to separate the dependent clause from the independent clause.

    C. The student does not need to spell out the words *five* and *three* in sentences 1 and 3.

    D. The student should use replace the words *does not* with the contraction *doesn't* in sentence 2.

4. Which **TWO** of the following explains when a colon can be used in a sentence?

    ☐ A. To separate two independent clauses.

    ☐ B. To separate an independent clause from a definition.

    ☐ C. To connect an introductory clause with the independent clause.

    ☐ D. To separate an independent clause from a list.

    ☐ E. To separate an independent clause from a coordinating conjunction.

5. Which of the following would be the <u>best</u> change to the sentence below?

    A teacher must submit their lesson plans each month by uploading the documents to the district website.

    A. Add a comma to the sentence after the word *month*.

    B. Change the word *their* to *his or her*.

    C. Add a hyphen to make the word *district-website*.

    D. Change the subject of the sentence to *teachers*.

6. Jose is reading the passage below. He reads through it accurately. When he gets to the word *impeccable*, he decodes the word properly but stops and asks the teacher what it means.

   What would be the most effective strategy to help Jose figure out the meaning of the word?

   > Jenny was always working on her homework. She wanted it to be *impeccable* before turning it in. This caused her much anxiety because she could never get it perfect enough.

   A. Have him find synonyms of the word in a thesaurus and apply them to the sentence.

   B. Have him use the restatement context clue in the sentence to determine a synonym for the word.

   C. Have him use the contrast clues in the sentence to determine an antonym for the word.

   D. Have him skip over the word and continue reading and look up the word after the reading is finished.

7. Which of the following strategies would be most effective in promoting word consciousness?

   A. Have students look up words they do not know in the dictionary and share the words with a partner.

   B. Model sophisticated language by substituting everyday words with complex vocabulary.

   C. Use regular vocabulary tests to assess students' knowledge and intervene when necessary.

   D. Have students work regularly in cooperative groups to practice new vocabulary for a set of predetermined words.

8. Which of the following activities is most effective when teaching English learners to advance from Tier I words to Tier II words?

   A. Have students analyze both common and applied definitions for new words.

   B. Have students complete word lists for homework.

   C. Have students memorize the Tier II words.

   D. Have students match common words to pictures.

9. Which of the following describes Tier III words?

   A. These words should be memorized because they occur in almost every text. These words do not always follow phonics rules.

   B. These words occur across contexts. More common in writing and everyday speech, these words enhance comprehension of a text.

   C. These words are used in everyday speech. These words are learned in conversation. They rarely require direct instruction.

   D. These words often pertain to a specific content area. They are best learned within the content of the lesson or subject matter.

10. Which of the following is most effective for a student who is struggling with a word in the textbook?

    A. Look the word up in the glossary.

    B. Use context clues.

    C. Write the word down.

    D. Skip the word.

11. Which of the following would be the most appropriate activity for students working on their receptive vocabulary?

    A. Conduct a presentation.

    B. Listen to a story on tape.

    C. Discuss stories in literature circles.

    D. Engage in a role-play conversation.

12. Which of the following would be the most appropriate activity for students working on their expressive vocabulary?

    A. Read a book.

    B. Listen to a story on tape.

    C. Discuss stories in literature circles.

    D. Look up vocabulary words.

13. Which of the following activities would be most appropriate for kindergarten students who are in the beginning stages of vocabulary development?

    A. Work on listening and speaking vocabulary.

    B. Work on reading and writing vocabulary.

    C. Work on using context to figure out difficult words.

    D. Work on incidental vocabulary in context.

14. A teacher has multiple centers set up around the room. At each station, there are words on index cards; each card has a new vocabulary word on the front of the card and its simple definition on the back of the card. At each center, groups of four students interact with the words and sort them according to the students' own criteria. Once they are done sorting the words, students then explain and defend why they chose to sort the words as they did. This activity is likely to promote:

    A. Systematic word recognition

    B. Semantic cueing in context

    C. Syntactic cueing in context

    D. Word consciousness

15. Which of the following would be most effective in helping English learners whose first language is Spanish understand idioms and proverbs commonly used in English?

    A. Have students look up common idioms on the Internet and then use them in their cooperative groups.

    B. Have students work in pairs to use common idioms in conversation in English and then compare them to common idioms used in Spanish.

    C. Have students use context to figure out the idioms when they are presented in text.

    D. Have students work in cooperative groups where they identify common idioms in English and define them.

16. Mrs. Garcia, a third-grade English language arts teacher, is discussing the concept of dialect with her students. She provides them with a passage from a novel where the characters speak in a distinct dialect. What is the primary purpose of teaching dialect?

A. To emphasize correct grammar and standard English usage.

B. To encourage students to adopt different accents.

C. To expose students to the cultural diversity and variations in language.

D. To discourage the use of non-standard English dialects.

17. A teacher is helping her students combine simple sentences to form compound sentences. She presents the students with two separate sentences and asks them to identify the correctly combined compound sentence. Which option correctly combines the two sentences into a compound sentence?

A. John likes to play basketball. He also enjoys swimming.

B. John likes to play basketball, but he also enjoys swimming.

C. John likes to play basketball and he also enjoys swimming.

D. John likes to play basketball, he also enjoys swimming.

18. For each row, categorize the sentence as either simple or compound.

Sentence	Simple	Compound
She was traveling just five miles over the speed limit, but she received a citation anyway.		
The two girls went to spend time with their grandmother and cousins.		
Marley was upset when she didn't win the race, but she was a good sport about it.		

Number	Answer	Explanation
1.	A	Answer choice A is the only answer choice where students are evaluating sentence structure and how it can be used to increase sentence variety. This is the most effective approach.
2.	C	The paragraph is robotic and uses short sentences. To give the writing more flow and readability, the student could add conjunctions to combine sentences.
3.	B	Sentence 3 uses an introductory clause and an independent clause. Therefore, a comma is needed to separate the two. *If we're being honest, we can learn what we need to in just three days.*
4	B & D	The only way a colon should be used in a sentence is to separate an independent clause from a definition or to separate an independent clause from a list. *The teacher focused on the most important aspect of her job: student achievement.* In the above sentence, the independent clause is *The teacher focused on the most important aspect of her job.* The words that follow the colon, *student achievement*, describe or define the most important aspect of her job. *She went to the store and bought several items for the party: party bags, paper plates, plastic cutlery, and decorations.* In this example, the independent clause is *She went to the store and bought several items for the party.* The list follows the colon.
5.	D	The way the sentence is written, the subject, *teacher*, is singular but the pronoun, *they*, is plural. This means the sentence does not have pronoun antecedent agreement. To fix this, make the subject plural so that there is pronoun/antecedent agreement. You may be tempted to change the pronoun *they* to *his or her*. However, this makes the writing awkward. The question asks for the <u>best</u> revision. Answer D is the best revision.
6.	B	In this case, the word *perfect* is a synonym context clue. Therefore, the most appropriate action is to use the restatement or synonym context approach to figuring out the word.
7.	B	Modeling is always an effective practice. In addition, modeling the use of erudite words in the classroom will pique students' interest in the words, promoting word consciousness.
8.	A	Tier II words are words that occur across contexts. More common in writing and everyday speech, these words enhance comprehension of a text. These words are best used for targeted explicit vocabulary instruction. Answer A is the best choice. You may be tempted to choose answer D. However, matching pictures to words is a beginning skill and the teacher is moving students from tier I words to tier II words. Answer A is most effective.

Number	Answer	Explanation
9.	D	Tier III words are low-frequency words. They are limited to a specific domain. They often pertain to a specific content area. They are best learned within the content of the lesson or subject matter. Examples: molecule, mitochondria
10.	B	Using context is one of the best ways to help students understand complex vocabulary. In addition, it makes the most sense when a student is reading. All the other answer choices break up the reading.
11.	B	Receptive vocabulary includes reading and listening skills. The only activity where students are using receptive vocabulary is listening to a story on tape. All the other answer choices work on expressive vocabulary.
12.	C	Expressive vocabulary includes speaking and writing skills. The only activity where students are using expressive vocabulary is discussion. All the other answer choices work on receptive vocabulary.
13.	A	Listening and speaking vocabulary are the beginning skills students acquire first, making Answer A most appropriate for these students.
14.	D	Allowing the students to sort the words according to their own criteria helps them come up with their own system of interacting with the words, which promotes word consciousness. Semantic cueing would be if the teacher told students they must sort by meaning. Syntactic cueing would be if the teacher told students they must sort by word structure. Systematic word recognition would be if students were memorizing the words and then recognizing them as they read.
15.	B	Allowing students to use idioms in conversation is providing students with a real-world application, which is always a best practice. In addition, the students find common idioms in their own language to help them understand meaning. None of the other answer choices are as effective as Answer B. You may be tempted to use context. However, idioms don't use context. For example, context cannot be applied to the common idiom *it was raining cats and dogs*.
16.	C	The primary purpose of teaching dialect in English language arts class is to expose students to the cultural diversity and variations in language. Dialects reflect regional, social, and cultural differences, and studying dialects helps students appreciate and understand the rich linguistic diversity present in different communities. It encourages empathy, respect, and recognition of the value of various dialects, rather than promoting the idea that one dialect is superior to others.
17.	B	Answer B correctly joins two independent clauses with a comma and a conjunction. Answer A contains two simple sentences. Answer C incorrectly combines two sentences with only a conjunction. A comma is also needed for this to be correct. Answer D contains a comma splice, which is when two independent clauses are incorrectly combined with only a comma. In this case, a comma plus conjunction is needed.

Number	Answer	Explanation

Sentence	Simple	Compound
She was traveling just five miles over the speed limit, but she received a citation anyway.		X
The two girls went to spend time with their grandmother and their cousins.	X	
Marley was upset when she didn't win the race, but she was a good sport about it.		X

18. See Chart

This page intentionally left blank.

III. Constructing Meaning

The following topics are aligned with the test specifications of the Praxis 7812. It is important that you examine these closely because these are the skills assessed on the exam.

A. Key Ideas and Details

B. Author's Craft and Text Structure

C. Integration and Application of Knowledge

D. Text Types

E. Text Production

F. Research Skills

G. Discussion and Collaboration

H. Presenting Ideas and Knowledge

A. Key Ideas and Details

Effective educators teach students how to read closely to determine explicit meaning from text. In addition, students must be able to make logical inferences and to cite specific textual evidence in support of conclusions. Requiring students to use evidence from the text to support their claims is an overarching theme in all English language arts instructional standards.

The following table contains strategies used to help students develop both literary and informational reading skills. The following strategies also help students develop metacognition, which is essential in reading comprehension and understanding key ideas and details in text.

Activity	Definition	Example
Jigsaw	A cooperative learning activity in which each student or groups of students read and analyze a small piece of information that is part of a much larger piece. They share what they learned with the class.	Teachers arrange students in groups. Each group reads and analyzes a piece of a text. Group members then join with members of other groups, and each student shares and discusses his or her section of the text. As the group shares, the entire text is covered. It is referred to as *Jigsaw* because students complete the puzzle when they share their individual pieces.
Chunking	A reading activity that involves breaking down a difficult text into manageable pieces.	In a science class, students break down a lengthy and complex chapter on genetics by focusing on pieces of the text. The teacher has planned for students to read and analyze the text one paragraph at a time.
Close Reading	Involves the use of evidence-based comprehension strategies embedded in teacher-guided discussions that are planned around repeated readings of a text.	Teacher reads the text aloud and models metacognitive strategies. Students and teacher read the text aloud together and answer guiding questions. In cooperative groups, students reread the text, analyzing it for different elements.

Activity	Definition	Example
Think-Pair-Share	A cooperative learning activity in which students work together to solve a problem or answer a question.	**Think** – The teacher asks a specific question about the text. Students "think" about what they know or have learned about the topic. **Pair** – Students pair up to read and discuss. **Share** - Students share what they've learned in their pairs. Teachers can then expand the "share" into a whole-class discussion.
Reading Response Journals	A writing activity where students use journals to react to what they read by expressing how they feel and asking questions about the text.	After reading a chapter of a book in class, the teacher asks students to use their reading response journals to respond to the story emotionally, make associations between ideas in the text and their own ideas, and record questions they may have about the story.
Evidence-Based Discussion	The teacher sets the expectation that students use evidence in the text to support claims they make during the discussion.	The class is discussing World War II. Students are asking and answering questions. When making claims, students identify support for those claims in the text.
Literature Circles	A small-group, cooperative learning activity where students engage and discuss a piece of literature/text.	In their cooperative groups, students read and analyze text together. Each student contributes to the learning. There is an administrator who decides when to read and when to stop and discuss. There is a note taker who writes down important information. There are two readers who take turns reading the text based on the administrator's suggestions.
Reciprocal Teaching	An instructional activity in which students become the teacher in small group reading sessions.	After engaging in a close read of a piece of literary text, students facilitate questions, exercises, and discussion in small groups.

Question-Answer Relationships (QAR)

Students can categorize the types of questions they engage in before, during, and after reading. When students us the strategy question-answer relationships (QAR) they categorize questions in four ways:

1. **Right there.** These are literal questions with answers that can be found directly in the text. Teachers will often say, "You can point to these answers directly in the text."

2. **Think and search.** Answers are gathered from several parts of the text and put together to make meaning.

3. **Author and you.** For these questions, students are required to relate their own experience to the reading. This can also be referred to as text-to-self. They have to use their schema or background knowledge to answer these questions.

4. **On my own.** Students must use their background or prior knowledge to answer these types of questions.

SQ3R

This is a comprehensive reading activity that stands for:

- **Survey.** Students scan titles, headings, charts, graphs, etc. to get a feel for the entire text.
- **Question.** Students turn the headings and subheadings into questions and answer these questions as they read.
- **Read.** Students read the text for comprehension.
- **Recite.** Students begin to answer the questions they generated.
- **Review.** Students summarize what they have read.

Cooperative learning

Cooperative learning is when students work in small groups to read and analyze text. Cooperative learning is most effective when it is structured and when every student has a role in the outcome of the reading activity.

Apply strategies that promote close reading of text.

Close reading requires students to read and reread text for different purposes. Below is just one method that teachers and students can use to close. Keep in mind, the teacher and the students are using the same piece of text during multiple reads.

1. Review the objective of the reading.
2. Quickly scan the page for headings or bolded words. Discuss those.
3. Teacher reads as students follow along, circling any confusing words.
4. The teacher rereads and thinks aloud about any confusing words.
5. Students then read to determine if the passage is expository, persuasive, narrative, or descriptive.
6. Students then partner read using accuracy, prosody, and automaticity.

Notice that the students have read the same passage 3-4 times for different reasons.

Test Tip

Close reading is considered a best practice for reading comprehension. If you see close reading as an option in an answer choice, it is most likely the correct answer. In addition, it may not say close reading and may instead describe close reading. Therefore, you should be able to identify it based on a description of the strategy.

Analysis is a high-level skill that involves several processes in the brain. Teaching students to analyze text is a complex process involving comprehension and metacognition. At times, students struggle to read for surface comprehension, so when they are asked to analyze text, they struggle to know what that means and how to do it. There is no simple checklist to give students for analytical reading. Teachers must model the skills.

Analysis of text involves two crucial processes: metacognition and comprehension.

Metacognition is thinking about thinking or being aware of the thought process. When students have metacognition, they understand the processes in their minds and can employ a variety of techniques to understand text. The most effective way to model metacognition in English language arts is through a read aloud/think aloud strategy. Below are two examples of a read aloud/think aloud strategy. In both scenarios, the teacher is sharing the thought process aloud as she reads.

- A teacher is reading aloud an excerpt from *Brave New World* by Aldous Huxley. When she gets to complex vocabulary, she stops and shares her thought process. "That's a word I've never seen before. Let me read around it to see if I can figure it out."
- A teacher is reading *Macbeth* by William Shakespeare. When she discovers a connection to the real world, she stops and talks about it. She models the connection between text and the real world.

Comprehension is a high-level cognitive skill essential in analyzing text. Students must make connections, access and apply prior knowledge, and think deeply about the text. This type of critical thinking while reading involves moving beyond memorization; it involves evaluating all elements of the text and deriving meaning from them. Reading comprehension skills include questioning, summarizing, and predicting.

- **Questioning.** Having students ask questions based on what they are reading.

- **Summarizing.** Asking students to summarize what they just read in their own words.

- **Predicting.** Asking students what they think will happen next.

*All the above strategies are considered higher order/critical thinking and can be employed before, during, and after reading.

Quick Tip

Modeling is an effective practice for helping students comprehend complex text. When teachers model how to approach difficult text and demonstrate their thought process to students (also known as a read aloud/ think aloud), students can then employ those practices during independent reading.

Sematic and syntactic structures, imagery, and diction

Analysis of text also requires students to understand semantic and syntactic structures, imagery, and diction. These elements of text can help students derive complex meanings from text.

Attribute	Definition	Classroom Scenario
Semantic structures	Semantics is the study of meaning in language.	A teacher would like students to determine the connotative meaning of words. She writes the following sentences on board and asks students to analyze the meaning of the word *black*. *The issue was black and white.* *The future is Black.*
Syntactic structures	Grammatical/ sentence structure	A teacher would like to illustrate how syntax can help the reader determine emotion in a text. She asks students to analyze repetition and sentence length. In groups, students try to determine the meaning of a repetitive syntactic structure and change in sentence length (e.g., from long to short sentences).
Imagery	Appealing to a reader's senses by using descriptive, sensory language	Students are asked to write a paragraph describing an experience in which they felt scared. To appeal to the reader's senses, one student writes the following sentence: *"The room was dark and cold."*
Diction	The style of speaking and writing; the choice of words	The teacher is instructing students on informal and formal diction. She asks students to write on one distinct topic in two different ways. She shows the following sentences to the class to illustrate the difference: Formal: "I am not optimistic about this new opportunity." Informal: "I'm not cool with this new situation."

Learning how to construct meaning is a significant step of the reading process. Students can use a variety of strategies to improve understanding while reading. To become strategic readers, students need to be explicitly taught how to use their thinking to understand text.

Strategy	Description
Activating prior knowledge	This pre-reading strategy asks students what they already know about a topic to provide a framework, or schema, to tie the new information to. A KWL chart— What do you know (K), what do you want to know (W), what did you learn (L)— is helpful for this strategy.
Schema building	Schema is stored clusters of concepts or knowledge from previous experiences. Schema and background knowledge are synonymous. Schema building can be applied in the classroom to improve the learning experience. One way to build schema is to help readers actively relate their own knowledge to ideas in the text.
Clarifying	Also called the "fix up" strategy, this is a during-reading strategy where students monitor their comprehension by asking questions, re-reading, and searching for context clues when the text is confusing.
Generating questions	Students ask and answer questions at key points in the text in this during-reading strategy. This strategy is also effective for facilitating discussion about the text.
Paraphrasing	This can happen at key points during reading or after reading. It is similar to retelling and summarizing but takes those strategies a step further by incorporating the new knowledge into student thinking. It is effective for monitoring comprehension because the student cannot reword what the author said if he or she does not understand what the author said. It is an easy formative assessment to guide future instructional support.
Analyzing	Analysis happens during close reads and after the reading is over. Students reread key pieces of text with a specific task or question in mind, developing deeper levels of understanding.
Summarizing	This after-reading strategy requires the student to synthesize the details and information presented in the text into a statement that sums up the main idea.

Graphic organizers

A graphic organizer is a visual and graphic display that depicts the relationships between facts, terms, and ideas within a text. Most English language arts teachers use graphic organizers to help students organize information as they read. Graphic organizers are effective for all students, but they are especially effective for visual learners. Common types of graphic organizers include:

KWL charts are used to activate or build background knowledge. KWL stands for:

- **(K)** What do you know?
- **(W)** What do you want to know?
- **(L)** What did you learn?

K Before reading	W Before and during reading	L After reading

Venn diagrams are used to compare and contrast characters, content, or events in the text.

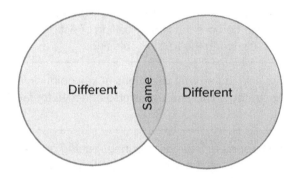

Mind maps are diagrams to visually organize ideas and concepts. The central idea or concept is placed in the center of the diagram, and then related ideas are added.

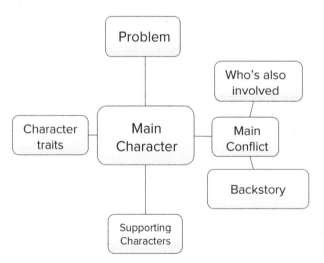

B. Author's Craft and Text Structure

Understanding structural elements of text can positively impact students' literacy skills. When students understand the structure of text, they can construct, examine, and extend the meaning, which leads to a depth of understanding of the text.

Text structure refers to how the information is organized in the text and can help students identify the following elements of the text.

- **Main Idea and Details.** The story or passage has an overarching viewpoint or idea and then supports that idea with details throughout the text.
- **Compare and Contrast.** The story or text finds similarities and differences between and among people, places, and situations.
- **Chronological.** The story or passage goes in order by time.
- **Cause and Effect.** The story or passage presents something that happens and then the result or effect of an action.
- **Problem and Solution.** The story or passage presents a problem and then possible solutions to the problem.
- **Inferences.** The story contains a conclusion based on evidence and reasoning. A logical "guess" based on something that is happening in the story.
- **Key Details.** The story contains words or phrases that help the reader answer questions about the text. Key details give information by asking questions like who, what, where, when, and why.

C. Integration and Application of Knowledge

Teachers must show students how to integrate and evaluate information and ideas across various texts, formats, and media. This includes critiquing the legitimacy of arguments by evaluating the validity of reasoning and the relevance and sufficiency of evidence. More importantly, this includes identifying the relationship between evidence and a claim.

Students can do this in a variety of ways. First, they should integrate information across multiple texts to synthesize it. For example, students can use newspaper articles, firsthand accounts, research, and stories to evaluate the validity of the ideas presented.

Example Question:

A third-grade class is reading a story about the Great Depression. The teacher wants to help students to gain a broad understanding of what it was like during this time in history. Which of the following would be most effective in meeting this goal?

A. Use a variety of texts, such as newspaper articles, stories, and letters from that time and have students explain how each one conveys meaning.

B. Allow students to watch a video on the Great Depression before reading the text to activate background knowledge.

C. Have students work in groups so they can express to each other how the text makes them feel about the Great Depression.

D. Use the textbook as the main source of information so students can identify facts first before they come to any conclusions.

Correct Answer: A

Using a variety of text types to gain a broader understanding of the Great Depression is most effective for the goal. Students can analyze the ways in which each type of text conveys the feelings of those who lived the experience. Students can also cross reference these sources to validate ideas.

Students can also compare different author approaches or ideas and analyze how various formats contribute to meaning, tone, or beauty of text. For example, students might look at the format of a letter and identify ways it is different from an expository text on the same topic.

Test Tip

The term *text variety* is a good word on any English language arts exam. This means the teacher is using a selection of narrative, expository, persuasive, cause and effect, chronological text to help students gain a broader understanding of the ideas expressed. Using the textbook as the primary mode of information is never the correct answer.

Finally, illustrations and other visual representations within a text support reader understanding.

Example Question

Which of the following would be most effective in helping kindergarten students read and understand text?

   A. The teacher reads the text aloud for students.

   B. The teacher has students work in pairs to read the text.

   C. The teacher goes over the vocab in the text before reading.

   D. The teacher uses images to support information in the text.

Correct Answer: D

Using images to support the text is the best answer, especially for early readers. Visuals that accompany test help to increase students' understanding.

D. Text Types

Using a balanced literary approach is key when teaching students how to read. A balanced literacy program uses a combination of informational and literary texts.

Text Type	Examples
Informational Text	Written primarily to inform Literary nonfiction History/social science texts Science/technical texts Digital texts
Literary Text	Adventure Folktales Legends Fables Fantasy Realistic fiction

Text structure and comprehension

Text structure refers to how the information is organized in the text. Understanding text structure and text features can help students with their comprehension. Effective English language arts teachers implement strategies for text analysis in their English language arts curriculum and instruction. If students can identify the clues that tell them the structure of the passage, they can make more sense of the information presented. The following are the main types of text structures.

Text Structure	Description	Clue Words/Phrases
Narrative	The purpose of narrative text is to entertain or present a personal story.	Written in first-person narrative (I, me, us, we)
Expository	This type of text explains a phenomenon or situation without personal option. It is informational.	Written in third-person narrative (he, she, they, them)
Argumentative/ Persuasive	This includes writing that is for or against an issue.	Persuasive text includes certain elements: claim, reason, evidence, counterclaim, and rebuttal.
Cause/effect	Authors use this structure when they want to establish a causal relationship between an event and the events that come after.	because of, as a result of, due to, for this reason, in order to, since, the cause, as a result, therefore, then/so, this led to, thus, so, consequently
Chronological/ sequential	Events in this structure are organized in chronological order (and sometimes reverse chronological order).	after, at, before, during, finally, first, second, third, last, next, then, until
Compare/ contrast	Authors communicate the similarities and differences between a set of events, concepts, ideas, or people.	more/less, in contrast to, in spite of, instead of, nevertheless, on the other hand, rather than, similarly, still, though, unlike, as, as opposed to, however, despite, likewise, either/or
Descriptive	Authors use descriptive language to paint a picture for the reader.	for example, for instance, looks like, sounds like, feels like, any descriptive adjectives
Problem/ solution	Authors present an issue or set of issues and possible solutions, then examine the effects of the solutions presented.	because, one part of, as a result, consequently, if/then, remedy, solution, problem, issue
Question/ answer	A question is posed at the beginning, and the author answers the question during the text.	answer, it could be that, one may conclude, perhaps, problem, question, solution, the best estimate, how, what, when, who, why

Note: In addition to using the clue words to identify text structure, students can also analyze a chapter or a stanza and determine how it fits into the overall text structure.

Components of informational text

There are several tools authors use to help organize and support the central idea of informational text. These include:

- **Table of contents** – Outline of the text with page references
- **Headings** – Bold words or phrases that separate the text by main idea
- **Diagrams and pictures** – Visual aids to support the text
- **Glossary** – Definitions of key terms used in the text
- **Index** – Page references for key terms used in the text

E. Text Production

Writing clearly and coherently can be challenging for elementary-age students. Therefore, teachers must provide students with tools to help with the writing process. There are several ways teachers can help students write clearly and coherently.

- **Organization.** It is important that students organize their writing by first mapping what they are going to write. Mind maps and other graphic organizers can help students do this.
- **Transition words.** These words connect parts of a paragraph to one another. Helping students identify the right transitional words is useful in coherent writing.
- **Cooperative learning.** These writing workshops help students revise their writing. Peer reviews, brainstorming sessions, and editing roundtables can help students revise their writing in an effective manner. It is important to remember that for cooperative learning to be effective, it must be organized, and everyone in the group must have a role.
- **Frameworks.** These formulas allow students to follow a step-by-step structure as they write. This allows students to plug their information into the pre-established formula. As the students get more proficient in writing, they can modify or abandon the formula.
- **Rubrics.** These assessment tools outline expectations for student writing. Students should not have to guess what the teacher wants to see in the writing assignment. Rubrics outline a set of parameters that help students focus their writing.

On the exam, you will be required to identify effective instructional methods for teaching writer's craft. Writer's craft is the techniques, language, and approaches used in writing to make the writing appealing to the reader. Writer's craft includes using:

Linking words (transition words) – These are words that link two ideas and are used to provide sentence variety in writing. Linking words include:

- For example
- In addition
- However
- Therefore

Precise language – Language that clarifies or identifies specific details. When students use precise language, they are using details that allow the reader or listener to understand the story.

Figurative language – Using metaphor, imagery, hyperbole, etc. in writing to make the writing interesting. Examples include:

Examples Literary Devices

Device	Definition	Examples
Simile	Using *like* or *as*	*She was as thin as a rail.*
Imagery	A description that conveys a clear picture to the reader	*The big, juicy burger with its melted cheese and ripe tomatoes made my mouth water.*
Metaphor	Applying word or phrase to an individual or thing	*He was a lion filled with rage.*
Personification	Attributing human characteristics to something not human	*The cat judged me from across the room.*
Onomatopoeia	The formation of a word from a sound associated with it	*Sizzle, kurplunk, POW!, BAM!*
Hyperbole	Exaggerated statements or claims not meant to be taken literally.	*The cake must have weighed 500 pounds!*
Idioms	A word or phrase that means something different from its literal meaning	*It's raining cats and dogs.*
Alliteration	When words that start with the same sound are used repeatedly in a phrase or sentence.	*Paul picked purple pickles in pink pants.*
Irony	Expression of one's meaning by using language that normally signifies the opposite, typically for humorous or emphatic effect.	*It was raining on National Picnic Day.*
Foreshadow	When the author uses clues or imagery to express what might happen next.	*The dark spot on the ceiling grew bigger and bigger.* This is written before a pipe bursts and floods the house.

Temporal words– These are used to indicate time. These words include:

- Meanwhile
- At that moment
- Before
- After
- Then
- Next

Dialogue – Use to show a conversation or verbal exchange between characters.

- The woman ran into the room shouting, "They've robbed the bank!"

Sentence variety – Refers to the practice of varying the length and structure of sentences to avoid monotony and provide appropriate emphasis on certain words. It makes the writing lively and unpredictable, which is pleasing to the reader. Using transition words, punctuation, and complex sentences all contribute to sentence variety.

- These sentences lack variety: *He went to the store. He bought a candy bar. He was happy.*

- This sentence has variety: *He went to the story and bought a candy bar, which made him happy.*

Test Tip

The term sentence variety is a good phrase on the exam. Teachers must teach students to move from robotic, short sentences to nuanced .

Effective writing teachers guide students through the stages of writing by using appropriate strategies and practices in the classroom.

Stages of the writing process

- **Pre-writing** – Brainstorming, considering purpose and goals for writing, using graphic organizers to connect ideas, and designing a coherent structure for a writing piece.
- **Drafting** – Working independently to draft the sentence, essay, or paper.
- **Peer review** – Students evaluate each other's writing in the peer review process.
- **Revising** – Reworking a piece of writing based on structure, tone, and clear connections.
- **Editing** – Editing based on conventions and mechanics.
- **Rewriting** – Incorporating changes as they carefully write or type their final drafts.
- **Publishing** – Producing and disseminating the work in a variety of ways, such as a class book, bulletin board, letters to the editor, school newsletter, or website.

Appropriate modes of writing

According to the Common Core State Standards for English language arts, students must demonstrate the following:

- Adapt their communication in relation to audience, task, purpose, and discipline.
- Set and adjust purpose from reading, writing, speaking, listening, and language use as warranted by the task.
- Appreciate nuances, such as how the composition of an audience should affect tone when speaking and how the connotations of words affect meaning.
- Know that different disciplines call for different types of evidence.

Teachers can help students meet these standards by supporting students' use of tone and purpose. Students must also use appropriate writing for the intended audience.

- **Tone.** This refers to the overall feeling of the piece of writing. When writing a narrative vs. an opinion, the tone or position may be different depending on the content. The tone will convey a specific attitude toward the audience and the subject. For example, *Pete the Cat* by Eric Litwin and James Dean expresses an optimistic tone. Pete the Cat runs into various obstacles but eventually prevails by having a positive attitude.

- **Purpose.** This refers to the reason for the piece of writing. Is the student writing to persuade, to entertain, or to explain? For example, if a student is writing to her state representative to pass a new law, the student should write a persuasive essay. However, if a student is writing to her grandmother to describe how summer camp is going, the student should write a narrative. Establishing a purpose for the piece of writing is an important step in the writing process.

- **Audience.** This refers to the individuals reading the piece of writing. As explained above, a student will write very differently in a letter to her grandmother than in a letter to her congressional representative. Understanding the audience is a key component of the writing process.

Rubrics

Rubrics are used to convey expectations and criteria of an assessment. Rubrics are often used to grade students' writing. Rubrics provide an explicit breakdown of the elements assessed. Rubrics also provide teachers with a framework to implement specific and meaningful feedback.

Rubrics should be given to students:

- **Before** writing to convey explicit expectations.

- **During** writing so students can check their progress.

- **After** writing to communicate grades/progress.

Example Rubric			
	1 – Minimal	**2 – Meets**	**3 – Exceeds**
Mechanics (Syntactic)	Many spelling, grammar, and punctuation errors; sentence fragments; incorrect use of capitalization.	Some spelling and grammar errors; most sentences have punctuation and are complete; uses uppercase and lowercase letters.	Correct spelling, grammar, and punctuation; complete sentences; correct use of capitalization.
Ideas and Content (Semantic)	Key words are not near the beginning; no clear topic; no beginning, middle, and end; ideas are not ordered.	Main idea or topic is in first sentence; semi-defined topic; attempts beginning, middle and end sections; some order of main idea and details in sequence.	Interesting, well-stated main idea or topic sentence; uses logical plan with an effective beginning, middle, and end; good flow of ideas from topic sentence to details in sequence.
Organization	Very unorganized and confusing.	Organized enough to read and understand the ideas.	Very organized and easy to understand.

Writing Workshops

Writing workshops provide a student-centered approach where students are given time, choice, and voice in their learning. Students will read each other's work and provide feedback on content, organization, and structure.

It is important that the teacher models and practices how to use writing workshops. This activity takes time to master and to use properly. The steps for writing workshops include:

- **Mini lesson.** A brief, focused, explicit lesson that helps children understand and apply the characteristics of effective writing. This is teacher-led and includes going over the workshop expectations and steps, modeling proper writing, and using examples to clarify information.
- **Work time.** A session when students work on their writing. This is usually done individually. Students will draft and briefly proof their work.
- **Share time.** This is when students work with a partner or in small groups to read over each other's work and provide feedback. It is helpful to provide students a rubric for this portion of the workshop because they will need guidance on what to provide feedback on.

F.   Research Skills

Effective teachers help students conduct research and gather relevant information. The focus of this instruction should be associated with a question, topic, or other form of inquiry. Teachers do this by helping students:

- Locate, select, and gather relevant information from reputable sources.
- Recall and organize information from relevant informational and literary text.
- Use evidence to support analysis.
- Analyze and reflect on evidence in literary text by comparing and contrasting characters, settings, and events.
- Analyze and reflect on evidence in informational text by explaining how an author uses reasons and evidence to support claims.
- Determine the credibility, accuracy, and biases of sources.

Text Credibility

Students should be given the opportunity to examine all kinds of information—newspaper articles, blogs, academic journals, stories, and more. However, teachers must help students discern what sources are credible and what sources might contain bias information.

Quick Tip

The most credible resources for students to use when conducting research are peer-reviewed academic journals— sources that have been rigorously reviewed by experts in the field. These publications present evidence free from bias. They also contain a bibliography that further supports the information in the writing.

Example Question:

If students want to evaluate the credibility of a source, which of the following would be most effective?

    A. Look over the table of contents.

    B. Determine if the author is well known.

    C. Evaluate the bibliography or references in the text.

    D. See if other researchers agree with what is presented in the text.

Correct Answer: C

The bibliography and references of where the author of the text found the information will help students analyze the information presented. Also, when a text contains a bibliography, it means that the author used other sources to support claims in the text.

Primary and Secondary Sources

Teachers must use a combination of primary and secondary sources to help students evaluate information.

Primary sources are firsthand accounts from people who had direct contact with the event. Examples of primary sources are:

- Autobiographies (written by the person who experienced the event)
- Oral histories
- Memoirs
- Letters
- Diaries
- Speeches
- Photographs

Secondary sources attempt to explain the primary source. For example, a newspaper article about Martin Luther King's "I Have a Dream" speech is a secondary source. The speech itself is the primary source. Secondary sources include:

- Biographies (written by someone other than the person who experienced the events)
- Newspaper articles
- Textbooks
- Political commentary
- Dictionaries
- Encyclopedias

Citations

Teaching students to properly cite their sources should start early. Even elementary teachers can help students develop these good habits. There will not be very many questions on this specific concept, but be sure to understand the following table.

Source	Format	Bibliography/Works Cited	In-Text Citation
Book	APA	Gleick, James. *Chaos: Making a New Science*. Penguin, 1987.	(Tolstoy, 1969)
	MLA	Tolstoy, L. (1869). War and peace. Moscow: Viking.	(Sullivan 120)

Source	Format	Bibliography/Works Cited	In-Text Citation
Journal article	APA	Wegener, D. T., & Petty, R. E. (1994). Mood management across affective states: The hedonic contingency hypothesis. *Journal of Personality and Social Psychology, 66*, 1034-1048.	(Wegener & Petty, 1994)
	MLA	Burgess, Anthony. "Politics in the Novels of Graham Greene." Literature and Society, special issue of Journal of Contemporary History, vol. 2, no. 2, 1967, pp. 93-99.	(Burgess 94)
Website	APA	Purr, J. (2019). *How to get certified*. Retrieved from https://www.website.com on August 10, 2023	(Purr, 2019)
	MLA	Dunn, Sally. "Pass Your English Test." www.website.com/ Accessed 5 August 23.	(Dunn, "Pass Your English Test")

Quick Tip

Websites provide a lot of relevant information for research. Remember, when students cite websites, they must include the date the website was accessed. That is a distinguishing part of citing online sources versus print sources.

G. Discussion and Collaboration

On the exam, you will have to identify ways to help students use social cues in discourse to communicate clearly and persuasively. You will also have to identify the best way to help students develop active listening skills.

This includes teaching students how to:

- Take turns to speak.
- Be respectful to others who are speaking.
- Acknowledge others when they are speaking.
- Clarify information.
- Build on other students' ideas when responding in discussion.
- Ask and answer clarifying questions.
- Paraphrase what other students have said before responding.
- Use evidence from the text to support discussion points.

Characteristics of Active Listening

Active listening is engaging in the conversation by asking questions and restating parts of the conversation. This shows comprehension or understanding of what the speaker is saying. There are questions a teacher can ask to show that she is listening to what the speaker is saying. A teacher can use this technique to improve relationships, make students feel cared for, make students feel understood, and make learning easier. Feedback is a big part of active listening.

Steps in the active listening process are as follows:

- Look at the person. Put everything else away and pay attention to the speaker.
- Listen to the words and understand how the speaker is feeling.
- Be interested in what the person is talking about.
- Restate what is being said.
- Ask questions for clarification.
- Be aware of your own opinions and feelings on the subject.
- Restate what the speaker has said. For example, "I hear you when you say, 'I think the story is about...'"

Appropriate feedback for active listening can be done verbally and nonverbally.

Verbal Signals	Non-Verbal Signals
"I'm listening"	Appropriate eye contact (when culturally appropriate)
Disclosures	Facial expressions
Statements of validation	Body language
Support statements	Silence
Reflecting/mirroring statements	Nodding

Technology

The goal of technology integration is always to improve students' analytical skills. They will need experience and assistance with this. Some strategies for using technology include the following:

- Databases for research sources
- Collaborative activities using document sharing software, such as Google Docs
- Virtual field trips to build background knowledge and schema
- Class blogs to communicate personal experiences
- Digital publishing tools for yearbooks and school newspapers

H. Presenting Ideas and Knowledge

Effective teachers help students organize and present information in a style appropriate for the audience and purpose. This includes the ability to:

- Sequence ideas logically. This helps students to organize and present ideas in a comprehensible manner. This is done through writing and speaking.
- Use the text to present facts and relevant details to support claims. Students can have opinions about a topic, but they should be encouraged to support those opinions with the text.
- Speak clearly and at an understandable pace. Teaching students how to think about their ideas and communicate them effectively is important.

- Use a speaking style, register, and dialect appropriate for the given context. Students must learn how to adapt their speaking style based on the audience.
- Use digital and visual media to express ideas. Teachers must help students use pictures, charts, graphs, and video that enhance their presentations.

Example Question

A fifth-grade teacher is helping students develop speeches about the current dress code that they will conduct at the next school board meeting. The following is an excerpt from a student's speech.

The current dress code is unfair and does not allow us to express ourselves. My friends and I use our clothes to show who we are. Being restricted to just long pants and collared shirts is unfair. We want to wear fun clothes. I know we will do better in school if we are allowed to wear what we want.

Which **TWO** of the following should the teacher focus on to help this student revise this piece of written for its intended audience.

- ☐ A. Use relevant evidence to support how a more relaxed dress code leads to more student engagement.
- ☐ B. Change the speech from first-person to third-person narrative.
- ☐ C. Use more description about what types of clothes are permitted under the current dress code.
- ☐ D. Use transitional words to connect sentences in the speech.
- ☐ E. Use pictures to enhance the student's position and to make the presentation more relatable.

Correct Answer: A & B

The student asserts that students will do better in school if they are permitted to wear what they want. This is a claim that is unsupported. Using relevant information to support that claim would help the intended audience to consider the assertion. In addition, first-person narrative is informal and typically used in narrative and editorial writing and speaking. Changing the speech to third-person narrative will give the student's position more legitimacy, especially since the intended audience is the school board.

Articulation

Students must develop proper articulation when they are speaking and presenting. Articulation is the formation of clear and distinct sounds in speech. This can be practiced a variety of ways:

- The teacher can model proper articulation.
- The teacher can highlight target sounds.
- Students can practice reading aloud rhyming poems.
- Students can use repeated reading focusing on targeted sounds.

Constructing Meaning Practice Questions

1. Which of the following should the teacher consider when using media literacy in the classroom?

    A. Who authored the media?

    B. Who is speaking in the media?

    C. What is the appropriate age of the media?

    D. Is the media aligned to the state standards?

2. A teacher is helping students understand the writing process and the organization of ideas within an essay. What should be her instructional focus?

    A. Grammar

    B. Revision

    C. Brainstorming

    D. Peer review

3. Which of the following question guides would be most helpful for students conducting peer-reviews in their writing workshops?

    A. The title of the story was _____.

    B. I liked this _____ part because _____.

    C. The author of the story is _____.

    D. The number of sentences in the story is _____.

4. Which of the following is the benefit of using document-sharing software instead of using word processing software?

    A. Document-sharing software allows the students to see their grammar and spelling mistakes in real time.

    B. Document-sharing software allows the teacher to determine easily if a student has plagiarized material from the Internet.

    C. Document-sharing software allows the student to incorporate a rubric into the writing assignment.

    D. Document-sharing software allows several students to collaborate on a piece of writing in real time.

5. Students are deciding whether to write a persuasive essay or an expository essay. What should students consider first?

    A. Audience

    B. Length

    C. Publication

    D. Genre

6. Which **TWO** of the following would be most effective for fourth-grade students who are working on an expository essay in social studies about the Great Depression?

   ☐ A. Internet search engine guidelines for appropriate websites

   ☐ B. Writing workshops where students can peer-review each other's papers

   ☐ C. Self-evaluation checklist that outlines proper expository writing practices

   ☐ D. A video on how to write an expository essay

   ☐ D. Newspaper articles that show political cartoons from that time.

7. At the beginning of the year, the fifth-grade language arts teachers worked in their professional learning communities to outline practices that would help their students move to an independent writing process. In which of the following practices are students involved in the writing process at the most independent level?

   A. Teacher and students think aloud as students brainstorm topics.

   B. Students work in groups to review each other's essays.

   C. Students watch videos on how to effectively proof and revise essays.

   D. Students use a graphic organizer to organize their essays while the teacher observes.

8. Which **THREE** of the following would be the most relevant example of how persuasive writing is used?

   ☐ A. An advertisement on the latest cell phone

   ☐ B. An editorial in the local newspaper

   ☐ C. A news article on the Internet

   ☐ D. A political ad for an upcoming election

   ☐ E. A biography of a controversial figure

9. Third-grade students are working on personal narratives about their summer. The teacher realizes that they need some support regarding description and organization in their writing. Which **TWO** of the following would help students most in this situation?

   ☐ A. Provide the student with a list of descriptive words and phrases they can use in their writing.

   ☐ B. Have students use a graphic organizer to categorize events in their writing.

   ☐ C. Remind students that description is important and to focus on variety in their writing.

   ☐ D. Tell students to read their essays aloud to a partner and suggest revisions.

   ☐ E. Provide students with extra time to organize their essays.

10. A teacher is modeling the process of reading comprehension. The teacher uses context clues to figure out difficult words. The teacher stops to think aloud and predict, summarize, and ask questions. What skill is the teacher modeling?

    A. Fluency

    B. Vocabulary

    C. Metacognition

    D. Reading aloud

Number	Answer	Explanation
1.	D	Alignment to the state standards is most important when choosing activities and materials for the classroom.
2.	B	Because the teacher is helping students work on reorganization of ideas, revision is the most effective focus. Grammar is about mechanics, brainstorming is about generating ideas, and peer review is when students review each other's work. Remember, *revision* is a good word in writing instruction.
3.	B	Peer reviews are used for content and understanding, and answer B is the most appropriate guide for this purpose.
4.	D	Document-sharing software is beneficial because students can collaborate on a piece of writing in real time. This is why teachers use Google Docs. You will not see the words Google Docs on the test because that is a brand name.
5.	A	One of the most important components of writing is the ability to adapt communication in relation to audience, task, purpose, and discipline. Length, publication, and genre are not important considerations.
6.	B & C	Both writing workshops and a self-evaluation checklist are beneficial for this task. A writing workshop with a peer review will help students with their overall ideas and structure of their writing. A self-evaluation checklist that outlines expository text does two things: reinforces recursive practices in writing and helps students stay on track with what is expected.
7.	D	In answer D, the teacher is observing, and students are working on their own. Out of all the answer choices, students are most independent in answer D.
8.	A, B & D	Answers A, B, and D are the most related to the real world and are the best examples of persuasive writing in our everyday lives.
9.	A & B	Providing students with a list of descriptive words is effective in helping them come up with ideas for their writing. A graphic organizer would help students organize their essays. These are the two skills the teacher is trying to help students strengthen in this scenario. Answers C, D, and E are not as helpful or as related to the task as answers A and B.
10.	C	The teacher is modeling her thinking process and showing students how to think about their thinking. This is metacognition.

This page intentionally left blank.

1. Which of the following sets of words has identical rime?

    A. *chair* and *stain*

    B. *steam* and *step*

    C. *play* and *pay*

    D. *post* and *pest*

2. A teacher asks a student, Jose, to read aloud in class. As Jose reads aloud, he reads accurately and rarely misses a word. However, he reads so quickly that other students who follow along struggle to keep up with his pace. At the end of the reading, the teacher asks Jose some questions about the text. However, he has difficulty answering questions about what he has just read. Identify the deficit in reading Jose is displaying.

    A. While Jose has automaticity and fluency, he struggles with reading comprehension.

    B. While Jose has comprehension, he struggles with his reading rate.

    C. While Jose can read quickly, he is struggling with automaticity and prosody.

    D. While Jose has accuracy, he is struggling with fluency and word recognition.

3. A kindergarten teacher is working on the alphabetic principle with students. They are learning that letters make sounds. She starts with the letter A and then B, but when she gets to the letter C, she notices some of her students are confused. Why might her kindergarten students have difficulty decoding the letter C?

    A. The letter C can be decoded differently depending on its phoneme-grapheme correspondence.

    B. Students have difficulty tracing the letter C because of their underdeveloped fine motor skills.

    C. Most students cannot pronounce the letter C until third grade.

    D. English language learners pronounce the /c/ sound differently.

Questions 4-6 refer to the following scenario.

A teacher uses the following passage with students to read and discuss different elements of the work.

As technology continues to advance, the way people communicate and connect with each other has significantly changed. The rise of social media platforms and instant messaging apps has made technology immersive and changed the way individuals interact and share information. Today, people can connect with friends and family across the globe, join online communities based on shared interests, and engage in virtual discussions and debates.

The accessibility of information has revolutionized how people consume information. People now have access to a vast array of knowledge at their fingertips. Online wikis, educational websites, and digital libraries provide a wealth of information on various subjects. With just a few clicks, individuals can explore topics of interest, conduct research, and deepen their understanding of the world.

In addition to communication and information access, technology has also transformed the way people entertain themselves. Streaming services and online platforms offer a wide range of movies, TV shows, and music, allowing individuals to enjoy their favorite content at their convenience. In addition, online gaming has gained immense popularity, providing interactive and immersive experiences for players worldwide.

With the continuous advancements in technology, the ways people communicate, learn, and entertain themselves will continue to evolve, shaping the future of human interactions and experiences.

4. Identify the words in the passage the teacher can use to reinforce tier II vocabulary words.

   ☐   A.   revolutionized

   ☐   B.   immersive

   ☐   C.   wikis

   ☐   D.   accessibility

   ☐   E.   learn

   ☐   F.   future

5. Identify the context clue used in the passage to help students figure out the meaning of *immersive*.

   A.   A definition

   B.   A contrast

   C.   Examples

   D.   A synonym

6. The teacher asks students to identify the text structure the passage follows. Which student answered correctly?

   A.   Student A: Chronological

   B.   Student B: Descriptive

   C.   Student C: Cause and effect

   D.   Student D: Compare and contrast

7. A teacher is using an encoding activity where students write what the teacher says. The teacher uses simple sentences.

   The teacher says the following.

   I like to go to the beach.

   I will swim and play in the sand.

   One student writes the following.

   I lik to go to the bech

   I will sim and pl in the snd,

   Identify **TWO** words from the student's writing that indicate the student has phonemic awareness and has applied that skill to the spelling of the words chosen.

   ☐   A.   *lik* for *like*

   ☐   B.   *bech* for *beach*

   ☐   C.   *sim* for *swim*

   ☐   D.   *pl* for *play*

   ☐   E.   *snd* for *sand*

8. A teacher is helping students develop their personal narratives during a prewriting workshop. The teacher uses the following graphic organizer as an example for the lesson.

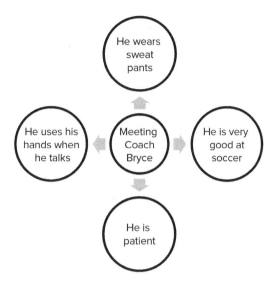

Identify the writing skills the teacher is focusing on for a personal narrative.

A. Narrowing the focus

B. Sequence

C. Developing conflict

D. Character development

Use the following poem, "Dreams" by Langston Hughes, for questions 9-10.

Hold fast to dreams
For if dreams die
Life is a broken-winged bird
That cannot fly.

Hold fast to dreams
For when dreams go
Life is a barren field
Frozen with snow.

9. In the poem "Dreams," the line "Life is a broken-winged bird" is an example of which type of figurative language?

A. Simile

B. Personification

C. Metaphor

D. Hyperbole

10. What is the central theme or message conveyed in the poem "Dreams"?

A. Dreams provide a sense of hope and inspiration.

B. Life without dreams is meaningless and unfulfilling.

C. Dreams have the power to make life extraordinary.

D. Holding onto dreams ensures a life of happiness and success.

11. Which literary device is used in the poem, "Dreams"?

    A. Repetition

    B. Alliteration

    C. Hyperbole

    D. Onomatopoeia

Use the following passage, "The Wind in the Willows" by Kenneth Grahame, for questions 12-14

One bright spring day, Mole decided to do something different. Tired of his underground home, he ventured outside to explore the world above. As he stepped onto the riverbank, he couldn't help but feel a sense of excitement and curiosity. The sights and sounds of nature surrounded him—the gentle rustling of leaves, the cheerful chirping of birds, and the sparkling blue waters of the river.

Mole's first encounter was with a friendly water rat named Rat, who was enjoying a leisurely boat ride. Rat invited Mole to join him, and they set off down the river, chatting and laughing along the way. Mole was captivated by the beauty of the countryside and the thrill of the river's current. He had never experienced anything quite like it before.

As they continued their journey, Rat introduced Mole to his dear friend Toad, a rather eccentric and impulsive creature. Toad was always seeking new adventures, but his latest obsession was motorcars. Toad whisked them away in his shiny new vehicle, laughing and shouting as they sped down the road. Mole held on tight, his heart pounding with both fear and exhilaration.

In the company of Rat and Toad, Mole discovered a world beyond his burrow that was filled with friendship, excitement, and unexpected escapades. Little did he know that this was just the beginning of their incredible adventures together.

12. Which of the following statements best describes the character of Mole based on the passage?

    A. Mole is a cautious and home-loving creature who rarely ventures outside.

    B. Mole is a daring and adventurous animal who loves exploring new places.

    C. Mole is a quiet and solitary creature who prefers the company of nature.

    D. Mole is a reckless and impulsive character who often gets into trouble.

13. Which evidence from the passage supports the answer to the previous question about Mole's character?

    A. "Mole's first encounter was with a friendly water rat named Rat."

    B. "He had never experienced anything quite like it before."

    C. "As they continued their journey, Rat introduced Mole to his dear friend Toad."

    D. "Tired of his underground home, he ventured outside to explore the world above."

14. The teacher recognizes that students might be unfamiliar with the term *eccentric*. Which context clues would students need to use to figure out this word?

    A. Synonym

    B. Antonym

    C. Definition

    D. Inference

Use the following passage for questions 15-18.

When we venture into the ocean's open waters, we are often greeted by the majestic presence of killer whales. These powerful creatures glide effortlessly through the waves, displaying their remarkable abilities and captivating our attention. How do they navigate the depths of the ocean with such grace and precision?

The answer lies in the unique adaptations of killer whales. From their streamlined bodies to their specialized respiratory system, every aspect of the killer whale helps it thrive in the marine environment.

Streamlined Bodies

Killer whales possess sleek and streamlined bodies, perfectly crafted for efficient swimming. Their elongated shape, tapered at the ends, reduces drag and allows them to glide through the water with minimal effort. This streamlined design enables them to conserve energy and reach impressive speeds as they navigate the vast ocean.

Respiratory System

Unlike human scuba divers who rely on tanks for oxygen supply, killer whales have developed a sophisticated respiratory system. Their blowholes, located on top of their heads, allow them to take in air without breaking the water's surface. This remarkable adaptation enables them to breathe seamlessly without the need for scuba gear or masks.

Additionally, killer whales possess a high capacity for oxygen storage in their blood and muscles. Their blood contains a significant number of oxygen-carrying molecules, such as hemoglobin and myoglobin, ensuring a steady supply of oxygen during their dives. This efficient respiratory system and oxygen storage capacity enable killer whales to explore the depths of the ocean for extended periods.

Intricate Communication

Another remarkable aspect of killer whales is their complex communication system, which is more sophisticated than that of most animals, even humans. These intelligent creatures use a variety of vocalizations, including clicks, whistles, and calls, to communicate and navigate their underwater world. Their ability to emit and interpret these intricate sounds allows them to coordinate hunting strategies, maintain social bonds, and convey important information within their pods.

Witnessing the extraordinary grace and skill of killer whales in their natural habitat is a humbling experience. Their remarkable adaptations and unique behaviors make them true masters of the ocean, captivating the awe and admiration of those fortunate enough to observe them.

15. Identify **ALL** the techniques the writer uses to create reader interest in the first two paragraphs of the passage.

☐ A. Description and imagery to create a sense of wonder

☐ B. Specific details to explain some of the characteristics of killer whales

☐ C. Synonyms to define killer whales' characteristics

☐ D. Personal experiences of interacting with killer whales

16. The teacher wants to extend the activity to show students how an author's writing style can enhance the work and make it more interesting to read. Which of the following styles should the teacher focus on when using the passage about killer whales?

A. Narrative and persuasive

B. Narrative and description

C. Expository and description

D. Expository and problem/solution

17. The teacher ends the lesson with how to use context clues to figure out complex vocabulary while reading. Identify **THREE** words in the passage that would most effectively show students how to use context clues while reading.

☐ A. elongated

☐ B. minimal

☐ C. vocalizations

☐ D. adaptations

☐ E. fortunate

18. The teacher asks students to summarize the passage using two sentences. Which of the following is the most effective summarization of the passage?

A. "Whales have complex communication systems. This helps whales talk to one another through clicks and whistles."

B. "Killer whales have sophisticated bodies, breathing techniques, and communication. This makes them one of the most majestic animals in the sea."

C. "Killer whales have more blood in their system. This allows them to stay underwater for long periods of time."

D. "Why do killer whales thrive in their environment? The answer is they have streamlined bodies and can breathe underwater."

Use the following 2 pieces of text to answer questions 19-21

The Seed and the Tree

Once upon a time, in a beautiful forest, there was a tiny seed. The seed dreamed of growing tall and strong, reaching up towards the sunlight. It was determined to become a magnificent tree one day.

The seed was planted in fertile soil, and with each passing day, it absorbed nutrients and water from the earth. It sprouted roots and slowly started to push through the ground. As time went on, the seedling grew taller and its branches stretched towards the sky.

Seasons came and went, and the little tree faced challenges along the way—storms, harsh winters, and scorching summers. But it persevered, adapting to the changing conditions. With each challenge, the tree grew stronger, its trunk thickening and its branches spreading wider.

Years passed, and the tiny seed had transformed into a grand and majestic tree. Its canopy provided shade and shelter for animals, and its branches were adorned with vibrant leaves and beautiful blossoms. The tree stood tall and proud, a testament to the power of growth and resilience.

"The Mighty Tree"

In the heart of the forest, Stands a tree so tall and grand.

Its branches reach out like arms, Creating a vast, leafy land.

Through wind and storm, it stands strong, With roots buried deep and wide.

Its trunk, so thick and sturdy, Defies the forces that collide.

From tiny seed to towering tree, It grew with strength and grace. Each ring within its mighty trunk,

Marks time and its steadfast pace.

Animals find shelter in its shade, Birds build nests up high.

The tree provides a home for all, Beneath the endless sky.

19. As students discuss the meaning of the two texts, the teacher asks them to use evidence to support their claims. Identify **TWO** student responses that most effectively use text evidence to defend the claim.

☐ A. "The seed in the story faced challenges like storms and harsh winters. This shows that even though it was small, it never gave up and kept growing."

☐ B. "The seed in the story wanted to become a tree, and it succeeded. This proves that we can achieve our goals if we have dreams and work hard."

☐ C. "In the poem, the tree faced challenges. For example, it endured storms, harsh winters, and scorching summers."

☐ D. "The tree provided shade for animals. The animals were happy because it was hot."

☐ E. "Even though the tree starts out small, it grows bigger and bigger. This helped it survive harsh winters."

20. The teacher asks students to write a summary of "The Mighty Tree." Below is one response from a student.

A tree stands tall in the forest and grows big and strong. It grows deep roots that help it survive. The poem describes the tree as strong but shows grace by providing space for smaller animals to live. Even though the tree stands alone, the tree is where all animals come.

Identify **TWO** strengths the student displays in the summary.

☐ A. The comparison of strength and grace in the poem

☐ B. The use of metaphor

☐ C. The use of vivid description

☐ D. The interpretation of the tree's feelings

☐ E. The clarification of the tree being alone and where other animals come

21. The teacher writes the following on the board and has students write their answers in their reading journals:

What does the story and the poem focus on, and why is it important? Use evidence from both texts to support your answer.

One student writes the following:

The story and the poem are really about the tree's determination to survive and the grace the tree shows other animals. For example, the poem and the story say that the tree stands alone and grows big and strong. In the story, the tree is alone when it is growing and surviving storms, harsh winters, and scorching summers. In the poem, the tree stands strong through wind and storm. In the story and the poem, other animals find shelter in the tree. This makes me think that the tree is not only strong but also kind and graceful because even though it had to endure all those tough elements, it still shares its branches and shade.

Identify the statements that show that the student achieved the objective of the assignment.

☐ A. It provides a backstory as evidence to support the student's claim.

☐ B. It shows the sequence of events as evidence to support the student's claim.

☐ C. It uses direct quotes from the poem and the story as evidence to support the student's response.

☐ D. It uses specific details from the story and the poem to support the student's claim.

☐ E. It uses several examples from the story and the poem to support the student's claim.

22. Based on the excerpt below, Identify **TWO** areas of instruction that would benefit this student.

    Sally mad a drnk stnd and pepl got lmnad.

    ☐ A. Consonant blends

    ☐ B. Consonant digraphs

    ☐ C. Common affixes

    ☐ D. Vowel, consonant, silent *e* (VCE)

    ☐ E. Representing medial vowel sounds

23. Identify the pair of words containing a $/ʒ/$ sound that cannot be represented by any one letter.

    A. *said* and *have*

    B. *tail* and *sail*

    C. *pleasure* and *usual*

    D. *what* and *gnaw*

24. Identify **ALL** the words that contain an open syllable.

    ☐ A. Recent

    ☐ B. Spade

    ☐ C. Fantastic

    ☐ D. Able

    ☐ E. Replay

25. A teacher says the following words during an encoding lesson:

    coat, *tick*, and *fine*

    The student writes:

    cot, *tik*, and *fin*.

    Identify **ALL** the areas in which the student needs support.

    ☐ A. Understanding that two vowels can represent one sound.

    ☐ B. Understanding onsets of words.

    ☐ C. Understand the vowel-consent pattern CVCe.

    ☐ D. Identifying consonant blends in rimes of words

26. Identify the word that contains a diphthong.

    A. Cave

    B. Flower

    C. Standing

    D. Phone

27. Ms. Johnson and her students are working on identifying affixes in words. Identify the set of words that would be most appropriate for this activity.

    A. Fearless, compatible, irreplaceable.

    B. Coin, joy, cow

    C. Terrain, artillery, commune

    D. mitochondria, ribosomes, nucleus

28. A third-grade teacher assesses a student's fluency skills during a running record. Which of the following are notes the teacher might make about these skills? Choose **ALL** that apply.

    ☐ A. The student pauses at commas and stops at ending punctuation.

    ☐ B. The student reads with intonation and prosody.

    ☐ C. The student recalls and properly identifies characters, setting, and plot.

    ☐ D. The student uses phoneme-grapheme correspondences to decode unknown words.

    ☐ E. The student reads at an appropriate pace with accuracy.

29. A teacher asks students to identify the individual sounds in the word *stand.* The teacher is working with students on:

    A. phoneme identity

    B. phoneme categorization

    C. phoneme blending

    D. phoneme segmentation

30. A sixth-grade language arts teacher emphasizes the importance of the revision stage of writing because she wants students to understand that final drafts result from writing and rewriting to achieve a cohesive essay. While explaining the revision process, the teacher should emphasize:

    A. fixing the structure and content

    B. editing errors in spelling and punctuation

    C. developing a focused topic

    D. using descriptive words

31. Before reading a new text, the teacher helps students set the purpose of reading. The teacher uses a KWL chart to activate background knowledge about the information in the text. These strategies will best help the students improve their:

    A. rate

    B. accuracy

    C. prosody

    D. comprehension

32. Identify **ALL** the words that contain a digraph.

☐ A. True

☐ B. Chip

☐ C. Path

☐ D. Bead

☐ E. Thick

33. Identify **THREE** words most appropriate for an emergent literacy decoding activity.

☐ A. Few

☐ B. Dog

☐ C. Pie

☐ D. Bat

☐ E. Put

34. During a small-group discussion, the teacher wants students to engage in active listening while students discuss parts of the text they just read. The teacher has students take turns sharing their perspectives. Identify **ALL** the ways in which students can show they are using their active listening skills.

☐ A. Julie reads ahead in the book during the discussion to find the part of the text she wants to talk about.

☐ B. Jose asks Jocelyn to clarify a perspective she shares about a portion of the text.

☐ C. Milly and Jacob nod when they agree with another student's perspective.

☐ D. Jackson chats with another student about his perspective of the text.

☐ E. Several of the group members maintain eye contact with the speaker.

35. Students in fifth-grade language arts are adapting their expository essays on cells into a group presentation. The following excerpt is from one student's essay.

The cell is the basic unit of life. However, it is not basic at all. Cells contain organelles that perform many functions that keep us alive. For example, the cellular membrane regulates what comes in and out of the cell. The nucleus is the cell's brain, and that's where our DNA is. The mitochondria is the powerhouse of the cell that gives the cell energy. The human body has 100 trillion of these cells working to keep us alive!

The teacher wants the students to choose a single visual aid that will enhance their presentation and help the audience comprehend the information presented. Identify the most effective visual this student can use to enhance the presentation.

A. An image of a cell with different vibrant colors

B. A video depicting millions of cells in the human body.

C. A diagram showing the parts of a cell and their functions

D. A picture of the mitochondria of the cell

Use the following poem by Edward Lear for questions 36-38.

There was an Old Man with a beard,

Who said, "It is just how I feared—Two Owls and a hen,

Four Larks and a wren,

Have all built their nests in my beard!"

36. The teacher projects the poem in large print in the front of the room. The teacher reads the poem to the students and points to each word she reads. Then, the teacher and the students do a choral reading of the poem. Again, she points to each word they read. The teacher is:

    A. Developing sight word recognition

    B. Modeling fluency

    C. Introducing words with digraphs and diphthongs

    D. Increasing metacognition

37. After the choral reading, the teacher posts the poem in the front of the room with several words highlighted.

There was an Old Man with a beard,

Who said, "It is just how I feared— Two Owls and a hen,

Four Larks and a wren,

Have all built their nests in my beard!"

The highlighted words would be most appropriate for:

    A. Clapping open syllables

    B. Identifying CVCe words

    C. Explicit instruction on vowel teams

    D. Blending consonant sounds

38. Which word in the poem is considered a high-frequency word that cannot be decoded using phoneme-grapheme correspondence?

    A. hen

    B. nests

    C. man

    D. said

39. Identify the sentence that demonstrates proper comma usage to separate a dependent introductory clause from an independent clause.

    A. I made myself a big, delicious sandwich.

    B. Jumping, running, and playing are all important parts of recess.

    C. Julie worked and saved the money she needed, and she went on the trip.

    D. While waiting for the bus, Jenny took time to read her book.

40. A third-grade teacher is helping students break down complex words. The teacher helps students locate the root word and then detach the prefix and suffix so the word is divided into chunks. The chart below shows a few examples.

Sentence from the text	Root	Prefix	Suffix	Meaning
It was <u>unbelievable</u> how fast the girl was.	believe	un-	-able	Not able to believe
The board was <u>pliable</u>.	pli		-able	Able to bend
She lived in a building <u>complex</u>.	plex	com	--	Made of many parts

Describe the method the teacher is using in this activity.

A. Using phonological awareness to break words up by their syllable parts.

B. Using explicit morphological analysis to understand word parts and their meanings.

C. Using phonemic awareness to help students identify individual sounds in words.

D. Helping students use sight word recognition to map words orthographically.

41. The following excerpt is from *Huckleberry Finn* by Mark Twain.

"I wisht old Boggss'd threaten me, 'cuz then I'd know I warn't gwyne to die for a thousan' years." Which of the following best describes how the language in the excerpt is used?

A. The imagery in the excerpt helps the reader visualize the conversation.

B. The figurative language in the excerpt enhances the conversation.

C. The dialect in the passage provides perspective into where the speaker is from.

D. The dialogue in the passage makes the reader aware of the character's mood.

42. Evaluate the following sentence:

She was exhausted when she got home. However, she knew she still had to cook dinner.

In the sentence, the word *however* acts as:

A. An adjective

B. An interjection

C. A coordinating conjunction

D. A conjunctive adverb

43. Evaluate the following sentence.

She ran quickly to her car.

In the sentence, the word "quickly" functions as a/n:

A. Verb

B. Adverb

C. Adjective

D. Noun

44. A teacher presents a student with the following sentence and asks the student to read it aloud.

I check the mail every day with my dad.

Student: *"I check the mall every with my dad."*

Teacher: "Does that make sense?"

What cueing system is the teacher using to help the student correct the mistake?

A. Syntactic

B. Semantic

C. Graphophonic

D. Phonological

Use the following passage to answer questions 44-45.

(1) I would like to get a job as soon as I can. (2) I want to make my own money. (3) I want to be responsible. (4) The sky is the limit when you know how to work hard. (5) I know that when I have my own job, I will have choices. (6) I can go where I want and do what I want.

45. Which suggested revisions to the paragraph would provide varied sentence structure necessary for reader interest?

A. Blend sentences 1, 2, and 3 using punctuation and linking words.

B. Eliminate sentence 5 because it is not related.

C. Use figurative language to increase description in the paragraph.

D. Add a closing sentence to the paragraph that sums up the meaning.

46. A student rewrites sentence 4 to the following:

The possibilities are infinite when you know how to work.

The student has improved the sentence by adding which of the following?

A. Replacing the cliché with an analogy

B. Replacing the cliché with a hyperbole

C. Replacing the metaphor with a simile

D. Replacing a basic description with an onomatopoeia

47. A fifth-grade teacher uses sentence frames to show contrast in writing. Identify **ALL** the frames that would be useful for this purpose.

☐ A. She was scared _____ . However, _____ .

☐ B. Many scientists agree _____ . Although, _____ .

☐ C. Also, _____ . For example, _____ .

☐ D. The reason _____ . This causes _____ .

☐ E. The steps are _____ . Consequently, _____ .

48. Which transitional words are used to signal cause and effect in text structure?

   A. For example, such as, near

   B. Then, next, first

   C. However, although

   D. As a result, because, therefore

49. A student is taking a spelling test and is struggling with a few words. Look at the spelling words and the student's encoding of the words and determine what interventions the student would benefit from most.

Spelling Word	Student Answer
sign	sing
depend	depned
girl	gril

   A. Syllables

   B. Phoneme sequencing

   C. Onset and rime

   D. Silent letters

50. A teacher is deciding what graphic organizer to use with the class. They are reading the literary passage below.

> The two sisters seemed extremely different. Jenny loved sports, while Shelia loved books. Shelia would often dress up, while Jenny would go days without changing her outfit. However, both girls loved their parents and looked forward to the vacations they took in the spring and summer.

Which of the following graphic organizers would be most appropriate for the following passage?

   A. Sequence map

   B. KWL Chart

   C. Timeline

   D. Venn Diagram

51. Which of the following questions would be most effective in helping students understand the literary device used in the passage?

> A Giant Oak stood near a brook in which grew some slender Reeds. When the wind blew, the great Oak stood proudly upright with its hundred arms lifted to the sky. (1) But the Reeds bowed low in the wind and sang a sad and mournful song.
>
> "You have reason to complain," said the Oak. "The slightest breeze that ruffles the surface of the water makes you bow your heads, while I, the mighty Oak, stand upright and firm before the howling tempest."
>
> "Do not worry about us," replied the Reeds. (2) "The winds do not harm us. We bow before them and so we do not break. (3) You, in all your pride and strength, have so far resisted their blows. But the end is coming."
>
> As the Reeds spoke a great hurricane rushed out of the north. The Oak stood proudly and fought against the storm, while the yielding Reeds bowed low. (4) The wind redoubled in fury, and all at once the great tree fell, torn up by the roots, and lay among the pitying Reeds.

A. What is the tone of the passage?

B. How does the author use personification in the passage?

C. Identify elements of allusion in the third paragraph.

D. What could be an alternate ending to this passage?

52. A storm can hit at any minute, and it is important to have provisions. Without extra food, toilet paper, water, and batteries, people will not have what they need to survive long periods of power outages. Many people fail to prepare properly, which leads to them having to go to shelters when a major storm hits.

Which of the following explains how the author uses context clues to provide the meaning of the word *provisions* in the preceding passage?

A. By using examples

B. By providing a definition

C. By using descriptive words

D. By using opposites

Use the following Aesop Fable to answer questions 53-54

Two Goats, frisking gayly on the rocky steeps of a mountain valley, chanced to meet, one on each side of a deep chasm through which poured a mighty mountain torrent. The trunk of a fallen tree formed the only means of crossing the chasm, and on this, not even two squirrels could have passed each other in safety. The narrow path would have made the bravest tremble. Not so our Goats. Their pride would not permit either to stand aside for the other.

One set her foot on the log. The other did likewise. In the middle, they met horn to horn. Neither would give way, so they both fell, to be swept away by the roaring torrent below.

53. Based on the passage, the reader can infer:

A. The Goats thought their plan all the way through.

B. The Goats had been enemies for a long while.

C. The Goats were afraid to cross the water alone.

D. The Goats were arrogant even in the face of danger.

54. Which of the following best paraphrases the moral of the fable?

   A. There are many who pretend to despise and belittle that which is beyond their reach.

   B. Expect no reward for serving the wicked.

   C. We are often of greater importance in our own eyes than in the eyes of our neighbors.

   D. It is better to yield than to come to misfortune through stubbornness.

55. A teacher is helping students first-grade students develop articulation skills needed to conduct presentations in class. Which activity would benefit students most in developing articulation for their oral presentations?

   A. Read long passages silently that include persuasive rhetoric and then generate questions about the passage.

   B. Read aloud to their partners using short rhyming poems and focusing on individual sounds within words.

   C. Read a script from a famous speech and focus on the tone and delivery of the words used.

   D. Read aloud incomplete sentences and quickly fill in the missing words without miscuing.

56. An elementary teacher selects a lengthy text about plate tectonics to use in her fifth-grade class. The text is too large to read all at once. She decides to break the reading up. She puts students in cooperative groups and assigns each group a section from the text. The teacher instructs students to become experts on their sections and topics. After students read and examine the text, she then breaks them into different discussion groups, where each student shares the expertise gained in the first reading groups. Which of the following collaborative strategies is the teacher implementing in the scenario?

   A. Literature circles

   B. Reader's Theater

   C. Jigsaw

   D. Reciprocal teaching

57. A fourth-grade teacher focuses on reading informational text. The teacher helps students identify signal words that frame the text's structure. The class analyzes the following text.

   The city in the story has a pollution problem. Many residents complain about the air quality and garbage on the streets. Many said that the town used to be a beautiful place where you could swim in the lake and picnic outside. For the town to return to this, the people must commit to recycling trash and driving low-emissions cars. This will help reduce pollution and garbage in the area. Everyone will have to work together.

   Identify the organizational structure used in this text.

   A. Description

   B. Problem/solution

   C. Spatial

   D. Compare/contrast

58. A student is writing a narrative about visiting the beach with his family. During the revision stage, he improved his first draft significantly. Below are the first and second drafts.

First draft:

We packed our picnic lunch and headed towards the beach. I was excited to fish and play in the water. My brother hates sand and would probably cry as soon as we got there. To my surprise, he didn't. We found a spot and put our stuff down. Before we left we did many fun things like play paddle ball, throw the cast net, make sand castles, and collect shells. I was happy and want to go back

Second draft:

It was a sunny day in June, and my family and I planned to go to the beach. We packed a picnic lunch of bologna sandwiches, chips, and watermelon pieces. I love eating cold watermelon on a steamy day at the beach.

I figured my little brother would cry as soon as his feet hit the sand because he cries over everything, and it annoys me. He usually gets excited when I play with him, so I included him in all the activities I did so he wouldn't ruin my day. We built a sandcastle together, and it wasn't so bad playing with him. We also played paddleball. He had a hard time with it, but I was patient. I even taught him how to throw the cast net. After we collected shells, we walked home. I was proud of my brother.

Identify **TWO** elements implemented in the second draft that improved the piece's overall effect.

- ☐ A. plot development
- ☐ B. mood
- ☐ C. description
- ☐ D. character development
- ☐ E. theme

59. After reading about the Civil War, students will evaluate several pieces of informational text about the topic. The teacher provides students with the graphic organizer below to help them organize their writing about key details that led to the Civil War and the war's outcomes.

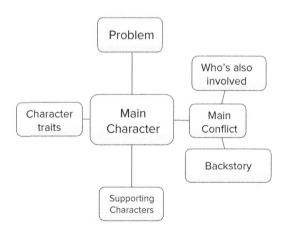

Identify **ALL** the reasons this graphic organizer would not help students with this type of analysis.

- ☐ A. It is more appropriate for describing literary text than informational text.
- ☐ B. It lacks a place to record facts about the Civil War.
- ☐ C. It focuses mainly on characterization and not on cause and effect.
- ☐ D. It is best suited for sequence rather than cause and effect.
- ☐ E. It is unfocused and has too many elements for students to focus on cause and effect.

Use the following student writing example to answer questions 60-62

1) The American alligator is a reptile. 2) The American alligator is an apex predator. 3) An apex predator is a predator at the top of the food chain. 4) Other apex predators are lions and tigers. 5) The American alligator lays eggs in sticks, leaves and mud.

60. Which of the following would strengthen the paragraph in terms of complex sentences?

    A. Change sentences 1 and 2 by combining them with punctuation.

    B. Delete sentence 4.

    C. Use varied vocabulary for the term *predator*.

    D. Add a comma after *leaves* in sentence 5.

61. What would be appropriate feedback to share with the student who wrote the paragraph above?

    A. "You use the term American alligator a lot. Try combining sentences to give the paragraph varied language."

    B. "Your writing does a great job describing your knowledge about the American alligator. Consider deleting sentence 4 so it doesn't take away from your overall theme."

    C. "Good job! Keep up the great work!"

    D. "Consider using a closing statement at the end."

62. Which of the following activities would benefit the student who wrote the essay above?

    A. Showing a video tutorial on how to format a research paper.

    B. Allowing the student to use spell check.

    C. Using small group instruction on combining sentences with different punctuation.

    D. Facilitating a whole-group presentation on vocabulary.

63. Read the following paragraph and determine the text structure.

    A powerful tornado appeared out of nowhere. It was a tri-state tornado with high winds going about 200 mph. The townspeople were terrified because they'd never seen a tornado of that size. Over 200 homes were destroyed that day.

    A. Problem and solution

    B. Chronological and sequential

    C. Narrative

    D. Cause and effect

Number	Answer	Category	Explanation
1.	C	I	The rime is the vowel and consonants that follow the onset consonant cluster. In this case, both words, *play* and *pay*, have the rime *ay*.
2.	A	I	In this example, Jose can read quickly and with automaticity. However, he does not remember or understand what he just read. Therefore, the deficit Jose is displaying when reading is comprehension.
3.	A	I	The letter c can have a /k/ sound or an /s/ sound depending on the letters that follow the C. This can be difficult for emergent readers to understand.
4.	A, B, D	II	Tier II words are general academic words that appear across different content areas and are important for understanding complex texts. In the given options, "revolutionized," "immersive," and "accessibility" are commonly used in various contexts and do not fall under tier I (basic) or tier III (discipline-specific) vocabulary. Wikis is a tier III word because it is domain-specific. The words "learn" and "future" are tier I words—they are high-frequency words.
5.	C	II	The first paragraph provides examples of how technology has revolutionized communication and connection, indicating the context in which "immersive" is used. The passage mentions online communities, virtual discussions, and the rise of online gaming. These examples give students clues to understand the meaning of "immersive" as being deeply engaging or involving. There is no contrast or definition used. Synonyms are also not used.
6.	B	III	The passage primarily describes the ways in which technology has impacted communication, information access, and entertainment. It provides details and examples to illustrate these changes without focusing on a specific sequence, cause-and-effect relationships, or comparisons and contrasts. Therefore, the passage follows a descriptive text structure, and student B answered correctly.
7.	A & B	I	The student represents the beginning, medial, and ending sounds in the words *like* and *beach*. In the other answer choices, the medial vowel sounds are missing. In the word *swim*, the student left out the /w/ sound. In the words *play* and *sand*, the student left, the student left out the /a/ sound.
8.	D	III	The graphic organizer has Coach Bryce in the middle and all the attributes that describe Coach Bryce in the bubbles around the center bubble. This is a character development exercise.

Number	Answer	Category	Explanation
9.	C	III	Hughes directly compares life to a broken-winged bird to describe how it would be if dreams do not live. Hughes does not use the words *like* or *as*. Therefore, this is a metaphor.
10.	B	III	The central theme or message of the poem "Dreams" is that without dreams, life becomes empty and lacks purpose. The poet emphasizes the importance of holding onto dreams as they bring vitality and meaning to one's existence.
11.	A	III	Repetition is a literary device that involves the repeated use of words, phrases, or lines to create emphasis or reinforce a specific idea. In the poem "Dreams," the repetition of the phrase "Hold fast to dreams" throughout the poem serves to emphasize the poet's message and encourage readers to remember the importance of dreams.
12.	A	III	The passage describes Mole as being tired of his underground home and deciding to explore the world above. However, his venture outside is portrayed as something different and exciting for him, suggesting that he is usually cautious and prefers the safety of his home.
13.	D	III	The evidence provided in option A supports the characterization of Mole as cautious and home-loving. The phrase "tired of his underground home" suggests that Mole is not accustomed to leaving his safe environment, reinforcing the idea that he is cautious and prefers the comfort of his burrow.
14.	D	III	There are no synonyms or antonyms directly stated in the passage. However, the reader can infer what eccentric (unconventional) means by evaluating the sentence: *Toad whisked them away in his shiny new vehicle, laughing and shouting as they sped down the road.*
15.	A & B	III	The description in the first two paragraphs is vivid and helps intrigue the reader. In addition, the author uses details to give context and support the vocabulary used in the piece. No synonyms are used in the first two paragraphs. In addition, the author does not use personal experience.
16.	C	III	The text is informational, not narrative. Therefore, answers A and B can be eliminated. The text is expository and uses details to enhance the writing. There is no problem or solution presented in the piece.
17.	A, C & D	II	Elongated can be used with inference clues because it is followed by *tapered at the ends, reduces drag, and allows them to glide through the water with minimal effort.* The word *vocalizations* can be used because it is followed by examples *clicks, whistles, and calls, to communicate and navigate their underwater world.* Finally, the word *adaptations* can be used because students can use inference clues by reading the sentence before the word and after the word to extract meaning. The words *minimal* and *fortunate* do not have any context clues to use to figure out the words' meanings.

Number	Answer	Category	Explanation
18.	B	III	Answer B includes information from the entire passage, which is most effective. Answer A and C are too specific to only a portion of the information. Answer D contains a misconception. Killer whales do not breath under water.
19.	A & C	III	Choices A and C are the only two responses that provide specific examples and evidence from the text. The other answers do not.
20.	A & E	III	The student summary indicates the student understands nuance in the poem. Answers A and E describe this. The student doesn't really use descriptive words or metaphor. There is no interpretation of the tree's feelings.
21.	D & E	III	The student uses examples from the story and the poem to support the claim. The student also uses language like, *for example*, to show the different instances in both pieces that support the student's claim. The student provides no backstory, sequence of events, or direct quotes, eliminating Choices A, B, and C.
22.	D & E	III	The student is missing the medial vowels in the words and the silent e in *made*.
23.	C	I	In the words *pleasure* and *usual*, the ending sound is not something that can be represented by any one letter. It is the /ʒ/ which makes a /zh/ sound. Other words that have this are *measure*, *visual*, and *decision*.
24.	A, D & E	I	An open syllable is one that ends with a single vowel sound. The vowel is not closed in by a consonant sound. In an open syllable, the vowel is usually long. In the word *recent*, the beginning syllable *re* is open. In the word *able*, the beginning syllable *a* is open. Finally, in the word *replay*, both syllables, *re* and *play* are open—the letter *y* acts as a vowel.
25.	A, C & E	I	The student has identified the correct sounds and has written them in the right order, but in each of the words, the student makes an error in using only one letter where a blend or digraph is required. Therefore, the student would benefit from a vowel team lesson. Also, in the word *fine*, the student writes *fin,* omitting the silent e. Finally, the student missed the consent blend in the rime of the word *tick*. The student correctly identified the onsets of all the words, eliminating answer B.
26.	B	I	Diphthongs are two vowels that work together to make a unique sound. The sound begins as one vowel sound and moves towards another. In the word *flower,* the "ow" is considered a diphthong.

Number	Answer	Category	Explanation
27.	A	I	Affixes are prefixes and suffixes. Choice A contains words with affixes, while the other words do not. Choice B are words that contain diphthongs. Choice C and D would be considered tier III words that are domain specific and would be best used for a vocabulary lesson.
28.	A, B & E	I	A running record is used to measure a student's fluency. Adhering to punctuation, as in answer choice A, reading with intonation, as in answer choice B, and using appropriate pace, as in answer choice E, are all part of fluency. Answer choice C involves comprehension. Answer choice D is decoding, which is phonics.
29.	D	I	The clue in the question is *individual sounds*. When students identify and pronounce individual sounds, they are preforming phoneme segmentation. Remember individual sounds in words are phonemes.
30.	A	II	The revision stage is when students fix the big issues in their writing, which includes structure, order, and mistakes in logic. These edits encompass the entire piece, which is what the revision stage is for. Replacing overused words and fixing punctuation errors happens is the line editing phase. Developing a focused topic is part of the pre-drafting and drafting stage. That happens at the very beginning.
31.	C	I	Activating background knowledge and setting the purpose for reading is a comprehension strategy. When students engage in these pre-reading strategies, it sets them up to better understand the text. Understanding the text is comprhension.
32.	A, B, C, D & E	I	Digraphs are two-letter (di-) combinations that create one phoneme (sound). Digraphs can be vowels or consonants. All the answer choices have digraphs—two-letter combinations that make one sound. In the word *true*, the *ue* makes one sound. In the word *chip*, the *ch* makes one sound. In the word *path*, the *th* makes one sound. In the word *bead*, the *ea* makes one sound. In the word *thick*, there are two digraphs: *th* and *ck*.
33.	B, D & E	I	The words *dog, bat,* and *put* are the most basic of the words listed. In addition, these words have consonant and short, single-letter vowel sounds. The words *you* and *few* contain vowel teams and are more complex. Emergent literacy is the very beginning stage of literacy. Therefore, choices B, D, and E are most appropriate.
34.	B, C & E	III	Clarifying (verbal cues), nodding (nonverbal cues), and maintaining eye contact (nonverbal cues) are all active listening skills.
35.	C	III	Because the excerpt talks about the different organelles and their functions, a diagram with those attributes labeled would be most beneficial to this presentation.

Number	Answer	Category	Explanation
36.	B	I	In this example, the teacher is modeling how to read the poem. Modeling is a very effective strategy to show students how to read fluently. Then, they engage in choral reading, which strengthens fluency skills. The poem's focus is not on sight words. In addition, while some of the words in the poem contain diphthongs and digraphs, this activity is not focused on those skills. If the class were thinking aloud about the poem, that would be metacognition; however, they are not doing that in the scenario.
37.	C	I	The words *beard*, *feared*, and *four* all contain long vowel teams—two vowels that make one long vowel sound. Therefore, the teacher is conducting explicit instruction on vowel teams.
38.	D	I	The word *said* does not follow the rules of phonics. Therefore, students should memorize this high-frequency word rather than attempting to decode the word by using phoneme-grapheme correspondence.
39.	D	II	The comma in answer choice D is separating the introductory clause—*While waiting for the bus*—from the independent clause—*Jenny took time to read her book*.
40.	B	I	Breaking the words down by prefixes, suffixes, and roots is using morphology. The chart is best used for a morphological analysis. Phonological awareness focuses on sounds in words. Phonics focuses on letter-sound correspondence. Orthographic mapping is using stored information in the brain to identify words. It involves developing phonological awareness and word-level reading skills.
41.	C	II	The novel *Huckleberry Finn* by Mark Twain uses lots of dialect to show the reader where the characters are from. In the dialogue in this example, lots of dialect is used.
42.	D	II	The word *however* is a conjunctive adverb that signals a contrast.
43.	B	II	An adverb is a word that modifies a verb. In this case, *quickly* is modifying the verb *ran*. Typically, words that end in *ly* are adverbs.
44.	B	I	Semantic cues are those that help students use meaning to figure out words in a sentence or passage. In this case, when the teacher asks, "Does that make sense?" it indicates the teacher is using meaning to help the student understand the mistake.
45.	A	II	Combining the short, robotic sentences by using commas and conjunctions will give the piece more readability and cohesion. This enhances sentence variety and makes the writing more enjoyable to read.

Number	Answer	Category	Explanation
46.	B	II	Teachers must show students how to avoid using clichés, or overly used phrases. Instead, the student can use figurative language. In this case, the student replaced the cliché with a hyperbole—an exaggeration.
47.	A & B	III	Transition words that show contrast in the frames are *however* and *although*.
48.	D	II	All the answer choices are transition words. However, answer D contains words that signal cause and effect.
49.	B	I	Because the student wrote the letters out of order, the student is struggling with phoneme sequencing.
50.	D	III	A Venn diagram is most appropriate here because the two characters have similarities and differences. Nothing is happening chronologically, eliminating a timeline or sequence map. Finally, a KWL chart is not being used here because there is no definitive need to focus on prior knowledge.
51.	B	III	The main literary device used in this passage is personification. The reeds and the trees are acting like people. Therefore, Answer B is the best choice.
52.	A	III	The author uses the examples in the text: extra food, toilet paper, water, and batteries. This helps the reader understand that the word *provisions* is another word for supplies.
53.	D	III	We can infer from the fable that the Goats were prideful and unwilling to bend, even if their safety was compromised.
54.	D	III	The Goats' stubbornness led to their demise. Had they waited and let the other go first, they would have had a better chance of crossing safely.
55.	B	III	The question emphasizes articulation, which is a skill that focuses on sounds. Answer choice B would best improve students' skills in this area because rhymes that build sound awareness will help students reinforce word patterns. You may be tempted to choose answer C; however these are first-grade students, and reading a script is too advanced.
56.	C	III	A jigsaw activity is when students are given pieces of a longer text to read in groups. They become experts on their part of the text. Then each group shares what they've learned in the reading. This is an effective way of taking a large piece of text and segmenting it into smaller, more digestible pieces. When the students come together to discuss their parts, it pieces the puzzle together, which is why the activity is named *jigsaw*.

Number	Answer	Category	Explanation
57.	B	III	The passage mentions the problem—pollution. At the end of the passage, the author offers a solution. Therefore, this passage has a problem/solution text structure.
58.	C & D	III	In the second draft, the student uses more description about the beach and watermelon. The student also develops the main character and his brother through their interactions. The plot, mood, and theme all remain consistent between the two drafts.
59.	A, C & E	III	The teacher wants students to understand what led to the war and the outcomes, which are causes and effects.

That being the goal, there are three problems with this graphic organizer. First, it focuses on the main character, which is most appropriate for literary rather than informational text. The next issue is that the organizer is mainly geared towards characterization, not the causes and outcomes of the Civil War. Finally, too many elements are included in the organizer, which could lead to confusion.

Students can use the organizer to write facts about the war. For example, in the "battles" and "main conflict" sections, students can write facts about the war, eliminating choice B. The organizer is not sequential, eliminating choice D. |
60.	A	III	Because the question is focused on complex sentence structure, combining sentences 1 and 2 is the best answer because it is concerned with complex sentences. Combining 1 and 2 would make it a complex sentence.
61.	B	III	When giving feedback on student writing, always start with a positive comment first, and then suggest ways to strengthen the piece. Answer B does that.
62.	C	III	A workshop on complex sentences and combining sentences with punctuation would be most beneficial to this student based on the writing.
63.	D	III	This is an example of the tornado (cause) impacting a town and homes (effect). No solutions are discussed, which eliminates answer A. The passage is not in chronological order. Finally, this is an expository piece not a narrative piece.

This page intentionally left blank.

7813 Mathematics

This page intentionally left blank.

About the Mathematics CKT – 7813

The Praxis 7813 Mathematics Content Knowledge for Teaching (CKT) test assesses the knowledge and skills of prospective educators in the field of mathematics instruction. You must understand mathematical concepts and be able to apply this knowledge teaching scenarios. The exam covers various areas of mathematics, including number sense and operations, algebraic thinking, geometry, measurement, data analysis, and probability.

Success on the Praxis 7813 Mathematics test indicates a strong foundation in mathematical principles and the ability to effectively teach this subject to students of different levels and abilities.

*A four-function, on-screen calculator is provided for the 7813 exam.

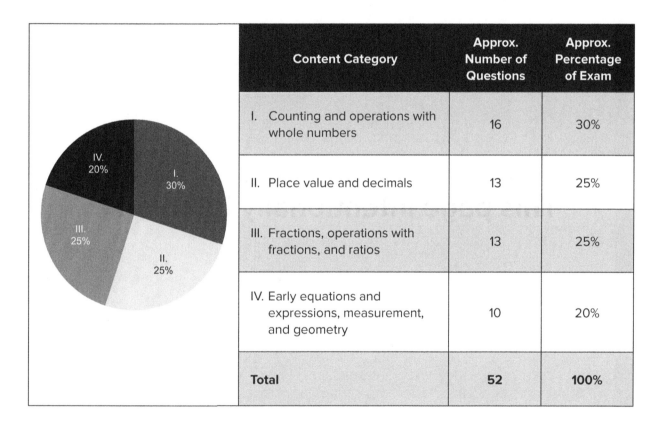

Content Category	Approx. Number of Questions	Approx. Percentage of Exam
I. Counting and operations with whole numbers	16	30%
II. Place value and decimals	13	25%
III. Fractions, operations with fractions, and ratios	13	25%
IV. Early equations and expressions, measurement, and geometry	10	20%
Total	**52**	**100%**

This page intentionally left blank.

I. Counting and Operations with Whole Numbers

The following topics are aligned with the test specifications of the Praxis 7813 exam. It is important that you examine these closely because these are the skills assessed on the exam.

A. Counting

B. Operations with Whole Numbers

A. Counting

Numbers are classified into various groups based on their properties. Notice that for each of the types of numbers defined in the table that follows, the numbers continue forever, hence the "..." at the end. The arrows at the end of a number line represent the concept of the numbers continuing forever. Numbers in the Real Number System that are addressed at various stages in grades K–6 are classified further into the groups shown in the table.

Classification of Numbers	
Real Number System	
Counting Numbers	$1, 2, 3, 4, 5, 6, \ldots$
Whole Numbers	$0, 1, 2, 3, 4, 5, 6, \ldots$
Integers	$-5, -4, -3, -2, -1, 0, 1, 2, 3, 4, 5, \ldots$
Rational Numbers	Any number that can be written as a fraction $\frac{a}{b}$, where a and b are any integer. Rational numbers include all terminating and repeating decimals. Example: $0.2, 4\frac{1}{2}, 7, \frac{1}{3}$

Cardinal & Ordinal Numbers

A **cardinal number** is a number that says how many of something there are. Cardinal numbers are used specifically for counting.

An **ordinal number** is a number that tells the position of something in a list. Ordinal numbers are used specifically when referring to the order of an object.

Cardinal Numbers	Ordinal Numbers
1	1st
2	2nd
3	3rd
4	4th
5	5th

Example: The following statements can be made about the puppies below.

- Statement 1: There are **4** puppies in the line.
- Statement 2: The dachshund is the **2nd** puppy in line.

Solution: Statement 1 uses the cardinal number *4* to convey the number of puppies in the line. Statement 2 uses the ordinal number *2nd* to convey the dachshund's position in the line of puppies.

Base-10 Number System

Our number system is called the **base-10 number system**, which is a system based on the digits 0, 1, 2, 3, 4, 5, 6, 7, 8, and 9.

Snap cubes and a place value mat are useful for making meaning of the base-10 system. The example below shows 7 cubes, representing 7 digits, in the 1s place.

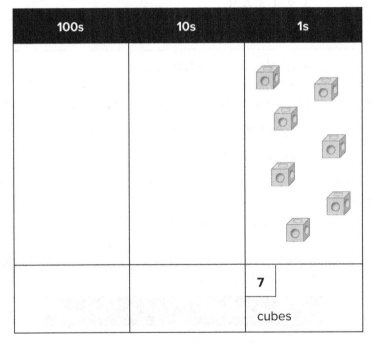

100s	10s	1s
		7
		cubes

When using snap cubes, remember that the base-10 system contains the digits 0 through 9, so if 10 cubes are in the 1s column, they connect to form 1 group in the 10s column. Once a group of 10 is formed, single digits can then be added again to the 1s column. The number represented on the left is 10, and the number represented on the right is 14. We could continue this pattern into the 100s column if we reached 10 groups in the 10s column, making 1 group of 100.

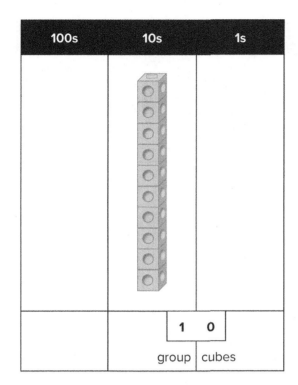

100s	10s	1s
	1	**0**
	group	cubes

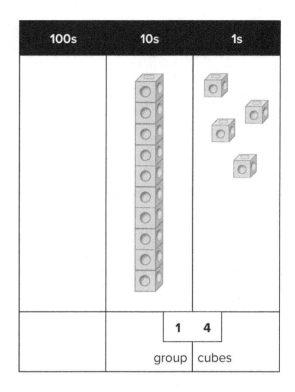

100s	10s	1s
	1	**4**
	group	cubes

B. Operations with Whole Numbers

Elementary students conduct operations of whole numbers using a variety of methods and manipulatives. It is important to recognize, analyze, and apply different methods for teaching mathematical concepts and procedures.

Manipulatives (physical models)

Manipulatives are used to represent counting, patterns, operations, physical attributes of geometric figures, and formulas. It's not enough to know that snap cubes exist; you also need to be aware of how they are used. Below is a list of commonly used manipulatives.

1. **Attribute blocks.** These come in five different geometric shapes and different colors. Attribute blocks can be used for sorting, patterns, and teaching attributes of geometric figures.

2. **Base-10 blocks**. These are visual models in powers of 10 that represent ones, tens, hundreds, and thousands. These blocks can be used to teach place value, regrouping with addition or subtraction, fractions, decimals, percents, and area and volume.

3. **Bar diagrams.** These are used to represent parts and whole and are often used with finding a missing value in a number sentence (e.g., $5 + ? = 12$).

4. **Counters.** These come in different shapes and colors (e.g., bears, bugs, chips) and are used for sorting and counting.

5. **Geoboards.** These are pegboard grids to which students stretch rubber bands to make geometric shapes. They are used to teach basic shapes, symmetry, congruency, perimeter, and area.

6. **Fraction strips** help to show the relationship between the numerator (top number of a fraction) and denominator (bottom number of a fraction) of a fraction and how parts relate to the whole.

7. **Snap cubes** are cubes that come in various colors that can be snapped together from any face. Snap cubes can be used to teach number sense, basic operations, counting, patterns, and place value.

8. **Tiles** are 1-inch squares that come in different colors. Some of the topics for which tiles can be used as a teaching aide include counting, estimating, place value, multiplication, fractions, and probability.

Manipulative Representations		
Attribute blocks	• Sorting • Patterns • Attributes of figures	
Base-10 blocks	• Place value • Whole number operations • Comparing numbers • Regrouping with addition and subtraction • Area and volume	
Bar diagram	• Solve for an unknown value using one of the four operations • Solve word problems	Kelly added 6 more stamps to her collection. Now she has 18 stamps. How many did she have before? 18 | ? | 6 |
Counters	• Sorting • Counting	
Geoboard	• Perimeter • Area • Properties of basic shapes • Congruency and Similarity	
Fraction strips	• Perform operations with fractions • Represent fractional parts	1 $1/2$ $1/2$ $1/4$ $1/4$ $1/4$ $1/4$ $1/8$ $1/8$ $1/8$ $1/8$ $1/8$ $1/8$ $1/8$ $1/8$ $1/2 = 1/4 + 1/4 = 1/8 + 1/8 + 1/8 + 1/8$
Snap cubes	• Combine like terms • Represent ratios • Distributive property • Multiply polynomials • Factoring polynomials	

Manipulative Representations		
Tiles	• Perform operations with fractions • Represent fractional parts	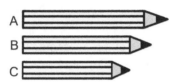

Subitize

When a student can subitize, the student can quickly identify several items in a small group without having to count them, regardless of the arrangement of items. For example, when I student looks at the dice below, the student can quickly recognize the three and the four on each die.

Transitivity

The transitivity principle states that if A is related to B and B is related to C in that same way, then A is also related to C. The transitivity principle can be applied when using indirect measurement. For the picture that follows, pencil B is shorter than pencil A and pencil C is shorter than pencil B. It follows then that pencil C is also shorter than pencil A.

Iteration

Iteration is repeatedly performing the same process by using the result, or output, of the first step to perform the operation on the next step. Listing multiples by adding the same number to the number before each time is an example of iteration.

Multiples of 3:

3

$3 + 3 = 6$

$6 + 3 = 9$

$9 + 3 = 12$

$12 + 3 = 15$

Each time we are adding 3 to the previous output to get the next number in the sequence.

Inventive strategies are methods in which students invent ways to solve complex problems. They involve using reason and understanding to get to the result. Here are some examples of inventive strategies students use:

- **Partitioning.** Taking large numbers and splitting them into small, manageable units.
- **Compensation.** Borrowing pieces of one number to compensate for another to make it easier to solve.

Standard algorithm is a specific method of computation that is conventionally taught for solving mathematical problem using standard notation in:

- Exchanging
- Regrouping
- Long division
- Long multiplication
- Average
- Area
- Volume

Partitioning
467 – 122 =
400 – 100 = 300
60 – 20 = 40
7 – 2 = 5
345

Compensation
46 + 38 =
Take **4** from **38** and give it to **46**.
50 + 34 =
84

Area model

In an area model, fractions are represented as part of a region. Think of a 10 by 10 grid with some of the squares shaded. The shaded squares represent a fractional part of the whole.

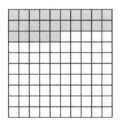

Linear model

In a linear model, the lengths of objects are compared to one another.

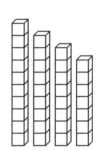

For example, think about 4 red snap cubes snapped together in a row and 3 green snap cubes snapped together to form another row. The green cubes are the length of the red cubes.

Set model

In a set model, a number of individual objects make up one whole.

For example, 8 counters could make up the entire set of counters; then 4 black counters would represent $\frac{4}{8}$ or $\frac{1}{2}$ of the set.

Tiling

Tiling is a geometric visual that uses patterns with no gaps to assist a student in calculating a value, such as area. The area of the shape that follows is 25 units.

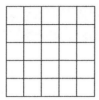

Performing Addition, Subtraction, and Comparison with Whole Numbers

When learning to add and subtract in kindergarten through second grade, students learn to approach a problem from different points of view. Various points of view help the student to better understand operations and number facts and is also preparing them for solving for an unknown value in later grades.

Add to

A number is given, and more is being added to the number to find a **sum**.

Result Unknown	Change Unknown	Start Unknown
Jon had two books. Kevin gave him 4 more books. How many books does Jon have now? $2 + 4 = ?$	Manda has three pencils. She found some more pencils in her room. Now she has seven pencils. How many pencils did she find in her room? $3 + ? = 7$	There are some birds resting on a fountain wall. Two more birds just joined them. Now there are five birds. How many birds were there on the wall to start? $? + 2 = 5$

Take from

A number is given, and some is being taken from this number to find a **difference**.

Result Unknown	Change Unknown	Start Unknown
Tory had five pieces of candy. She gave away 2 pieces. How many pieces does she have now? $5 - 2 = ?$	Six baseballs were on the ground. Evan picked some of them up to throw to a friend. There were three balls still on the ground. How many baseballs did Evan take? $6 - ? = 3$	There were some cookies on a plate. Scotty ate four of the cookies. Then there was one cookie on the plate. How many cookies were on the plate before Scott ate some? $? - 4 = 1$

Put together and take apart

This is often referred to as part-part-whole. Part of the number is given, then another part is given to make a total amount.

Total Unknown	Addend Unknown	Both Addends Unknown
There were four cups on the table. Jamie put one more cup on the table. How many cups are on the table? $4 + 1 = ?$	Darrell has seven pairs of socks. Three pairs are blue, and the rest are white. How many pairs of socks are white? $3 + ? = 7$ $7 - 3 = ?$	Brock has four tickets to place into two buckets, bucket A and bucket B. How many tickets can he put in A, and how many can he put in B? $? + ? = 4$ $1 + 3$ and $3 + 1$ are different when listing all the possibilities.

Compare addition and subtraction

Two values are given for a total, with the size of one being compared to the size of the other.

Difference Unknown	Bigger Unknown	Smaller Unknown
How many more?	**"More" Version**	**"More" Version**
There are five butterflies on a purple flowering bush. There are three butterflies on a yellow flowering bush. How many more butterflies are on the purple flowering bush? $3 + ? = 5$	Tory has four more tickets than Paula. Paula has 3 tickets. How many tickets does Tory have? $3 + 4 = ?$	Joseph has two more dollars than Stephen. Joseph has five dollars. How many dollars does Stephen have? $5 - 2 = ?$
How many fewer?	**"Fewer" Version**	**"Fewer" Version**
Kevon has three oranges. Natasha has six oranges. How many fewer oranges does Kevon have than Natasha? $6 - 3 = ?$	Elvin has one fewer notebook than Josiah. Elvin has four notebooks. How many notebooks does Josiah have? $? - 1 = 4$	Petra has three fewer fish than Deana. Deana has eight fish. How many fish does Petra have? $? + 3 = 8$

Equal groups

Beginning in third grade, students work with multiplication and division as an extension of addition and subtraction. The tables that follow outline how students learn multiplication and division. Be familiar with the terms in the chart and the type and composition of problems that each scenario represents.

Unknown Product	Group Size Unknown	Number of Groups Unknown
Multiplication	**How many in each group?** Division	**How many groups?** Division
There are 3 bags with 6 plums in each bag. How many plums are there in all? $3 \times 6 = ?$	If 18 plums are shared equally into 3 bags, then how many plums will be in each bag? $3 \times ? = 18$ and $18 \div 3 = ?$	If 18 plums are to be packed 6 to a bag, then how many bags are needed? $? \times 6 = 18$ and $18 \div 6 = ?$
Measurement Example	Measurement Example	Measurement Example
You need 4 lengths of string, each 5 inches long. How much string will you need altogether? $4 \times 5 = ?$	You have 12 inches of string, which you will cut into 6 equal pieces. How long will each piece of string be? $6 \times ? = 12$ and $12 \div 6 = ?$	You have 14 inches of string, which you will cut into pieces that are 7 inches long. How many pieces of string will you have? $? \times 7 = 14$ and $14 \div 7 = ?$

Arrays and area

Unknown Product	Group Size Unknown	Number of Groups Unknown
Array Example	Array Example	Array Example
There are 3 rows of apples with 6 apples in each row. How many apples are there? $3 \times 6 = ?$	If 18 apples are arranged into 3 equal rows, how many apples will be in each row? $3 \times ? = 18$ and $18 \div 3 = ?$	If 18 apples are arranged into equal rows of 6 apples, how many rows will there be? $? \times 6 = 18$ and $18 \div 6 = ?$
Area Example	Area Example	Area Example
What is the area of a 4 cm by 5 cm rectangle? $4 \times 5 = ?$	A rectangle has area 12 square centimeters. If one side is 6 cm long, how long is a side next to it? $6 \times ? = 12$ and $12 \div 6 = ?$	A rectangle has area 14 square centimeters. If one side is 7 cm long, how long is a side next to it? $? \times 7 = 14$ and $14 \div 7 = ?$

Compare (multiplication and division)

Compare problems occur first with whole numbers (e.g., two times as much) and then phase in unit fractions (e.g., one-half as much) in the fifth grade. Either grade level scenario is a possibility on the test.

Unknown Product	Group Size Unknown	Number of Groups Unknown
Word Problem	Word Problem	Word Problem
A blue hat costs $6. A red hat costs 3 times as much as the blue hat. How much does the red hat cost? $$6 \times 3 = ?$$	A red hat costs $18, and that is 3 times as much as the cost of a blue hat. How much does a blue hat cost? $$3 \times ? = 18 \text{ and } 18 \div 3 = ?$$	A red hat costs $18, and a blue hat costs $6. How many times as much of the blue hat does the red hat cost? $$? \times 6 = 18 \text{ and } 18 \div 6 = ?$$
Measurement Example	Measurement Example	Measurement Example
A rubber band is 6 cm long. How long will the rubber band be when it is stretched to be 3 times as long? $$6 \times 3 = ?$$	A rubber band is stretched to be 18 cm long, and that is 3 times as long as it was at first. How long was the rubber band at first? $$3 \times ? = 18 \text{ and } 18 \div 3 = ?$$	A rubber band was 6 cm long at first. Now it is stretched to be 18 cm long. How many times longer is the rubber band now than it was at first? $$? \times 6 = 18 \text{ and } 18 \div 6 = ?$$
Unit Fraction Example	Unit Fraction Example	Unit Fraction Example
The oak tree is 15 feet tall. The palm tree is 1/5 as tall as the oak. How tall is the palm tree? $$15 \times \frac{1}{5} = ?$$	The palm tree is 3 feet tall. This is 1/5 as tall as the oak tree. How tall is the oak tree? $$? \times \frac{1}{5} = 3 \text{ and } 3 \div \frac{1}{5} = ?$$	The oak tree is 15 feet tall. The palm tree is 3 feet tall. What fraction of the height of the oak tree is the height of the palm tree? $$3 \times ? = 15 \text{ and } 3 \div 15 = ?$$

Properties of Operations

Know the properties of operations for the exam, including how and when they are used. As students become more proficient with addition and multiplication, these properties allow them to fluently change and simplify problems. The following table was taken from the National Governors Association Center for Best Practices, Council of Chief State School Officers.

Property of Operations	Rule	Description
Commutative Property of Addition	$a + b = b + a$	Changing the order of two numbers being added does not change the sum.
Commutative Property of Multiplication	$a \cdot b = b \cdot a$	Changing the order of two numbers being multiplied does not change the product.
Associative Property of Addition	$(a + b) + c = a + (b + c)$	Changing the grouping of the addends does not change the sum.
Associative Property of Multiplication	$a \cdot (b \cdot c) = (a \cdot b) \cdot c$	Changing the grouping of the factors does not change the product.
Additive Identity Property of 0	$a + 0 = 0 + a = a$	Adding 0 to a number does not change the value of that number.
Multiplicative Identity Property of 1	$a \cdot 1 = 1 \cdot a = a$	Multiplying a number by 1 does not change the value of that number.
Inverse Property of Addition	For every a, there exists a number $-a$ such that $a + (-a) = (-a) + a = 0$	Adding a number and its opposite results in a sum equal to 0.
Inverse Property of Multiplication	For every a, there exists a number $\dfrac{1}{a}$ such that $a \cdot \dfrac{1}{a} = \dfrac{1}{a} \cdot a = \dfrac{a}{a} = 1$	Multiplying a number and its multiplicative inverse results in a product equal to 1.
Distributive Property of Multiplication over Addition	$a \cdot (b + c) = a \cdot b + a \cdot c$	Multiplying a sum is the same as multiplying each addend by that number, then adding their products.
Distributive Property of Multiplication over Subtraction	$a \cdot (b - c) = a \cdot b - a \cdot c$	Multiplying a difference is the same as multiplying the minuend and subtrahend by that number, then subtracting their products.

Number Theory

Additional Classifications	
Prime	A positive integer that only has 1 and itself as factors. Example: 2, 3, 13, 29 ***Note: 1 is neither prime nor composite, and 2 is the only even prime number.***
Composite	A positive integer that has factors other than 1 and itself. Example: 4, 12, 27, 44
Even	A number that is divisible by 2
Odd	A number that is not divisible by 2

Terms used to classify real numbers may be sprinkled throughout the test. Know what type of number each of these terms represent in the event the term is used in a problem.

It is possible that you get a question that tests your knowledge of number sense. For example, why $\frac{0}{1}$ is a number but $\frac{1}{0}$ not defined?

For the first fraction, we can say that 1 goes into 0 zero times, so the result is 0. For the second fraction, a number cannot be divided into 0 parts, so a denominator of zero makes no sense and is not possible.

Test Tip

Remember these important number facts:

- 1 is neither prime nor composite.
- 2 is the only even prime number.
- 0 is an even number.
- The sum of two even numbers is always even.
- The sum of two odd numbers is always even.
- The sum of an even number and an odd number is always odd.
- Zero can never be in the denominator.

Math Fluency

Math fluency, much like literacy, is the ability to perform mathematical operations accurately, efficiently, and with flexibility. It involves understanding and using numbers confidently, and being able to apply mathematical skills to solve problems. Here are some general steps that can help build math fluency:

1. **Foundational Knowledge**. Understanding basic math concepts is the first step. This includes learning about numbers, shapes, basic operations (like addition and subtraction), and other foundational math concepts.

2. **Skill Practice**. Regular practice is important for fluency in any area, including math. Worksheets, flashcards, math games, and other activities can help reinforce math skills and increase speed and accuracy.

3. **Concrete to Abstract**. This starts with physical, tangible representations and moving towards more abstract, symbolic understanding. This progression is key in developing a deep and meaningful understanding of mathematics.

4. **Understanding**. Going beyond rote memorization to understand why math works the way it does can significantly improve fluency. Understanding the "why" behind an operation can make it easier to remember and apply.

5. **Problem Solving**. Applying math skills to solve problems helps deepen understanding and increase fluency. This can involve word problems, puzzles, or real-world situations that require mathematical reasoning.

6. **Number Sense**. This is an intuitive understanding of numbers, their magnitude, relationships, and how they are affected by operations. Building number sense can help with mental math and estimation skills, both of which contribute to math fluency.

7. **Mental Math**. Practicing mental math can enhance fluency by improving speed, accuracy, and flexibility in thinking. It also builds confidence in one's ability to work with numbers.

8. **Progressive Difficulty**. As skills improve, the difficulty of the problems should gradually increase. This keeps learners challenged and promotes continued growth and fluency.

9. **Consistency**. Regular and consistent practice is key to becoming fluent in math. Daily practice, even for a few minutes, can make a big difference over time.

10. **Patience and Persistence**. Finally, it's important to remember that fluency takes time and perseverance. Everyone learns at their own pace, so patience and persistence are crucial.

Remember that math fluency is not just about speed, but also about accuracy, efficiency, and flexibility in thinking. The goal is to be able to use math effectively in various situations, both in school and in everyday life.

This page intentionally left blank.

Counting and Operations Practice Questions

1. A teacher has several paper plates with dots to represent numbers. She shows a plate to a student who quickly and accurately identifies how many dots are on the paper plate. Which of the following describes the process the student is displaying?

    A. Transitivity

    B. Cognitive complexity

    C. Flexibility

    D. Subitizing

2. A teacher gives her students the following problem.

    There are six coconuts on a palm tree in the front yard. There are two coconuts on a palm tree in the back yard. How many more coconuts are there on the palm tree in the front yard?

    Which of the following best describes the structure of this problem?

    A. Add to, change unknown

    B. Compare, difference unknown

    C. Take apart, addend unknown

    D. Put together, total unknown

3. A teacher is conducting a lesson on perimeter. Which one of the following manipulatives would NOT be a good choice for the teacher to use for teaching this lesson?

    A. Snap cubes

    B. Geoboard

    C. Pattern blocks

    D. Base ten blocks

4. While completing an addition problem, the teacher is having students use snap cubes to find the sum. Which instructional approach is the teacher using?

    A. Abstract

    B. Fluency

    C. Concrete

    D. Representational

5. A 5th grade teacher is beginning a lesson on the attributes of two-dimensional figures. Which of the following would be an appropriate strategy for the teacher to use to begin the lesson?

    A. Use dot paper or a geoboard to explore attributes of figures.

    B. Make a table and list the attributes of two-dimensional figures.

    C. Use geometric formulas to determine the attributes of two-dimensional figures.

    D. Use base ten blocks to explore the attributes of two-dimensional figures.

6. Which of the following best depicts why $3 \times 5 = 15$?

A.
```
• • • • •
• • • • •
• • • • •
```

B.
```
• • • •
• • • •
• • • •
```

C.
```
• • • •
• • • •
• • • •
• • • •
```

D.
```
• • •
• • •
• • •
• • •
• • •
• • •
```

7. A 3rd grade teacher gives a timed test of multiplication facts through 10. The teacher is most likely testing for what?

A. Accuracy

B. Complexity

C. Flexibility

D. Fluency

Number	Answer	Explanation
1.	D	When a student can identify the number of items in a group without having to count them, this is known as subitizing.
2.	B	This is a subtraction problem where you are comparing two values with the difference between them unknown.
3.	D	Base ten blocks would not be the best choice for teaching perimeter because they do not change in dimension.
4.	C	Using a hands-on approach to learning is part of the concrete approach to math.
5.	A	To begin any lesson, a teacher should start at the concrete, hands-on phase of student learning before moving on to more abstract definitions and facts. Base ten blocks are not effective for this lesson.
6.	A	The concrete representation of the multiplication problem is a picture or array of 3 groups of 5 items. The array in option A contains 3 rows, each with 5 dots.
7.	D	Because the test is timed, the teacher is checking for fluency. Although the teacher would most likely also be checking for accuracy, accuracy is one of the steps of fluency, so D is the best answer choice.

7813
Mathematics

This page intentionally left blank.

II. Place Value and Decimals

The following topics are aligned with the test specifications of the Praxis 7813 exam. It is important that you examine these closely because these are the skills assessed on the exam.

1. Understand the value of the digits in a number
2. Compare multidigit and decimal numbers
3. Round multidigit and decimal numbers
4. Composes and decomposes multidigit numbers
5. Instructional strategies such as manipulatives to reinforce place value and decimals

Place Value

The value of a certain digit is determined by the place it resides in a number. In our number system, each "place" has a value of ten times the place to its right or $\frac{1}{10}$ of the number to its left. The place value of each digit in a number is included in the word form of a number.

Take the number 2,487,905.631 as an example.

This number is read as *two million, four hundred eighty-seven thousand, nine hundred five, and six hundred thirty-one thousandths.*

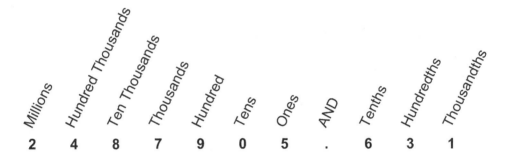

It is important to know how to manipulate a number using the base 10 system. Moving the decimal point to the left (to create a smaller number) is the same as dividing by increments of 10 or multiplying by increments of $\frac{1}{10}$. Conversely, moving the decimal point to the right (to create a larger number) is the same as multiplying by increments of 10. Increments of 10 include 10, 100, 1000, 10,000...etc.

Composing and Decomposing Numbers

Knowledge of place value helps students to compose and decompose larger numbers to better understand the size of the number.

Example question

For the number 42,103.68, the 4 is how many times larger than the 0?

   A. 4

   B. 100

   C. 1,000

   D. 40,000

Correct answer: C

The 0 is 3 places to the right of 4, which would be 10 × 10 × 10 = 1,000 times larger.

Example question

Select all the statements that are true about the number below.

23,401.07

   ☐ A. 2 is in the thousands place.

   ☐ B. 4 is in the hundreds place.

   ☐ C. There are no 10s in this number.

   ☐ D. 7 is in the tenths place.

   ☐ E. 2 is in the ten-thousands place.

Correct answer: B, C, and E

There is a 4 in the hundreds place, there are no 10s in the number, and the 2 is in the ten-thousands place. Answer choice A is not true because 3 is in the thousands place. Answer choice D is not true because 7 is in the hundredths place.

Rounding

In addition to being able to compose and decompose, students are expected to round to a given place value. Questions involving rounding will require students to know each of the place values. To round, look at the number to the right of the place value to which you are rounding. If the number to the right is between 0 and 4, keep the place value the same. If the number to the right is between 5 and 9, the place value is rounded up 1.

Example question

A teacher asked the class to round the number 507,291 to the nearest ten-thousands. Of the responses she received below, which one is correct?

   A. 507,000

   B. 508,000

   C. 510,000

   D. 600,000

Correct answer: C

We are rounding the 0 in the number 507,291. The number to its right, 7, is greater than 4, which means 0 is rounded up 1. Thus, the rounded number is 510,000.

Remember, after rounding to the correct place value, all the numbers to the right of the place value become zeros.

Strategies for problem solving

You should be familiar with a variety of strategies that students can use to solve problems and the best strategy for various problem types. Typically, test questions will expect you to *apply* a strategy rather than *identify* the strategy by name.

Examples of common problem-solving strategies:

- Draw a picture
- Find a pattern
- Guess and check
- Make a chart or table
- Work the problem backwards
- Act it out
- Estimating or rounding

When solving, focus on drawing pictures, estimating when it is reasonable to do so, and checking the reasonableness of your answer. Always double-check that your answer makes sense in the context of the problem. For example, if the problem asks you to find how many words per minute a person can type, an answer of 1,000 is unreasonable, whereas an answer of 100 makes sense.

Example: Robert was at a friend's house for three and a half hours. He left his friend's home at 6:15 p.m. What time did he arrive?

Solution: This is a good problem for using the problem-solving strategy of working backward. Starting with 6:15 and going back 30 minutes to account for the half hour puts the time at 5:45. Working backward another 3 hours to address his remaining time at his friend's house puts Robert arriving at 2:45.

This page intentionally left blank.

Place Value Practice Questions

1. While solving a multi-digit addition problem, Jessica decides to break the numbers up into easier numbers and add them in her head. Antwan decides to break the numbers up by place value and then add them all together. Yesenia uses the method of adding the ones and carrying any tens over to the next column, repeating this process until she is done. Which one of these students is using a standard algorithm?

   A. Jessica

   B. Antwan

   C. Yesenia

   D. Jessica and Antwan

2. Which set of numbers would be most helpful for students studying place value?

   A. 2, 4, 6, 8

   B. 10, 20, 30, 40

   C. 100, 200, 300, 400

   D. 1, 10, 100, 1,000

3. Sara solves the addition problem 43 + 54 by thinking, *I have 4 tens and 5 tens which is 9 tens, or 90. I also have 3 ones and 4 ones, which is 7 ones. Together, 90 plus 7 is 97.* This is an example of which type of strategy?

   A. Combining place values

   B. Compensation

   C. Decomposition

   D. Put-together

4. Place the numbers in order from least to greatest.

   $$-0.61, \quad -\frac{2}{3}, \quad -\frac{7}{11}, \quad -0.\overline{61}$$

   A. $-0.61, \quad -\frac{2}{3}, \quad -\frac{7}{11}, \quad -0.\overline{61}$

   B. $-\frac{2}{3}, \quad -\frac{7}{11}, \quad -0.\overline{61}, \quad -0.61$

   C. $-0.61, \quad -0.\overline{61}, \quad -\frac{7}{11}, \quad -\frac{2}{3}$

   D. $-\frac{2}{3}, \quad -\frac{7}{11}, \quad -0.61, \quad -0.\overline{61}$

5. A student writes a subtraction problem as shown.

$$\begin{array}{r} \overset{\overset{10}{}}{2\cancel{0}} \\ -\ 17 \\ \hline 13 \end{array}$$

What is the error in the student's thinking?

A. The student has no understanding of subtraction.

B. The student does not understand how to subtract numbers in the tens place.

C. The student does not know how to count to 20.

D. The student does not understand the algorithm for borrowing 10 from a higher place value.

Number	Answer	Explanation
1.	C	Yesenia is following a step-by-step procedure to arrive at the answer, which is the standard algorithm for adding.
2.	D	Answer choices A, B, and C all have numbers in the same place values and would not be effective sets of numbers to use. Answer choice D contains numbers with various place values and would be the best set to use.
3.	A	Notice that when solving, Sara is applying her knowledge of place value to add first the tens and then the ones. Thus, she is using combining place values to solve.
4.	B	When comparing numbers in different forms, convert them all to decimals of the same length. Three place values is a good length for comparison. When comparing negative numbers, the greater the negative number, the smaller its value is. $$-0.61 = -0.610$$ $$-\frac{2}{3} = -0.667$$ $$-\frac{7}{11} = -0.636$$ $$-0.\overline{61} = -0.616$$ From least to greatest we have $-\frac{2}{3}, -\frac{7}{11}, -0.\overline{61}, -0.61$
5.	D	The student crossed out the zero in the ones place and replaced it with a borrowed 10 from the tens place, but the student did not take the borrowed 10 away from the 20. The student subtracted the problem he wrote correctly, so we can eliminate answer choices A and B. We can also eliminate answer choice C because we cannot determine his ability to count from a subtraction problem. Answer choice D is the correct answer choice because the student did not correctly apply the standard algorithm for subtraction.

III. Fractions, Operations with Fractions, and Ratios

The following topics are aligned with the test specifications of the Praxis 7813 exam. It is important that you examine these closely because these are the skills assessed on the exam.

1. Understand fractions as part-whole relationships

2. Understand characteristics of fractions

3. Understand fraction equivalence

4. Instructional strategies for comparing fractions

5. Perform operations such as addition, subtraction, multiplication, and division with fractions

6. Understand applications of operations on fractions

A. Fractions and Operations with Fractions

Ordering and comparing various forms of numbers

In upper elementary grades and into middle school, students are presented with different ways to write the same number. This includes writing numbers as fractions, decimals, percents, scientific notation, and as a product using exponents. Therefore, on the test, you should be familiar with writing numbers in different forms and comparing the size of these numbers and where they are placed on the number line.

Test Tip

Memorize the decimal values of common fractions. Knowing the decimal conversions for fourths, thirds, fifths, eighths, and ninths will save valuable time. You will encounter several of these fractions to convert on the test.

Unit fractions

A unit fraction is any fraction with a numerator of 1. Students learn unit fractions using fractional pieces of circles or bars and by breaking up a number line into fractional pieces. From the number line, students learn the placement of fractions and their size relative to one another and to 0 and 1. The table that follows gives examples of some, not all, unit fractions.

Unit Fraction	Manipulative Representation	Number Line Representation
$\dfrac{1}{2}$	A circle divided into two halves, each labeled $\dfrac{1}{2}$. or A bar divided into two halves, each labeled $\dfrac{1}{2}$.	The fraction $\dfrac{1}{2}$ is the same distance from both 0 and 1. A number line from 0 to 1 with $\dfrac{1}{2}$ marked in the middle, showing $\dfrac{1}{2}$ distance from 0 to $\dfrac{1}{2}$ and $\dfrac{1}{2}$ distance from $\dfrac{1}{2}$ to 1.

Unit Fraction	Manipulative Representation	Number Line Representation
$\dfrac{1}{4}$	or	The fraction $\dfrac{1}{4}$ is closer to 0 than 1, and $\dfrac{1}{4}$ is less than $\dfrac{1}{2}$
$\dfrac{1}{5}$	or	The fraction $\dfrac{2}{5}$ is closer to 0 than 1, and $\dfrac{3}{5}$ is greater than $\dfrac{1}{2}$

Working with unit fractions leads to decomposing fractions and writing an equation to represent the decomposition. To **decompose** a fraction means to break it into parts.

Example question

Which of the following is a decomposition of $\dfrac{3}{4}$?

A. $\dfrac{1}{4} + \dfrac{1}{4} + \dfrac{1}{4} = \dfrac{3}{4}$

B. $\dfrac{3}{4} = 0.75 = 75\%$

C. $\dfrac{1}{4} + \dfrac{3}{4} = \dfrac{4}{4} = 1$

D. $\dfrac{1}{2} < \dfrac{3}{4}$

Correct answer: A

Decomposing a fraction means to break a fraction up into the sum of smaller parts with the same denominator. Options B, C, and D do not break the fraction into smaller parts.

Number representation

The same number can be written several ways. Be prepared to know how to write a number in different forms or recognize equivalent forms of the same number. Also, be prepared to compare numbers written in different forms.

Fractions, decimals, and percents are all interchangeable and are acceptable in any of the three forms. Each of these is a number out of 100, so base-10 blocks create an effective visual when first learning percents and decimals.

Form	Example
Base-10 blocks	When interchanging fractions, decimals, and percents, we think of this out of 100. To represent this pictorially, we can use a base-10 block with 100 squares. The image to the right has 30 squares shaded or 30 out of 100, which is $\dfrac{30}{100}$
Fraction	The fraction $\dfrac{30}{100}$ may also be written as $\dfrac{3}{10}$.
Decimal	To convert a fraction to a decimal, always divide the numerator (top number) by the denominator (bottom number); numerator ÷ denominator. $30 \div 100 = 0.30$ or 0.3
Percent	To convert a decimal to a percent, move the decimal point 2 place values to the right. This works because a fraction and its decimal are out of 1, and a percent is out of 100. Moving the decimal point two places to the right is the same as multiplying by 100. **Example:** To convert 0.30 to a percent, move the decimal 2 places to the right: $0.30 = 30\%$ This is the same as $0.30 \times 100 = 30$. Moving the decimal is the shortcut; make sure you always know the math behind the shortcuts.

Application problems for fraction, decimal, and percent conversions often include having to find the percent of a number. To find the percent of a number, change the percent to a decimal and multiply the decimal by the number. For example, 12% of 40 is $0.12 \times 40 = 4.8$.

Example question

Choose a number from the list that is greater than 70% but less than 80%.

    A. 0.85

    B. $\dfrac{65}{100}$

    C. 1

    D. 0.75

Correct response: D

To solve, rewrite each of the numbers as a decimal so that they are easy to compare. The correct choice should be between 0.7 and 0.8.

- 0.85 is greater than 0.8 so answer choice A can be eliminated.

- $\dfrac{65}{100} = 0.65$ is less than 0.7 so answer choice B can be eliminated.

- 1 is greater than 0.8 so answer choice C can be eliminated.

- 0.75 is between 0.7 and 0.8 so answer choice D is the correct answer.

Which of the following expressions is equivalent to 0.75? Select all that apply.

☐ A. $\dfrac{75}{100}$

☐ B. $\dfrac{3}{5}$

☐ C. 75%

☐ D. $5^2 + 50$

☐ E. 0.750

☐ F. $1 - \dfrac{1}{4}$

Correct response: A, C, E and F

To solve, rewrite each of the numbers as a decimal so that they are easy to compare.

☐ A. $\dfrac{75}{100} = 0.75$ (correct)

☐ B. $\dfrac{3}{5} = 0.6$ (incorrect)

☐ C. $75\% = 0.75$ (correct)

☐ D. $5^2 + 50 = 25 + 50 = 75$ (incorrect)

☐ E. $0.750 = 0.75$ (correct)

☐ F. $1 - \dfrac{1}{4} = \dfrac{3}{4} = 0.75$ (correct)

In a recent survey, 15% of 60 people eat dinner out more than twice a week. What fraction of people do **NOT** eat dinner out more than twice a week?

A. $\dfrac{85}{60}$

B. $\dfrac{45}{60}$

C. $\dfrac{15}{60}$

D. $\dfrac{51}{60}$

Correct answer: D

To find the fraction of people who do not eat dinner out more than twice a week, we need to know the actual number of people this represents. To find this number, we need to first find the percent of people who do not eat out more than twice a week. If 15% eat out more than twice a week, then $100\% - 15\% = 85\%$ represents those who do not eat out more than twice a week.

Next, find 85% of 60 people.

$0.85 \times 60 = 51$

Thus, 51 people do NOT eat out more than twice a week, which is $\dfrac{51}{60}$ as a fraction.

Integers and exponents

When placing negative numbers on a number line, be careful. It is easy to put them in the wrong place.

Integer. Positive and negative whole numbers. For example, $\ldots, -5, -4, -3, -2, -1, 0, 1, 2, 3, 4, 5, \ldots$

Integer with integer exponent. When an exponent is negative, rewrite the number as a fraction with one in the numerator and make exponent positive. For example:

$$3^2 = 3 \times 3$$

$$3^{-2} = \frac{1}{3^2} = \frac{1}{3 \cdot 3} = \frac{1}{9}$$

Test Tip

Know what the "set-up" of problems looks like. You will be required to identify expressions that could be used to find the percent of a number, the unit rate, the total cost, etc. Remember, there is more than one way to write expressions, so use the answer choices as a guide to help with what the problem is looking for.

For example:

To find the percent of a number, we typically convert the percent to a decimal, but on the test, a question may represent the decimal as a fraction. Both produce the same results.

0.85×60 as $\dfrac{85}{100} \times 60$.

B. Ratios

Proportional relationships

A **ratio** is a comparison of two numbers using a fraction, a colon, or the word *to*. **Rates** are ratios with different units, while ratios have the same units. Rates are often expressed as unit rates and are read using the word "per" instead of "to." It is common to reference a unit rate in everyday language.

Rates and Ratios	
Verbal statement	Four dogs for every three cats
Manipulatives/picture	
Fraction	$\dfrac{4 \text{ dogs}}{3 \text{ cats}}$
Colon	4 dogs: 3 cats or 4:3

A **unit rate** is a rate with a denominator of 1. Examples of unit rates include 60 miles per hour $\left(\dfrac{60\ \text{miles}}{1\ \text{hour}}\right)$, \$3 per box $\left(\dfrac{\$3}{1\ \text{box}}\right)$, or 22 students per teacher $\left(\dfrac{22\ \text{students}}{1\ \text{teacher}}\right)$. Any rate can be converted to a unit rate by dividing the numerator of the fraction by the denominator.

When two ratios are equivalent, they can be set equal to form a **proportion**.

Test items that contain proportional relationships may involve any of the following:

- A scale
- Equivalency statements
- Descriptions of similar figures

For this section, be prepared to identify the best option from a list of items and to set up proportions to solve word problems.

Proportions given a scale

A scale is typically given using a colon, and questions include a map or a model. The units may or may not be part of the scale, but they will be given in the problem or in an accompanying picture.

Example: A model of a new parking garage being built downtown has a height of 12.5 inches. If the scale of the model to the actual building is 2:15 and represents inches to feet, how tall is the actual parking garage?

Solution: Set up the first part of the proportion using the scale.

Quick Tip

Ratio: $\dfrac{2\ \text{feet}}{3\ \text{feet}}$ same units

Rate: $\dfrac{25\ \text{miles}}{3\ \text{hours}}$ different units

Proportion: $\dfrac{3\ \text{inches}}{14\ \text{miles}} = \dfrac{x\ \text{inches}}{84.5\ \text{miles}}$

How do you identify using a proportion?

✓ Contains a scale (2:15).

✓ Each of the numbers contains units.

✓ There are 3 numbers with units, and the problem asks for a 4th number with units.

$$\frac{2\ \text{inches}}{15\ \text{feet}}$$

Next, finish setting up the proportion by using what we call **_matchy-matchy_**. Match the units in the first fraction with the units in the second fraction; if inches are in the numerator in the first fraction, inches must also be in the numerator for the second fraction.

$$\frac{2\ \text{inches}}{15\ \text{feet}} = \frac{12.5\ \text{inches}}{x\ \text{feet}}$$

Last, cross multiply and solve the equation to find the value of the variable.

$2x = 12.5(15)$

Note: Once you cross-multiply, the fraction has been eliminated.

Now divide both sides by 2 to isolate the x.

$$\frac{2x}{2} = \frac{187.5}{2}$$

$x = 93.75$ feet

Proportions given an equivalency statement

An equivalency statement is a statement that describes a rate using words, such as a few envelopes stuffed every 20 minutes or a number of chaperones for every 15 students. Equivalency statements will have a constant rate and will also have three numbers with units and will ask for a fourth number.

Example: A pie crust machine can press 15 pie crusts into pie tins in 20 minutes. How many pie crusts can be pressed into pie tins in 4 hours?

Solution: Set up the first part of the proportion using the equivalency statement.

$$\frac{15 \text{ crusts}}{20 \text{ minutes}}$$

Next, finish setting up the proportion, remembering *matchy-matchy*. Be careful because the time for the second fraction is in hours. Convert hours to minutes so that the units are the same.

4 hours = 4 · 60 minutes = 240 minutes

$$\frac{15 \text{ crusts}}{20 \text{ minutes}} = \frac{x \text{ crusts}}{240 \text{ minutes}}$$

Last, cross-multiply and solve the equation to find the value of the variable.

$20x = 240(15)$

$20x = 3600$

Divide both sides by 20 to isolate the

$x = 180$ pie crusts

> **How do you identify using a proportion?**
> - ✓ Contains an equivalency statement that represents a rate
> - ✓ Each of the numbers contains units
> - ✓ There are 3 numbers with units, and the problem asks for a 4th number with units.

Proportions given a description of similar figures

Some word problems describe a situation that is proportional without explicitly giving this information. In this case, the situation may represent similar figures. The side lengths of similar figures are proportional, which is why the problem does not have to state anything about proportionality. If all the units are alike, this may indicate similar figures.

Example: The height of a tree can be found using similar triangles. A 12-foot-tall tree casts a 7-foot shadow. If a nearby tree casts a 5-foot shadow, how tall is the nearby tree?

Solution: Draw a picture and label the lengths.

> **How do you identify using a proportion?**
> - ✓ Contains similar figures that can be drawn
> - ✓ Each of the numbers contains units
> - ✓ There are 3 numbers with units, and the problem asks for a 4th number with units.

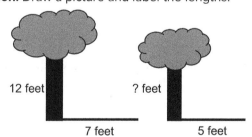

12 feet   ? feet

7 feet   5 feet

Next, use the picture to set up the proportion. Notice that the labels on the picture are already in the right place for a proportion.

$$\frac{12}{7} = \frac{x}{5}$$

Note: The units are not included here because they are all the same.

Last, cross-multiply and solve the proportion for the variable.

$$7x = 12(5)$$

$$7x = 60$$

Divide both sides by 7 to isolate the

$$x = 8\frac{4}{7} \text{ feet}$$

Proportions given similar figures

Questions that contain a proportional relationship may also be just a figure. In this instance, the shapes should be the same shape but a different size.

Example: The rectangles below are similar. What is the length of the missing side, x?

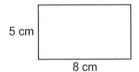

5 cm   8 cm   5 cm x cm

How do you identify using a proportion?

✓ The problem stated the figures are similar.

✓ There are 3 numbers with units, and the problem asks for a 4th number with units.

Solution: Be careful when setting up the proportion for this question because the second rectangle is rotated so that the shorter side is the length. When setting these up, think about matchy-matchy. If the first fraction in the proportion is set up as the shorter side over the longer side, make sure it is the same in the second fraction.

$$\frac{5}{8} = \frac{x}{5}$$

$$8x = 25$$

Divide both sides by 8 to isolate the x.

$$x = 3.125 \text{ cm}$$

Example question

An artist made a scale drawing of a mural he is painting on the side of a building that is 10 feet tall and 80 feet wide. The scale of inches to feet used to make the drawing is 3:40. How wide is the scale drawing?

   A. 6 inches

   B. 0.75 inches

   C. 24 inches

   D. 5 inches

Correct answer: A

The scale is one side of the proportion, and since the question is asking for the width of the scale drawing, the width of the actual building and the scale $3:40$ should be used.

$$\frac{3}{40} = \frac{x}{80}$$

$$40x = 240$$

$$x = 6 \text{ inches}$$

The height of building AB can be measured using similar triangles. A small puddle reflects the top of building AB so that a person standing on the top of ED can see the reflection of AB in the puddle. Using the information in the sketch below, find the height of building AB.

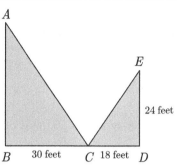

A. 36 feet

B. 39 feet

C. 40 feet

D. 45 feet

Correct answer: C

$$\frac{x}{30} = \frac{24}{18}$$

$$18x = 720$$

$$x = 40 \text{ feet}$$

Example question

A factory produces 10 pillows every 45 minutes. If the factory runs 8 hours each day, how many pillows will it produce in a 5-day work week?

A. 36

B. 106

C. 533

D. 888

Correct answer: C

The equivalency statement for this problem is 10 pillows every 45 minutes. The question asks for the final answer in hours, so first convert 45 minutes to hours, which is $45 \div 60 = 0.75$ hour. The final answer also asks for the number of pillows over 5 days. This problem can be solved by either using 40 hours in the proportion or using 8 and multiplying the answer by 5. To speed up the problem solving and not forget the last step, we suggest using 40 in the original problem.

$$\frac{10}{0.75} = \frac{x}{40}$$

$$0.75x = 400$$

$$x = 533.\overline{3}$$

The company cannot make 0.3 of a pillow, so C is the correct solution.

Percent of change (increase/decrease)

Questions that require finding the percent of increase or decrease will either ask for the percent of increase/decrease or the percent of change. To find the percent of change, first find the fraction:

$$\frac{\text{new number} - \text{original number}}{\text{original number}}.$$

Next, convert the fraction to a decimal and then to a percent. If the percent is positive, the change was an increase. If the percent is negative, the change is a decrease. The negative sign is not included in the answer of a percent decrease. It is instead denoted with the word *decrease*.

Example question

Last month, Michael ran an average of 5 miles per day. This month, he ran an average of 6 miles per day. Find the percent of increase for Michael's mileage.

    A. 16%

    B. 17%

    C. 20%

    D. 183%

Correct answer: C

$$\frac{\text{new} - \text{original}}{\text{original}} = \frac{6-5}{5} = \frac{1}{5} = 0.2 = 20\% \text{ increase.}$$

Percent of total

When a question asks what percent a situation represents, this requires writing numbers as a fraction, converting the numbers to decimals, and then converting the decimal to a percent.

Example question

At a local baseball tournament of 1,500 players, 500 of the players did not record a strikeout at the plate. What percent of the players, to the nearest whole percent, did record a strikeout during the tournament?

    A. 67%

    B. 96%

    C. 33%

    D. 46 %

Correct answer: A

First find the number of those striking out: $1500 - 500 = 1{,}000$

Next, write this number as a fraction out of the total number of players: $\dfrac{1000}{1500}$

Convert to a decimal and then a percent: $\dfrac{1000}{1500} = 0.6667 = 67\%$. The correct answer choice is A

Fractions, Operations with Fractions, and Ratios Practice Questions

1. The fraction of an hour it took four students to complete a test is listed in the table. What is the sum of the number of hours it took all four students to complete the test?

Student	Sara	Gary	Rudolph	Lorenzo
Time (hours)	$\dfrac{3}{5}$	$\dfrac{7}{10}$	$\dfrac{4}{5}$	$\dfrac{9}{10}$

   A. $\dfrac{23}{10}$

   B. $\dfrac{23}{15}$

   C. $\dfrac{23}{30}$

   D. $\dfrac{30}{10}$

2. A pizza restaurant gets an average of 250 orders on a weekend night. Of those orders 24% are for pickup, and the rest are for delivery. How many orders, to the nearest whole number, does the restaurant get for delivery on a weekend night?

   A. 60

   B. 100

   C. 180

   D. 190

3. Solve: $\dfrac{2}{9} + \dfrac{1}{3}$

   A. $\dfrac{1}{3}$

   B. $\dfrac{5}{9}$

   C. $\dfrac{5}{27}$

   D. $\dfrac{3}{9}$

4. Which of the following represents $-1\dfrac{3}{4}$ on the number line?

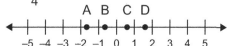

   A. A

   B. B

   C. C

   D. D

5. The two triangles are similar. What is the value of x?

A. 1

B. 2.8

C. 10

D. 28

6. Which of the following represents the largest value?

A. 842 thousandths

B. 82 hundredths

C. 8 tenths

D. 4 fifths

7. Which of the following represents the shaded region below?

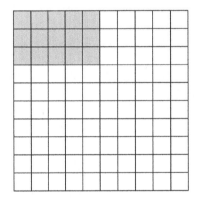

A. 10% or 0.10

B. 15% or 1.5

C. 25% or 0.25

D. 15% or 0.15

8. How many mini 4-ounce bags of snack mix can you make from a large 3.5 pound of snack mix?

A. 16

B. 14

C. 13

D. 12

9. Sam measured the length of the worms in his earthworm farm and recorded their lengths in inches below.

- 2.27

- $2\frac{1}{5}$

- $2\frac{2}{8}$

- 2.215

Which of the following shows the length of the worms in order from greatest to least?

A. $2\frac{1}{5}$, 2.215, $2\frac{2}{8}$, 2.27

B. 2.27, $2\frac{2}{8}$, $2\frac{1}{5}$, 2.215

C. 2.27, $2\frac{2}{8}$, 2.215, $2\frac{1}{5}$

D. 2.215, 2.27, $2\frac{2}{8}$, $2\frac{1}{5}$

10. A family wants to sod their 10 ft. by 50 ft. lawn, which is in the shape of a rectangle. If sod costs $3.00 per 10 ft^2, how much will it cost the family to sod their entire lawn?

A. $50.00

B. $1,500.00

C. $150.00

D. $300.00

This page intentionally left blank.

Number	Answer	Explanation
1.	D	Find a common denominator for all the fractions, then add the numerators. $\dfrac{3}{5} + \dfrac{7}{10} + \dfrac{4}{5} + \dfrac{9}{10}$ $= \dfrac{6}{10} + \dfrac{7}{10} + \dfrac{8}{10} + \dfrac{9}{10}$ $= \dfrac{30}{10}$
2.	D	Multiply 250×0.24 and get 60. Next subtract this from 250 to get the amount of pizzas for delivery. $250 - 60 = 190$
3.	B	$\dfrac{2}{9} + \dfrac{1}{3} = \dfrac{2}{9} + \dfrac{1 \times 3}{3 \times 3} = \dfrac{2}{9} + \dfrac{3}{9} = \dfrac{5}{9}$
4.	A	The point $-1\dfrac{3}{4}$ is between -1 and -2 on the number line, so point A is the correct answer choice.
5.	B	Set up a proportion to solve this problem. $\dfrac{10}{7} = \dfrac{4}{x}$ $\dfrac{10x}{10} = \dfrac{28}{10}$ $x = 2.8$ Remember, dividing by 10 is the same as moving the decimal point one place to the left.
6.	A	Writing out each of the values to 3 decimal places allows for a quick comparison. A. 0.842 B. 0.820 C. 0.800 D. 0.800 Answer choice A is the largest value.
7.	D	15 of the 100 squares are shaded, so this represents 15%. To change 15% to a decimal, move the decimal point two places to the left. 15% = 0.15.
8.	B	Because 1 pound = 16 ounces, you can make four 4-ounce bags for each pound and two 4-ounce bags for each half pound. Thus, for 3.5 pounds, you can make $12 + 2 = 14$ mini bags.

Number	Answer	Explanation
9.	C	Convert each of the lengths to decimals, writing each decimal out three places after the decimal point. $2.27 = 2.270$ $2\frac{1}{5} = 2.200$ $2\frac{2}{8} = 2.250$ $2.215 = 2.215$ The ones place and the tenths place are the same value for all numbers in the set. Using the hundredths place to put the values in order from greatest to least, we have: $2.27, \quad 2\frac{2}{8}, \quad 2.215, \quad 2\frac{1}{5}$
10.	C	Find the area of the rectangular lawn. $10 \cdot 50 = 500$ ft^2 Sod costs \$3.00 per 10 ft^2, so divide 500 by 10 to get the number of 10 ft^2 parcels of sod needed. $500 \div 10 = 50$ Last, multiply 50 by \$3.00 to get the cost of sodding the entire yard. $50 \cdot \$3 = \$150$

IV. Early Equations and Expressions, Measurement, and Geometry

The following topics are aligned with the test specifications of the Praxis 7813 exam. It is important that you examine these closely because these are the skills assessed on the exam.

A. Early Equations and Expressions

B. Measurement

C. Geometry

A. Early Equations and Expressions

Equations

The equations you will have to solve on the test are linear or a factored form of a quadratic, which is like solving a linear equation. A linear equation is an equation with all the variables having a power of 1. An example of a linear equation is $y = 2x + 4$. You do not need to identify whether an equation is linear.

A factored quadratic equation looks like $(x + 3)(x - 5) = 0$. If we performed the multiplication between the parentheses, the power of x would be 2, which is what makes it a quadratic equation. You do not need to know how to identify quadratic equations. These terms are discussed here to be able to note the differences when solving.

Translating verbal statements into expressions and equations

The following lists and examples include common math vocabulary used in verbal statements. Be familiar with these phrases. You may be expected to translate verbal expressions presented in different scenarios, so be prepared.

Verbal Statements			
Addition	• Sum • Plus • Add • Altogether • Total • Increased by	**Subtraction**	• Difference • Minus • Take Away • Less, Less than • Subtracted from • Decreased by
Multiplication	• Product • Times • Multiply • Of • Double, twice	**Division**	• Quotient • Divide • Ratio • Split into Parts
Equal	• Is • Equal • Equivalent to	**Grouping Symbols**	• Quantity • 2 Operations in a row (Example: times the sum of...)

The following terms are prevalent in assessment questions, so make sure you know these terms.

- Sum
- Product
- Of
- Is
- Difference
- Less than
- Subtracted from
- Quotient
- Quantity
- Times the sum of...

Example: Four times the quantity of a number, x, plus three.

Solution: $4(x + 3)$

Verbal expression breakdown:

four	4
times	$\times$
the quantity	$(\ )$
a number x	x
plus	$+$
three	3

The tricky part here is the phrase *the quantity.* When you have two operations in a row or the phrase *the quantity,* the numbers and operations following go into the parentheses because they are *the quantity.* The math statement that represents the verbal statement is $4(x + 3)$. (We don't need the multiplication symbol between the 4 and the parentheses).

Example: The quotient of double a number, y, and 15

Solution: $\dfrac{2y}{15}$ OR $2y \div 15$

Example: Eight subtracted from the product of 3 and m.

Solution: $3m - 8$

Subtracted from can be tricky because it switches the order of the terms given in the problem. Since 8 is subtracted from the product, the product of and needs to come first.

Example question

Four times the difference of a number and twelve is eighty-seven. Which of the following choices represents this equation?

    A. $4 \times x - 12 = 87$

    B. $4(x - 12) = 87$

    C. $4(12 - x) = 87$

    D. $12 - 4x = 87$

Correct answer: B

When two operations are in a verbal statement with no numbers in between, this represents a quantity. Four times the difference of two numbers should be interpreted as having to subtract two numbers in the order they appear before multiplying by 4, which would mean the subtraction problem has to be in parentheses so that it comes first in the order of operations.

Order of Operations

The acronym, PEMDAS, or the mnemonic *Please Excuse My Dear Aunt Sally*, is often used to remember the order of operations.

Please, or parentheses, includes all grouping symbols, which may include brackets [ ], braces { }, and absolute value bars | |. If there is math that can be computed inside grouping symbols, do that FIRST, then the grouping symbols may be removed.

Excuse, or exponents, means anything raised to a power should be simplified after there are no more parentheses.

My **D**ear, or multiplication or division, are essentially the same "type" of operation and are therefore done in order from left to right, just as you would read a book. All multiplication and division should be completed BEFORE any addition or subtraction that is not inside parentheses.

Aunt **S**ally, or addition and subtraction, are also essentially the same "type" of operation and are also done in order from left to right. These operations should always come last, unless they were inside parentheses.

P	Parentheses
E	Exponents
M D	Multiplication & Division
A S	Addition & Subtraction

Example question

Simplify the expression.

$(16 - 4) \div (5 - 2) \times (10 - 8)$

   A. 1

   B. 2

   C. 4

   D. 8

Correct answer: D

$(\mathbf{16 - 4}) \div (\mathbf{5 - 2}) \times (\mathbf{10 - 8})$ Problems in different parentheses can be solved at the same time.

$= \mathbf{12 \div 3} \times 2$ Parentheses are not necessary once all operations are completed.

$= 4 \times 2$

$= 8$

Example question

Jessica and Emily both collect coins. Emily has four less than twice as many coins as Jessica. If c represents the number of coins Jessica has, which expression represents the number of coins Emily has?

   A. $4 < 2c$

   B. $4 - 2c$

   C. $2(4 - c)$

   D. $2c - 4$

Correct answer: D

Four less than twice as many coins as Jessica is calculated by finding two times the number of coins Jessica has, then subtracting four. Remember, 1 less than 5 equals 4, and it is written as $5 - 1$. When you see *less than,* slow down and think about the order of the numbers being subtracted in the problem. The less than symbol is not an option because the word "is" would need to be present. For example, 4 is less than 5 is written as $4 < 5$ whereas 4 less than 5 is written as $5 - 4$.

Example question

Jarrod is using a verbal statement to represent the addition of two terms in an expression. Which word could he use to represent addition?

    A. Sum

    B. Product

    C. Difference

    D. Quotient

Correct answer: A

The solution to an addition problem is called the sum.

Write equations and inequalities given a word problem

In addition to translating verbal expressions, you will be expected to write an equation, inequality, or system of equations given a real-world scenario. The process is the same as translating a verbal expression, but you will have to make some inferences. For example, John earns $15 per hour will translate to 15.

Example question

Heather buys some tomatoes for $2 each and three onions for $1.25 each. She spent less than $9 on tomatoes and onions. Which option represents this scenario?

    A. $2t + 1.25 < 9$

    B. $2t + 1.25 > 9$

    C. $2t + 3.75 < 9$

    D. $2t + 3.75 \leq 9$

Correct answer: C

We don't know how many tomatoes Heather bought, so let t represent the number of tomatoes purchased. We do know the tomatoes were $2 each, so $2t$ represents the cost of the tomatoes. She purchased 3 onions for $1.25 each, making the cost of the onions $3 \times 1.25 = \$3.75$. If she spent less than $9, the total cost of the tomatoes and onions, $2t + 3.75$, is less than 9, or $2t + 3.75 < 9$. Therefore, C is the correct answer choice. Right away, we can eliminate answer B and D because the question says that Heather spent less than $9. Therefore, any equation without a less than sign can be eliminated.

A gym membership costs \$18 per month plus a \$10 application fee. Which equation represents the total cost of the membership after m number of months?

- A. $y = 18m + 10$
- B. $18m + y = 10$
- C. $10 - y = 18m$
- D. $18(y + m) = 10$

Correct answer: A

The application fee is a flat rate, so in an equation, it is simply adding 10. The cost per month can be represented by $18m$ because members pay 18 each month. The total paid after any given number of months can be found using the equation $y = 18m + 10$.

Solving for a variable

On the test, you will have to solve for a variable in a formula after substituting in given values. This means you will have to use inverse operations to solve.

The following table provides an example and the solution for many common formulas (e.g., temperature conversions, area, volume). Understanding these will prepare you for most formulas you may encounter on the test.

Formula	Example	Solution	
$V = lwh$	Find w if the length is 4 meters, the height is 6.5 meters, and the volume is 260 cubic inches.	$260 = (4)(w)(6.5)$	Substitute given values.
		$260 = 26w$	Simplify.
		$\dfrac{260}{26} = \dfrac{26w}{26}$	Divide both sides by 26.
		$10 = w$	Solution
$A = \dfrac{1}{2} bh$	Find the height of a triangle with a base of $12\dfrac{1}{2}$ inches and an area of 50 square inches.	$50 = (0.5)(12.5)(h)$	Substitute given values.
		$50 = 6.25h$	Simplify.
		$\dfrac{50}{6.25} = \dfrac{6.25h}{6.25}$	Divide both sides by 6.25.
		$8 = h$	Solution

Evaluating expressions and equations

Evaluating an expression or equation means to substitute given values into the variables and simplify the math expression. When evaluating, it is important to remember to follow order of operations and be very careful about negative signs.

Evaluate the expression for $x = -2$.

$-x^2 - 4x - 1$

    A. 2

    B. -2

    C. 3

    D. -3

Correct answer: C

Substitute -2 into the expression. Pay close attention to all the negative and minus signs.

$-(-2)^2 - 4(-2) - 1$

$= -(4) - 4(-2) - 1$

$= -4 - (-8) - 1$

$= -4 + 8 - 1$

$= 4 - 1 = 3$

Properties of equality

Properties of equality explain equivalent equations where two equations have the same solution.

Property of Equality	Rule	Example
Reflexive Property	$a = a$ *Most often used in geometric proofs*	 $AB \cong AB$
Symmetric Property	If $a = b$, then $b = a$	If $-3 > x$, then $x < -3$
Transitive Property	If $a = b$ and $b = c$, then $a = c$	If $y = x$ and $x = a$ then $y = a$
Addition property	If $a = b$, then $a + c = b + c$	If $a = 3$, then $a + c = 3 + c$
Subtraction property	If $a = b$, then $a - c = b - c$	If $a = 2$, then $a - c = 2 - c$
Multiplication property	If $a = b$, then $a \times c = b \times c$	If $a = 7$, then $a \times c = 7 \times c$
Division property	If $a = b$, and $c \neq 0$, then $a \div c = b \div c$	If $a = 4$, and $c \neq 0$, then $a \div c = 4 \div c$
Substitution property	If $a = b$, the b may be substituted for a in any expression containing a.	If $a = b$, and $b = x^2$, then $a + 7 = x^2 + 7$

Properties of inequality

	Rule	Example
Reversal Property	If $a > b$, $b < a$	$a > 3$, $3 < a$
Additive Inverse Property	If $a > b$, $-a < -b$	$4 > 3$, $-4 < -3$
Transitive Property	If $a > b$, and $b > c$, then $a > c$	If $4 > 3$, and $3 > 2$, then $4 > 2$
Addition property	If $a > b$, then $a + c > b + c$	If $5 > 3$, then $5 + c > 3 + c$
Subtraction property	If $a > b$, then $a - c > b - c$	If $7 > 2$, then $7 - c > 2 - c$
Multiplication property	If $a > b$, and $c > 0$, then $a \times c > b \times c$ If $a > b$, and $c < 0$, then $a \times c < b \times c$	If $9 > 4$, and $c > 0$, then $9 \times 2 > 4 \times 2$ If $9 > 5$, and $c < 0$, then $9 \times -2 < 5 \times -2$
Division property	If $a > b$, and $c > 0$, then $a \div c > b \div c$ If $a > b$, and $c > 0$, then $a \div c < b \div c$	If $6 > 4$, and $c > 0$, then $6 \div 2 > 4 \div 2$ If $8 > 6$, and $c < 0$, then $8 \div -2 < 6 \div -2$

Example question

Jack's mom gave him $10 to spend at the school store for spiral notebooks that cost $1.25 each and folders that cost $0.50 each. If he buys 3 spiral notebooks and x folders, which option represents how much money he can spend if his mom asked him to spend under $10?

    A. $0.5x + 3.75 < 10$

    B. $1.25x + 1.5 > 10$

    C. $0.5x + 3.75 \geq 10$

    D. $1.25x + 1.5 \leq 10$

Correct answer: A

Jack's mother asks him to spend *less than* $10. The only answer choice that depicts *less than* 10 is answer choice A. Additionally, the information provided says that Jack is getting 3 notebooks that cost $1.25 each, or 3($1.25) which equals $3.75. The number of folders for $0.50 is the unknown quantity, or $0.5x$. The equation becomes $0.5x + 3.75 < 10$.

Central tendency

Measures of center, or measures of central tendency, include mean, median, and mode. These statistical values are referred to as measures of center because they are symbolic of the values in the data set.

Measures of spread or **variability**, include range and mean absolute deviation. Absolute deviation is very tedious to find, so it is unlikely you will have to find this value.

Measures of Central Tendency		
Mean	Find the average; add all the numbers and divide by how many numbers were added. *We think of the mean as "mean" because it's mean to make you do so much work to get an answer.*	
Median	Place numbers in ascending order; find the middle number. If there are two middle numbers, add them and divide by 2. *Remember, median is in the middle, just like the median in the road.*	
Mode	The number or numbers that occur the most. *Mode and most both start with MO...__MODE__ __MO__ST.*	
Range	Subtract the smallest number in the set from the largest number in the set. *Range is always going to be a comparison of the largest and smallest numbers.*	

Example question

On a quiz in Mrs. Fingal's class, 8 students scored 70%, 12 students scored 80%, and 4 students scored 95%. What is the mean score for the quiz? Round to the nearest whole number.

A. 79

B. 82

C. 80

D. 85

Correct answer: A

To find the mean of a list that groups values in sets, it is not necessary to list out all the numbers. Instead, find the sum of each like group of values, then add the sums together and divide by the total number of values.

Partial sums:	Total sum:	Mean:
8 × 70 = 560 12 × 80 = 960 4 × 95 = 380	560 + 960 + 380 = 1,900	1,900 ÷ 24 = 79

Example question

Find the mode of the data: {3, 3, 5, 6, 4, 5, 6, 2, 4, 5, 1, 10}

A. 7

B. 5

C. 4

D. 3

Correct answer: B

To find the mode, first put the numbers in order, then find the number that is repeated the most.

{1, 2, 3, 3, 4, 4, 5, 5, 5, 6, 6, 10}. The number repeated the most is 5.

Test Tip

When finding the median and mode, make sure the data is in ascending order first.

Range

To find the range, arrange the numbers in the data set in ascending order, then subtract the smallest value from the largest value.

Example question

Find the range of the data set: {6, 3, 1, 10, 12, 4, 9}

A. 3

B. 10

C. 11

D. 12

Correct answer: C

Place the values in order, {1, 3, 4, 6, 9, 10, 12}, then subtract the smallest from the largest, 12 − 1 = 11.

B. Measurement

The measurement portion of the test includes conversions within the U.S. customary system, conversions within the metric system, and an understanding of the relative size of basic measurements.

Metric conversions

The metric system is based on units of 10. When converting within the metric system, you are only responsible for the basic units: kilo-, centi-, and milli-. The other units that are grayed out are to show the conversions by units of 10.

Metric Conversions						
Prefixes						
Kilo-	Hecto-	Deca-	**Basic Unit**	Deci-	**Centi-**	**Milli-**
Abbreviations						
km	hm	dkm	**meter (m)**	dm	**cm**	**mm**
kL	hL	dkL	**liter (L)**	dL	**cL**	**mL**
kg	hg	dkg	**gram (g)**	dg	**cg**	**mg**
0.001	0.01	0.1	**1**	10	**100**	**1,000**

There are two different ways to approach metric conversions: moving the decimal and using a proportion.

Convert by moving the decimal point.

If the conversion is from a **smaller unit to a larger unit**, move the decimal point **LEFT** the number of spaces between the two units.

If the conversion is from a **larger unit to a smaller unit**, move the decimal point **RIGHT** the number of spaces between the two units.

This method requires memorizing the abbreviations in order.

Example question

Complete the following.

4.5 L = _____ kL

    A. 0.0045 kL

    B. 45000 kL

    C. 450 kL

    D. 0.045 kL

Correct response: A

The conversion is going from a smaller unit to a larger unit. Therefore, the decimal point moves to the left. Liters is 3 units away from kiloliters, so the decimal point moves three places to the left.

kiloliter   hectoliter   decaliter   liter

You can also solve this by setting up a proportion.

Example question

Complete the following.

4 km = _____ mm

    A. 400 mm

    B. 0.4000 mm

    C. 4,000,000 mm

    D. 0.0004 mm

Correct answer: C

The conversion is going from a larger unit to a smaller unit. Therefore, the decimal point moves to the right. Kilometers and millimeters are six units apart, so the decimal point moves six places to the right.

4 km = 4,000,000 mm

Convert using a proportion.

To use a proportion, create a ratio from the problem and set up an equivalent ratio using the numbers in the table.

This method requires memorizing the abbreviations in order and knowing how to add in the numerical values.

Complete the following.

4L = _____ mL

    A.   40 mL

    B.   4000 mL

    C.   4,000,000 mL

    D.   0.0004 mL

Correct answer: B

The ratio created from the problem is $\dfrac{4L}{x\ \text{mL}}$, and the ratio created from the table would be $\dfrac{1L}{1000\ \text{mL}}$.

Choose the units from the problem to determine the units for the second ratio. The proportion would be:

$$\frac{4L}{x\ \text{mL}} = \frac{1L}{1000\ \text{mL}}$$

Cross-multiply and solve.

$4000 = 1x$

Standard conversions

Standard conversions require quite a bit of straight memorization, which is not the purpose of the exam. It is not likely (of course anything is possible) that a question asks for conversions across multiple units, such as cups to gallons.

Standard US Conversions	
1 foot = 12 inches	1 cup = 8 fluid ounces
1 yard = 3 feet = 36 inches	1 pint = 2 cups
1 mile = 5,280 feet = 1760 yards	1 quart = 2 pints
1 hour = 60 minutes	1 gallon = 4 quarts
1 minute = 60 seconds	1 pound = 16 ounces
	1 ton = 2,000 pounds

Standard conversions are often embedded in questions that contain measurements in two units but require only one unit to solve. For example, finding the area of a square that measures 8 inches by 2 feet.

C. Geometry

The possible scenarios of real-world geometry problems are endless. Test questions typically, but not always, include a combination of formulas so that multiple skills are assessed at one time. You will not have to recall every formula listed. Most formulas are intuitive. If you remember the basic formulas for area, it is much easier to find surface area and volume because surface area is just several basic area formulas added together, and volume is simply the area of the base times the height of the object.

Common formulas used on standardized math assessments

- Perimeter of a rectangle or square
- Area of a circle
- Area of a rectangle or square
- Area of a triangle
- Volume of a sphere
- Volume of a rectangular prism (box)
- Pythagorean Theorem

Measurement	Formula	Picture and Description
Perimeter Rectangle or Square	Rectangle: $$P = b + h + b + h = 2b + 2h$$ Square: $$P = 4s$$	Add all the sides of the figure for both the rectangle and square.
Area Rectangle	$$A = bh$$	The base (b) and height (h) are always perpendicular to one another for all figures.
Area Parallelogram	$$A = bh$$	The base (b) and height (h) are always perpendicular to one another, so a dotted line is added to show the height.
Area Trapezoid	$$A = \frac{1}{2}h(b_1 + b_2)$$	Because a trapezoid can have either base at the bottom, the base lengths are averaged, then multiplied by the height (h).
Area Triangle	$$A = \frac{1}{2}bh$$	The base and height are always perpendicular to one another, so a dotted line is added to show the height for different types of triangles.

Measurement	Formula	Picture and Description
Area Circle	$A = \pi r^2$	The area of a circle uses the radius, which is the length from the center of the circle to a point on the circle.
Circumference Circle	$C = \pi d = 2\pi r$	The circumference measures the distance around the outside of a circle.
Surface Area Prism	$SA = Ph + 2B$ P is perimeter of base; h is height of prism for 2nd formula	The surface area (SA) of a prism is found by finding the area of all six sides and adding these areas together.
Volume Prism	$V = lwh$ or $V = Bh$	Multiply all three sides together to find the volume of a prism.
Pythagorean Theorem	$a^2 + b^2 = c^2$	Used to find a missing side of a right triangle only.
Approximations of pi (π)	$\pi \approx 3.14$ OR $\dfrac{22}{7}$	Know both the decimal approximation and the fraction approximation for pi.

The examples below represent some of the common types of problems representative of those that appear most often on tests.

Example question

Find the perimeter of a square with an area of 100 square feet.

    A. 10 feet

    B. 20 feet

    C. 40 feet

    D. 1,000 feet

Correct answer: C

Because the sides are the same length, find what number was multiplied by itself to get the length of each side. In this case, 100 = 10 × 10, so the side lengths are 10 feet. Therefore, the perimeter is

$P = 4s$

$P = 4(10) = 40$ feet

A wastepaper basket is in the shape of a rectangular prism, as shown below. If the wastepaper basket is covered with decorative paper on the outside, what is the surface area of the faces with paper?

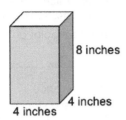

8 inches

4 inches

4 inches

A. 16 in²

B. 128 in²

C. 144 in²

D. 160 in²

Correct answer: C

The surface area of a rectangular prism is found by finding the area of each of the faces of the prism and adding these areas together. The trick for this problem is recognizing that a wastepaper basket has no top, so there are only five faces.

Surface area of wastepaper basket: (4 · 4) + 2(4 · 8) + 2(4 · 8) = 16 + 64 + 64 = 144 in².

Note: the first term is not multiplied by 2 because of the "missing" top.

Example question

Find the area of Box A.

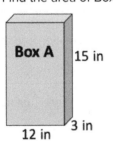

Box A   15 in

12 in   3 in

A. 480 in³

B. 540 in³

C. 600 in³

D. 720 in³

Correct answer: B

Box A: $V = lwh = 12 \times 3 \times 15 = 540$ in³

How a change in dimensions affects other measurements

When dimensions change by a given factor, area changes by the square of the factor, and volume changes by the cube of the factor. The example that follows shows why this happens.

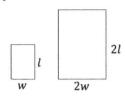

Area of a rectangle: $A = l \cdot w$

Area of a rectangle with sides doubled: $A = 2l \cdot 2w = \mathbf{2^2}(l \cdot w)$

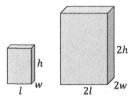

Volume of a rectangular solid: $V = l \cdot w \cdot h$

Volume of a rectangular solid with side doubled: $V = 2l \cdot 2w \cdot 2h = \mathbf{2^3}(l \cdot w \cdot h)$

Example question

Rhonda is having a small sign that measures 5 inches by 4 inches enlarged to create a poster. The dimensions will be increased by a scale factor of 3. What will be the area of the enlarged poster?

- A. 180 in²
- B. 60 in²
- C. 100 in²
- D. 240 in²

Correct answer: A

The area of the poster will increase by a factor or $3^{\$}$. Therefore, the area is $5 \times 4 \times 3^2 = 180$ in².

Quick Tip

When a figure is changed by a factor (i.e., increases by a factor of 4), the **area** of the figure is multiplied by the factor **squared (2 times)**. If you're finding **volume**, the volume of the figure is multiplied by the factor **cubed (3 times)**.

Attributes of two-dimensional and three-dimensional figures

To help solve problems on the test, knowing attributes of basic geometric figures will help you with problem-solving. When geometric figures are named, their unique properties are understood to be true by the reader. The most used figures and their attributes are given in the table that follows.

Figure Name	Image	Attributes
Rectangle		• All angles equal 90° • Opposite sides have the same length • A special type of parallelogram • Opposite sides are parallel
Square		• All angles equal 90° • All sides have the same length • A special type of parallelogram • A special type of rectangle • Opposite sides are parallel
Circle		• Diameter goes through the center of the circle to the edge of the circle • Radius starts at the center of the circle and ends on the edge of the circle • The radius is half the length of the diameter.
Cube		• All sides of a cube are squares • All sides have the same length • All angles equal 90°

Properties of Three-dimensional Shapes

Three-dimensional figures are solid shapes that have three dimensions, such as length, width, and height. These figures are comprised of polygons and all have faces, edges, and vertices.

Face. A two-dimensional figure that makes up the side of a three-dimensional figure.

Edge. The edge, or intersection, where two faces that make up a three-dimensional figure meet.

Vertices. The corners, or points, where edges of a three-dimensional figure meet.

Prism. Has two identical ends; the shape of the end is part of the name of the figure.

Pyramid. A three-dimensional figure with triangular faces that meet at a point; the base can be any shape and is used as part of the name of the pyramid.

Base. In a pyramid, the base is the side opposite the point; in a prism, either of the two identical ends.

Nets

A net is the two-dimensional shape when a three-dimensional figure is opened and laid flat; the net is the pattern for the three-dimensional figure. Nets are useful when teaching surface area and characteristics of three-dimensional figures. On the test, questions with a net will ask to pair a net with the name of the three-dimensional figure. To determine the name of a three-dimensional figure, use the following tips:

- A prism will have two bases. All other shapes are the sides of the prism.
- A pyramid will have one base. All other figures are the sides of the pyramid.
- The shape of the base is used to name the prism or pyramid.

Know the names of the figures below to use the base name to name the three-dimensional figure. The key to getting a question with a net correct is identifying and naming the base(s).

Figure	Name	Number of Sides
▲	Triangle	3
▬	Rectangle	4
■	Square	4
⬠	Pentagon	5
⬡	Hexagon	6
Heptagon shape	Heptagon	7
⯃	Octagon	8

The table that follows lists the name of prisms and pyramids and gives an example of a possible net. Sometimes the figure is turned on its side, and the bases are located on the sides of the figure (see the rectangular prism and triangular figures in the table).

Figure	Possible Net	Figure	Possible Net
Rectangular Prism		**Square Pyramid**	
Cube		**Triangular Pyramid**	
Triangular Prism		**Cylinder**	

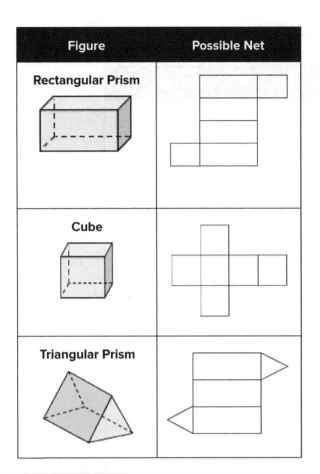

Example question

Which of the following is a possible net for a cube?

A.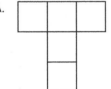

C.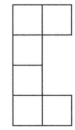

B.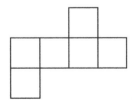

D.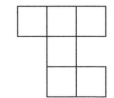

Correct answer: B

The net of a cube should have 4 squares in a row and squares that are able to be folded to create the top and bottom. Answer choice A does not have enough squares to create a cube, and answer choice D does not have 4 squares in a row to create the sides. Answer choice C needs the squares on the sides to be on opposite sides so one covers the top and the other covers the bottom.

Which of the following could be used to construct a triangular prism?

    A. 4 triangles

    B. 3 triangles, 4 squares

    C. 2 triangles, 3 rectangles

    D. 2 triangles, 4 rectangles

Correct answer: C

A prism has two identical ends, and the end shape is part of the name of the prism. In this case, triangles would be the two ends. Thus, three rectangles would connect the triangles to form a triangular prism.

Example question

Name the net.

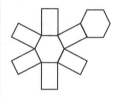

    A. Pentagonal prism

    B. Hexagonal prism

    C. Octagonal prism

    D. Hexagonal pyramid

Correct answer: B

The shape of the base is a hexagon, which is a 6-sided figure. Because the net has two bases, the figure is a prism. Therefore, the net makes a hexagonal prism, which is answer choice B.

Figure	Name	Faces	Edges	Vertices
	Rectangular prism	6	12	8
	Cube	6	12	8
	Triangular prism	5	9	6

Figure	Name	Faces	Edges	Vertices
	Square pyramid	5	8	5
	Triangular pyramid	4	6	4

Classify two-dimensional figures

Triangles are polygons with 3 edges and 3 vertices.

Triangle	Definition and Characteristics	Examples
Classification by Sides		
Scalene	A triangle with no congruent sides and no congruent angles.	
Isosceles	A triangle with two congruent sides. Angles opposite the congruent sides are also congruent.	
Equilateral	A triangle with all sides congruent. Angles in an equilateral triangle are all congruent, or equal to 60° (sometimes called equiangular).	

Triangle	Definition and Characteristics	Examples
Classification by Angles		
Acute	A triangle with all angle measures less than 90°	
Right	A triangle with one angle equal to 90°	
Obtuse	A triangle with one angle greater than 90°	

Polygons are plane figures with sides that are connected to form a shape. A **regular polygon** is a polygon with all sides congruent, or the same length.

Special quadrilaterals are polygons bounded by 4 line segments.

Figure	Name	Definition
	Parallelogram	A quadrilateral with • Opposite sides and opposite angles congruent • Opposite sides parallel
	Rhombus	A parallelogram with • All sides congruent • Opposite angles congruent (1 pair obtuse, 1 pair acute)
	Rectangle	A parallelogram with • Opposite sides congruent • All angles congruent
	Square	A parallelogram with • All sides congruent and all angles congruent (90°)
	Trapezoid	A quadrilateral with • One pair of parallel sides
	Kite	A quadrilateral with • 2 pairs of adjacent sides congruent

Four Quadrants of a Rectangular Coordinate System

The coordinate plane is made up of both a horizontal number line and a vertical number line, which split the coordinate plane into four quadrants. For the test, be able to identify the parts of the coordinate plane. Questions may reference any part of the coordinate plane with the definition being known by the test taker.

In addition to being able to identify parts of the coordinate plane, also be able to graph a point or identify in which quadrant a point lies. Knowing the signs of coordinates in each quadrant may help in answering test questions.

Parts of the Coordinate Plane

- x-axis
- y-axis
- Origin
- Quadrants I
- Quadrant II
- Quadrant III
- Quadrant IV

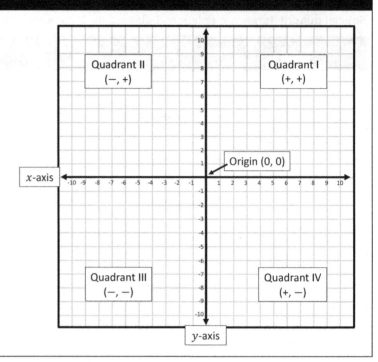

In addition to being able to identify parts of a coordinate plane and coordinates on the plane, you may be required to draw shapes and answer questions about shapes on a coordinate plane. This includes being able to find the perimeter or area of the figure.

Example question

A triangle has the coordinates $(2, 6)$, $(2, 1)$, and $(8, 1)$. What is the area of the triangle?

A. 15 square units

B. 20 square units

C. 25 square units

D. 30 square units

Correct answer: A

It is useful to draw a quick sketch of the triangle to help find the lengths of the base and height (the two sides that form a right angle). The base and height of the triangle are 5 units and 6 units.

The area of the triangle is $A = \frac{1}{2}bh = \frac{1}{2} \cdot 6 \cdot 5 = 3 \cdot 5 = 15$ square units.

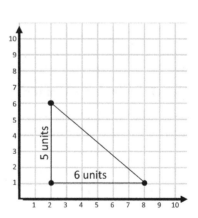

Given that the coordinates of a square are $(1, 5)$, $(4, 1)$, $(8, 4)$, and $(5, 8)$, find the perimeter of the square.

    A.   32 units

    B.   25 units

    C.   20 units

    D.   16 units

Solution: C

This question can be approached a few ways, but the fastest and easiest is to apply your knowledge of right triangles to quickly find the length of the sides of the square. First, quickly sketch the square on a coordinate plane.

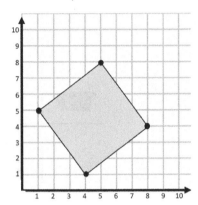

Because the square is drawn slightly rotated, we cannot count units from one point to the next to determine side lengths. What we can do, though, is see that we can sketch in a right triangle, with one of the sides of the square being the hypotenuse of the triangle. The triangle has two sides that are 3 units and 4 units. Now use the Pythagorean Theorem $a^2 + b^2 = c^2$, which makes the hypotenuse 5 units.

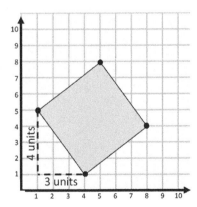

Because the hypotenuse of the triangle is also the side of the square, we can say that the sides of the square are each 5 units. Thus, the perimeter of the square is $P = 4(5)$, which 20 units.

Transformations

Transformations change the location or size of a figure. Types of transformations you will see on the test include translations, rotations, and reflections. Translations, rotations, and reflections create a new image that is *congruent* to, or the same size, the original image.

Transformations are typically done on a coordinate plane so that the exact changes are reflected in the coordinates of the vertices of the image. When a figure is transformed, the vertices contain a prime mark (like an apostrophe) to delineate between the original figure and the transformed figure. For example, if rectangle ABCD is rotated, the new rectangle will be named A'B'C'D'.

Translation. A translation changes the position of an image by moving it left, right, up, or down. The figure will look the same but in a different place. Another term for translation is slide.

Rotation. A rotation spins or rotates a figure about a point or line. A rotated figure will be in a different place and will have a different orientation.

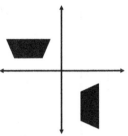

Reflection. Reflections "flip" an image over a line or axis. Each vertex point of the new figure will be the exact same distance from the line as the original image, in the direction of the reflection. You will have to be able to identify the axis over which the reflection occurred. The axis that the figures are on either side of will be the axis over which the figure was reflected. Another term for a reflection is flip or a mirror image.

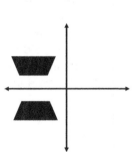

Example question

The coordinate plane below shows what type of transformation?

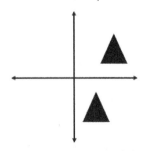

A. Translation

B. Rotation

C. Reflection over the-axis

D. Reflection over the -axis

Correct answer: A

Sliding one of the images up/down and left/right will produce the second image. Therefore, answer choice A is the correct answer.

What transformation occurred from one image to the other?

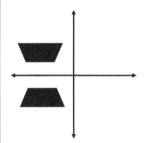

    A.   Reflection over the y-axis

    B.   Rotation about the origin

    C.   Reflection over the x-axis

    D.   Translation

Correct answer: C

The two images are mirror images of one another, or one is flipped over the x-axis to get the second image.

This page intentionally left blank.

Early Equations and Expressions, Measurement, and Geometry Practice Questions

1. What is the BEST way to classify the triangle below?

    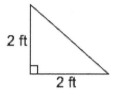

    A. Right, scalene

    B. Right, isosceles

    C. Acute, scalene

    D. Acute, equilateral

2. Which of the following is **NOT** a parallelogram?

    A. Rectangle

    B. Rhombus

    C. Kite

    D. Square

3. In what quadrant is the point $(2, -1)$?

    A. Quadrant I

    B. Quadrant II

    C. Quadrant III

    D. Quadrant IV

4. A triangle has the coordinates $(2, 6)$, $(2, 1)$, and $(8, 1)$. What is the area of the triangle?

    A. 15 square units

    B. 20 square units

    C. 25 square units

    D. 30 square units

5. A rectangular backyard is fenced in using 200 feet of fencing. All sides are fenced except the side against the house. If the width of the house is 80 feet, how long is the backyard?

    A. 32 feet

    B. 60 feet

    C. 120 feet

    D. 160 feet

6. In which quadrant is the point $(-3, -6)$?

    A. Quadrant I

    B. Quadrant II

    C. Quadrant III

    D. Quadrant IV

7. Find the area of the trapezoid.

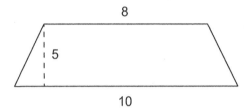

    A. 80

    B. 45

    C. 60

    D. 40

8. Which of the figures has 5 faces and 6 vertices?

    A. Triangular pyramid

    B. Triangular prism

    C. Rectangular prism

    D. Cylinder

9. A triangle has interior angle measurements of 20°, 50°, and 110°. Classify the triangle.

    A. Acute scalene

    B. Isosceles

    C. Equilateral

    D. Obtuse scalene

10. Which answer choice best describes a cube?

    A. 6 faces, 6 edges, 6 vertices

    B. 6 faces, 12 edges, 8 vertices

    C. 8 faces, 12 edges, 6 vertices

    D. 6 faces, 24 edges, 8 vertices

Number	Answer	Explanation
1.	B	Because the triangle has two congruent sides, it is isosceles, and because it contains a right angle, it is also a right triangle. The correct answer choice is B.
2.	C	A kite is not a type of parallelogram because it does not have 2 pairs of parallel sides with opposite sides and opposite angles congruent.
3.	D	A coordinate with a positive x value and a negative y value is in the 4th quadrant. II $(-,+)$ I $(+,+)$ III $(-,-)$ IV $(+,-)$
4.	A	A quick sketch of the triangle assists in finding the lengths of the sides of the base and height of the triangle (the two sides that form a right angle). The base and height of the triangle are 5 units and 6 units. Thus, the area of the triangle is $A = \frac{1}{2}bh = \frac{1}{2} \cdot 6 \cdot 5 = 3 \cdot 5 = 15$ square units, answer choice A. 5 units 6 units
5.	B	Even though the question says the backyard is a rectangle, you are only trying to find 3 sides of the fence. The 4th side is the house and does not need to be fenced. This means the 3 remaining sides of the fence must add up to 200 feet. Since the house represents the width of the fence, then the side opposite of the house is also 80 feet. Next you have to figure out the length. With a total of 200 feet of fencing, subtract 80 feet (the side opposite of the house) to get 120 feet (the remaining amount of fence). 200 – 80 = 120 Next, divide 120 by 2 since opposite sides of rectangles are the same length. 120 ÷ 2 = 60

7813
Mathematics

Number	Answer	Explanation
6.	C	The quadrants make a C if you start at quadrant I and go around the coordinate plane in order to quadrant IV. Thus, the point $(-3, -6)$ is in quadrant III.
7.	B	The formula for the area of a trapezoid is $A = \frac{1}{2}h(b_1 + b_2)$. $A = 0.5(5)(8 + 10) = 2.5(18) = 45$ square units.
8.	B	The faces of a three-dimensional figure are the sides and the vertices are the points where the edges of each side meet. The correct answer choice here is triangular prism.
9.	D	The largest angle will always identify the type of triangle. 110° is greater than 90°, so the triangle is obtuse. Also, since none of the angle measures are the same, none of the side lengths will be the same making the triangle scalene as well.
10.	B	A cube has 6 faces (each of the sides plus the top and bottom), 8 vertices (which are the points where the sides come together), and 12 edges (where each of the sides meet).

1. Jose is in the concrete phase of learning subtraction. What does Jose's learning look like?

   A. He memorizes $5 - 3 = 2$.

   B. He draws 5 blocks and crosses out 3.

   C. He remembers $3 + 2 = 5$.

   D. He puts 5 blocks on the table and then removes 3.

2. What strategies should a teacher use to help students increase automaticity of math facts?

   A. Memorization and repetition

   B. Evaluation and analyzation

   C. Compare and contrast

   D. Calculation and estimation

3. A student is solving the following equation: $4(x + 3) - 5(x + 3) = 0$

   At what step did the student make a mistake?

   Step 1: $4(x + 3) - 5(x + 3) = 0$

   Step 2: $4x + 12 - 5x - 15 = 0$

   Step 3: $x - 3 = 0$

   Step 4: $x = 3$

   A. Step 1

   B. Step 2

   C. Step 3

   D. Step 4

4. When considering the learning progression of students in a kindergarten classroom learning their numbers, which of the following skills should the teacher expect the students to master first?

   A. Comparing numbers

   B. Counting numbers

   C. Decomposing numbers

   D. Ordering numbers

5. Mr. Watson is preparing activities for small groups based on a recent formative assessment on fractions. The activities he planned are below.

   Group 1: Partners roll two fraction cubes five times and add the values together; the person with the highest total wins.

   Group 2: Color in fraction strips to represent various fractions.

   Group 3: Use fraction strips to add two fractions.

   Put the groups in order of cognitive complexity, from lowest to highest.

   A. Group 1, Group 2, Group 3

   B. Group 2, Group 3, Group 1

   C. Group 3, Group 2, Group 1

   D. Group 2, Group 1, Group 3

6. Which of the following assessments would **NOT** be used to inform instruction during the learning process?

A. State test

B. Diagnostic assessment

C. Formative assessment

D. Exit ticket

7. Which of the following are all components of math fluency?

A. Accuracy, automaticity, rate, complexity

B. Accuracy, automaticity, rate, flexibility

C. Rate, flexibility, composing, decomposing

D. Automaticity, rate, flexibility, speed

8. For which of the following concepts would a 10 by 10 grid be the most appropriate teaching tool?

A. Decimals and percents

B. Two-digit addition

C. Area of a circle

D. Modeling expressions

9. A student in class stated, "*If k equals m then m must equal k.*" This is an example of which property?

A. Transitive property

B. Commutative property

C. Symmetric property

D. Reflexive property

10. A flagpole is 12 feet tall, and it casts a shadow that is 8 feet long. A nearby light pole is 48 feet tall. What is the length, in feet, of the shadow of the light pole?

A. 32

B. 42

C. 56

D. 72

11. A teacher posed the question below, and a student's work for solving is shown. What could the teacher do to help the student correct their mistake?

Kelvin was at swim practice for 250 minutes last week and 324 minutes this week. How many more minutes did he practice this week than last week?

$$\begin{array}{r} 250 \\ + \ 324 \\ \hline 574 \end{array}$$

A. Give single digit numbers to make the math easier to solve.

B. Give a subtraction problem that does not require regrouping.

C. Tell the student to attempt the problem again because the answer is incorrect.

D. Clarify the problem by asking, "Which day did he practice more? By how much?"

12. In first and second grade, a student learns to use fraction language to describe the partition of shapes and to partition one whole into equal parts. In third grade, a student learns unit fractions and equal parts by using manipulatives, pictures, and number lines. What is the next skill in this learning progression?

    A. Finding common denominators

    B. Multiplying fractions

    C. Creating equivalent fractions

    D. Learning mixed numbers

13. A teacher is using tiling as a hands-on method for learning a new skill. What skill is the teacher most likely teaching?

    A. Counting

    B. Volume

    C. Area

    D. Place value

14. The structure "compare smaller unknown" is present in which of the following examples?

    A. There were 3 cookies on the plate. Kim ate one of the cookies. How many are left?

    B. Jacob has 3 more quarters than Molly. Molly has 2 quarters. How many quarters does Jacob have?

    C. Kevin has 2 more baseball cards than Preston. Kevin has 8 baseball cards. How many does Preston have?

    D. Johnny has 6 pairs of shoes. Four pair of shoes are sneakers, and the rest are dress shoes. How many pairs of dress shoes does Johnny have?

15. Ms. Johnson allows her students to add 2-digit numbers using a variety of methods. Which component of math fluency does this address?

    A. Accuracy

    B. Automaticity

    C. Rate

    D. Flexibility

16. Which of the following comes last in the learning progression of operations and algebraic thinking?

    A. Evaluating and interpreting numeric expressions.

    B. Using equal groups and arrays to solve problems.

    C. Solving multiplication compare problems.

    D. Understanding remainders when solving.

17. Which of the following is an example of automaticity?

    A. Solving a word problem that involves division.

    B. Recognizing that six buttons on a plate represents the number 6.

    C. Knowing how to solve an addition problem two different ways.

    D. Quickly being able to recite addition math facts.

18. When solving an addition problem, Marcus takes part of the first number and adds it to the second to make adding the numbers easier. What strategy is he using?

    A. Partitioning

    B. Compensation

    C. Making equal parts

    D. Tiling

19. Mr. Garry gives his students the problem below.

    There are 4 rows of boxes with 8 boxes in each row. How many boxes are there?

    This is an example of which type of problem structure?

    A. Arrays

    B. Compare

    C. Put-together

    D. Add-to

20. A teacher gives a mini assessment before starting a unit on multiplication and finds that 16 out of 20 students understand repeated addition and equal parts. How should the teacher proceed with teaching the unit?

    A. She should proceed as planned with teaching equal parts because not all students understand the concept.

    B. She should move forward, skipping over equal parts and repeated addition because most of the class understands the concept.

    C. She should give an example of each type of problem for the whole class, then move forward.

    D. She should create an extension activity for the students who understand and work with the others on repeated addition and equal parts.

21. Which equation below could be used to represent the phrase: *the height, h, is 7 more than twice the width, w?*

    A. $2h + 2 = w$

    B. $7w + 2 = h$

    C. $2w + 7 = w$

    D. $2w + 7 = h$

22. If $a = b$, then $a - c = b - c$ is an example of which property?

    A. Subtraction property of equality

    B. Reflexive property of equality

    C. Addition property of equality

    D. Division property of equality

23. Which of the following represents the largest value?

    A. 842 thousandths

    B. 92 hundredths

    C. 6 tenths

    D. 4 fifths

24. Solve: $3(x - 4) = 7x + 2$

    A. $x = -3.5$

    B. $x = -2.5$

    C. $x = -1.5$

    D. $x = -0.5$

25. Julie is shopping for school supplies. She spends $2.40 on paper, $5.00 on markers, $2.50 on glue, and $7.00 on a bookbag. She would like to know how much change she will receive from a $20.00 bill. Which operation will she do last?

    A. Add

    B. Subtract

    C. Multiply

    D. Divide

26. A car weighs 50 pounds less than a truck. Which of the following represents the weight of the car (c) in terms of the truck (t)?

    A. $t = c - 50$

    B. $t = 50 - c$

    C. $c = 50 - t$

    D. $c = t - 50$

27. Dane rewrites the expression $3 + 4x - 2$ as $4x + 3 - 2$ to make it easier to simplify. Which property did Dane apply when rewriting the expression?

    A. Distributive property

    B. Addition property of equality

    C. Commutative property of addition

    D. Associative property of addition

28. What operation should be performed first in the expression $1 + 2(18 - 9) \div 6$?

    A. Addition

    B. Subtraction

    C. Multiplication

    D. Division

29. Amarah told Rowan that she knows 4,215 is divisible by 3 without using a calculator. How did she apply the divisibility rule for 3 using mental math?

    A. She divided the last two digits, 15, by 3 and found that it divided evenly with no remainder.

    B. She added the digits 4, 2, 1, and 5 together and found that their sum is evenly divisible by 3.

    C. She knows that 5 is an odd number and 3 is an odd number, so 4,215 is divisible by 3.

    D. She multiplied 4, 2, 1, and 5 together and found that their product is evenly divisible by 3.

7813
Mathematics

30. Trystan bought a $20.00 shirt and received 20% off. Courtney bought a $25.00 shirt and received 10% off. Leo bought a $30.00 shirt and received 25% off. Drake bought an $18.00 shirt and received 15% off. Who paid the least amount for a shirt?

    A. Trystan

    B. Courtney

    C. Leo

    D. Drake

31. Julia is clearing her 7.5-acre plot of land. She rents a truck that can clear 1.5 acres in 60 minutes. How long will it take her to clear the entire 7.5-acre lot?

    A. 4 hours

    B. 5 hours

    C. 6 hours

    D. 300 hours

32. Mr. Mansell is teaching a lesson on fractions and wrote the following problem on the board.

    Terrance ate 3 pieces of pizza, and Gus ate 5 pieces of pizza. If the pizza was cut into 12 slices, what fraction of the pizza did the boys eat?

    He uses a drawing of a circular fraction set to help the students solve the problem. What type of fraction model is this?

    A. Linear model

    B. Tangram model

    C. Area model

    D. Set model

33. Which of the following is **NOT** equivalent to $3(a + 2b) - 5a + b$?

    A. $3a + 6b - 5a + b$

    B. $7b - 2a$

    C. $3a - 5a + 3b$

    D. $(3a - 5a) + (6b + b)$

34. If students are presenting their process for solving multi-step equations, they are using what type of math fluency?

    A. Automaticity

    B. Concrete skills

    C. Mental Math

    D. Abstract thinking

35. The steps to simplifying a problem are below. In which step was the distributive property used?

Step 1: $6x + 3 + 4(2x + 1)$

Step 2: $6x + 3 + 8x + 4$

Step 3: $(6x + 8x) + (3 + 4)$

Step 4: $14x + 7$

A. Step 1

B. Step 2

C. Step 3

D. Step 4

36. Which of the following points on the number line is closest to $\dfrac{5}{8}$?

A. A

B. B

C. C

D. D

37. Ms. Greenall is using fraction strips to model a problem. She uses the shaded regions to show relationships among fractions. Which of the following problems could she be modeling?

$\dfrac{1}{2}$		$\dfrac{1}{2}$	
$\dfrac{1}{4}$	$\dfrac{1}{4}$	$\dfrac{1}{4}$	$\dfrac{1}{4}$

A. $\dfrac{1}{2} + \dfrac{1}{2} = 1$

B. $\dfrac{1}{2} + \dfrac{1}{4} = \dfrac{3}{4}$

C. $\dfrac{1}{2} - \dfrac{1}{4} = \dfrac{1}{4}$

D. $\dfrac{1}{4} - \dfrac{1}{4} = \dfrac{1}{2}$

38. A prescription medicine bottle holds 15 grams of medicine. If 1 pill is equal to 250 milligrams, how many pills can the bottle hold?

A. 15

B. 40

C. 60

D. 80

39. The following pie chart shows the number of TV sets per household for 2,000 families. Given the data, how many households have at least three TV sets?

TV Sets Per Household

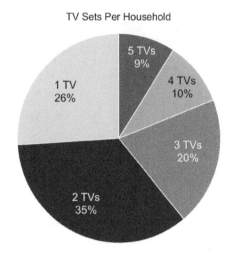

A. 400

B. 520

C. 780

D. 910

40. Which of the following student responses indicates the student understands the concept of calculating volume?

A. Student 1: Volume is used for three-dimensional figures and that's why cubic units are used.

B. Student 2: Volume is used for three-dimensional figures and that's why square units are used.

C. Student 3: Three dimensional shapes have three sides, and that's why cubic units are used.

D. Student 4: Three-dimensional objects can hold water, and that's why cubic units are used.

41. Which of the following statements indicates the student has a misconception regarding circles?

A. Student 1: The diameter goes through the center of the circle to the edge of the circle.

B. Student 2: The radius starts at the center of the circle and ends on the edge of the circle.

C. Student 3: The area of a circle can be found by squaring the radius and multiplying that by 3.14.

D. Student 4: Circles always form the base of a prism.

42. Based on the following descriptions, which quadrilateral is described below?

- Opposite sides are parallel.

- All four sides are equal.

- One set of opposite angles is acute.

A. Parallelogram

B. Rhombus

C. Square

D. Trapezoid

43. Clive is painting a design in the middle of a museum floor. His design consists of three triangles, each with a height of 6 feet and a base of 10 feet, and one rectangle with a height of $18\frac{1}{2}$ feet and a base of 10 feet. If one can of paint covers 250 square feet, what is the minimum number of cans of paint Clive will need to buy?

   A. 1

   B. 2

   C. 3

   D. 4

44. In what quadrant does the point $(-2, 9)$ lie?

   A. I

   B. II

   C. III

   D. IV

45. What is the perimeter of a square with an area of 49 square inches?

   A. 7 inches

   B. 24.5 inches

   C. 28 inches

   D. 98 inches

46. Find the area of the figure.

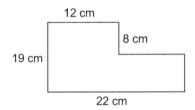

   A. 110 square cm

   B. 228 square cm

   C. 242 square cm

   D. 338 square cm

47. Which of the following could be used as the weight of a textbook?

   A. 10 grams

   B. 2 grams

   C. 22 kilograms

   D. 2 kilograms

48. Which measure might be used for a single serving of orange juice?

    A. Quart

    B. Pint

    C. Gallon

    D. Milliliter

49. Which of the conversions is **NOT** correct?

    A. 2.8 g = 280 cg

    B. 400 g = 400,000 mg

    C. 1.2 cg = 12 mg

    D. 0.4 kg = 40 g

50. Which of the following student statements indicates a misconception about the order of operations?

    A. Student 1: Operations inside parentheses should be done first.

    B. Student 2: The operation multiplication always comes before division.

    C. Student 3: The operation adding and subtracting should be done last.

    D. Student 4: Division can sometimes come before multiplication, depending on the problem.

51. A student's work for simplifying an expression is shown below. The student claims that he used the commutative property of addition, the associative property of addition, and the distributive property all in one problem. Is the student's statement correct?

Simplify: $3(x+2) + 6x - 1$

Step 1: $3x + 6 + 6x - 1$

Step 2: $3x + 6x + 6 - 1$

Step 3: $(3x + 6x) + 6 - 1$

Step 4: $9x + 5$

    A. Yes, because the properties were applied in steps 1, 2, and 3.

    B. Yes, because the properties were applied in steps 1, 2, and 4.

    C. No, because the student did not use the commutative property of addition.

    D. No, because the student did not use the associative property of addition.

52. A teacher is helping students calculate how many hours it will take a family traveling to a football game in another state. They want to figure out how long the 650-mile trip will take them if they travel at an average rate of 75 mph. Which equations would help students determine how many hours it will take the family to reach their destination?

    A. $75 = \dfrac{x}{650}$

    B. $650 = \dfrac{75}{x}$

    C. $x = \dfrac{75}{650}$

    D. $x = \dfrac{650}{75}$

Mathematics 7813 - Practice Test Answer Explanations

Number	Answer	Category	Answer Explanation
1	D	I	In the concrete stage, students are using physical models, such as blocks, to represent numbers and manipulating them to understand/demonstrate math operations. You may be tempted to choose answer B. However, drawing is in the representation stage. The concrete stage is physically touching something to learn concepts.
2	A	I	Automaticity is automatic thinking. Therefore, to increase automaticity of math facts, teachers should work on memorization of math facts and repetition to help with the memorization.
3	C	IV	The student did not combine like terms correctly in step 3. $4x - 5x = -x.$
4	B	I	Students need to learn to count before they can compare and order numbers, so we can eliminate answer choices A and D. Decomposing numbers requires an understanding and application of place value, which would come well after learning to count. Therefore, the correct answer choice is B.
5	B	I	The group performing the task with the lowest complexity is group 2 because they are identifying fractional parts. Next is group 3 because they not only have to understand fractional parts, but they also have to add fractions. The highest complexity is the students rolling the fraction cubes because once they add, they also have to compare fractions. Thus, answer choice B is the correct choice.
6	A	Assessments	A state test is a summative assessment which is a culminating assessment meant to determine where the student is at that time. It is not intended to provide specific diagnostic information for the teacher in order to make teaching decisions for specific students. The other assessments may all be used as a way to gather information/data about student learning to help guide the teacher's instruction.
7	B	Assessments	The four components of math fluency are accuracy, automaticity, rate, and flexibility.
8	A	II	A 10 by 10 grid is a good tool for modeling decimals and percents because the grid has 100 squares. Thus, the correct answer is choice A.

Number	Answer	Category	Answer Explanation
9	C	II	Written mathematically, the statement would read: If $m = k$, then $k = m$. This is an example of the symmetric property of equality.
10	A	III	When solving word problems, it is sometimes helpful to first sketch a picture of the situation. This is a proportional situation, so we can use a proportion to find the length of the light pole's shadow. $$\frac{12}{8} = \frac{48}{x}$$ Cross-multiply and solve for x. $$12x = 8(48)$$ $$12x = 384$$ $$x = 32$$
11	D	II	In this case, the student confuses the phrase, *how many more*, for addition. This can sometimes be a confusing statement, so clarifying by asking on which week Kelvin practiced more and by how much helps the student to see that the operation is actually subtraction, not addition. Because the confusion is with the wording of the problem, using simpler numbers does not aide in student understanding, which eliminates answer choices A and B. We can also eliminate answer choice C because simply telling a student they're wrong and to try again does not help the student with his understanding of the problem. Answer choice D is the correct answer choice.
12	C	I	Once students have a solid understanding of equal parts, they can begin to find equivalent fractions which will then lead into operations with fractions. Understanding equivalent fractions is an important prerequisite skill to fraction operations. Therefore, answer choice C is the correct answer.

Number	Answer	Category	Answer Explanation
13	C	I	Tiling is the process of covering up a space with tiles so that no tiles overlap or have gaps between them. The best use of this strategy is when teaching area. Therefore, the correct answer is choice C.
14	C	I	A compare problem means two values are being compared to one another. In answer choices A and D, the numbers are not being compared, so we can eliminate these answer choices. Answer choices B and C are both comparing two values, so we need to determine which one has the smaller number unknown. For answer choice B, Molly has the smaller amount, and her number of quarters is given, so we can eliminate this choice. In choice C, Kevin has more baseball cards, and we are given the amount Kevin has, so the smaller amount is unknown. Thus, answer choice C is the correct answer.
15	D	Assessments	By allowing her students to solve problems in a way that is best for their learning style, Mrs. Johnson is promoting flexibility in math fluency.
16	A	Assessments	Students begin learning multiplication by using arrays and equal groups to solve problems, so we can eliminate answer choice B. Once students understand multiplication, they move into multiplication compare, learning to evaluate situations such as *three times as many*. They then apply this to basic division and division with remainders. Last, students evaluate and interpret numeric expressions following order of operations in preparation for working with algebraic expressions. Therefore, the correct answer is choice A.
17	D	Assessments	Automaticity refers to the ability to retrieve basic math facts from memory with little to no effort. Therefore, answer choice D is the correct answer.
18	B	I	Taking part from one number and giving it another number to make solving easier is known as compensation. Thus, answer choice B is the correct answer choice.
19	A	I	Giving an arrangement of objects into rows and columns is an example of an array, making answer choice A the correct answer.

Number	Answer	Category	Answer Explanation
20	D	I	We can eliminate answer choices A and B because neither choice addresses the needs of all the students in the class. Answer choice C does not give the necessary attention to the students who need remediation and repeats already learned material for most of the class. With this answer choice, there is no way of knowing if the students who needed remediation understand the concept. Thus, answer choice C should be eliminated. Because most of the class is ready for the next step, the teacher should give them an extension activity to ensure that they are challenged and work with those who need remediation in a small group. Answer choice D is the correct answer.
21	D	I	When translating a verbal phrase into an algebraic phrase, *is* typically represents an equal sign, so *the height, h, is* can be represented by $h =$ *7 more than twice the width, w* means 7 is being added to 2 times the width. Putting it together we have $h = 2w + 7$, which is equivalent to answer choice D.
22	A	I	When determining which algebraic property a math sentence represents, determine what is changing from one line to the next, how one side of an equation changed from another, or what is the same on both sides of an equation. In this case, is being subtracted from both sides of an equation. We subtract the same thing from both sides of an equation to keep both sides equal. Thus, this is called the subtraction property of equality.
23	B	II	Writing out each of the values to 3 decimal places allows for a quick comparison. A. 0.842 B. 0.920 C. 0.600 D. 0.800 Answer choice B is the largest value.

Number	Answer	Category	Answer Explanation
24	A	IV	To solve, first distribute the 3, then move all the x terms to one side of the equation. Last, continue solving until the variable is isolated. $$3(x-4) = 7x + 2$$ $$3x - 12 = 7x + 2$$ $$-12 = 4x + 2$$ $$-14 = 4x$$ $$-3.5 = x \text{ or } x = -3.5$$
25	B	III	To determine her change, Julie will have to subtract each of the values from $20 or add all the items and then subtract their total from $20. Either way, the last operation she will perform is subtraction.
26	D	IV	Because the problem is asking for the weight of the car in terms of the weight of the truck, the equation is going to start with $c =$ Recall that the phrase *less than* switches the order of the numbers given, so 50 pounds less than a truck is written as $t - 50$. Putting it together, we have $c = t - 50$.
27	C	IV	Remember, when determining which algebraic property a math sentence represents, determine what is changing from one line to the next, how one side of an equation changed from another, or what is the same on both sides of an equation. In this case, Dane switched the order of the 3 and $4x$. Switching the order of two terms that are added together is an example of the commutative property of addition.
28	B	III	Following order of operations, we would first need to simplify the expression inside the parentheses, so subtraction should be the first operation performed.
29	B	II	The divisibility rule for 3 states that a number is divisible by 3 if the sum of its digits is divisible by 3. Thus, for 4,215, $4 + 2 + 1 + 5 = 12$, and 3 goes into 12 evenly, so 3 will also divide into 4,215 evenly.

Number	Answer	Category	Answer Explanation
30	D	III	Find the new cost of the shirt for each person by multiplying by the discount and subtracting this value from the original price. Trystan: $20 \times 0.20 = 4$; $20 - 4 = \$16$ Courtney: $25 \times 0.10 = 2.50$; $25 - 2.50 = \$22.50$ Leo: $30 \times 0.25 = 7.50$; $30 - 7.50 = \$22.50$ Drake: $18 \times 0.15 = 2.70$; $18 - 2.70 = \$15.30$ Drake paid the least amount.
31	B	III	The problem gives us a rate of 1.5 acres per 60 minutes, and we need to find an equivalent rate for 7.5 acres. In order to solve, set up a proportion, cross-multiply, and solve for the variable, which will represent the number of minutes. $$\frac{1.5 \text{ acres}}{60 \text{ minutes}} = \frac{7.5 \text{ acres}}{x \text{ minutes}}$$ $$\frac{1.5}{60} = \frac{7.5}{x}$$ $$1.5x = 60(7.5)$$ $$1.5x = 450$$ $$x = 300$$ Our answer is in minutes but notice that the multiple-choice answers given are all in hours. Divide 300 minutes by 60 to get the number of hours. $$300 \div 60 = 5$$
32	C	I	When students are given the whole as 1 piece that is separated into fractional parts, this is an example of the use of an area model (e.g., fraction circles or pattern blocks placed together to make a shape). This is slightly different from the set model in which the whole is assumed, and the pieces are individual (e.g., individual counting chips). A linear model would compare the lengths of straight fractional pieces. There is no such thing as a tangram model.

Number	Answer	Category	Answer Explanation
33	C	IV	Equivalent expressions may include the application of the distributive property with multiplication by 3, rearranging of terms, and combining like terms. When choosing equivalent expressions, it is a good idea to quickly simplify the expression on your scratch paper, showing all steps. $3(a + 2b) - 5a + b$ $3a + 6b - 5a + b$ $3a - 5a + 6b + b$ $-2a + 7b$ Notice that the second line is answer choice A. The third line is similar to answer choice D. Including the parentheses is acceptable because they do not change the value of the expression. The last line is similar to answer choice B, just switched around, which also does not change the value of the expression. Thus, the only option left is answer choice C. This option is not equivalent because when the b terms are combined, the result should be $7b$, not $3b$.
34	D	IV	Solving multi-step equations requires high-level, abstract math skills. All the other answer choices are low-level math skills. Therefore, answer D is the correct answer.
35	B	I	The distributive property was applied in Step 2 because the 4 was distributed/multiplied to each of the terms inside the parentheses.
36	C	III	The fraction $\frac{5}{8}$ is equivalent to 0.625, which is a little more than one-half. Therefore, point C is the correct answer choice.
37	B	III	Notice that the shading is equal to $\frac{3}{4}$, so this value should be part of the problem. The only answer choice with $\frac{3}{4}$ is B, which is the correct answer.
38	C	IV	We need to convert to milligrams so that all our numbers are in the same units. Recall that 1,000 milligrams are equal to 1 gram. Thus, 15 × 1,000 = 15,000 milligrams. If the pills are 250 milligrams each, we can divide the total number of milligrams the bottle holds by 250 to get the number of pills this equals. $$15,000 \div 250 = 60$$

Number	Answer	Category	Answer Explanation
39	C	III	First, add up the percents that have at least 3 TV sets (this includes both 4 and 5 TV sets as well). $$20\% + 10\% + 9\% = 39\%$$ Next find 39% of 2000 $$0.39 \times 2000 = 780$$
40	A	IV	The only correct statement is student 1, answer A.
41	D	IV	Circles form the base of cylinders not prisms. Therefore, student 4 has a misconception of circles.
42	B	IV	Let's look at each description. Opposite sides are parallel means the quadrilateral is a parallelogram, eliminating answer choice D. All four sides are equal means it is now either a square or a rhombus, eliminating choice A. One set of opposite angles is acute eliminates a square, choice C, because all the angles in a square are right angles. This leaves us with answer choice B as the correct answer.
43	B	IV	Find the area of the three triangles and the rectangle. Add the areas together to get the total square footage the design will cover. Next, divide the total area of the figure by 250 to get the number of paint cans needed. Round up to the next whole number, regardless of the decimal because a portion of a paint can cannot be purchased. Triangle Area: $3 \times \dfrac{1}{2} bh = 3 \times 0.5 \times 6 \times 10 = 90$ Rectangle Area: $bh = 18.5 \times 10 = 185$ Total area: $90 + 185 = 275$ $275 \div 250 = 1.1$ This rounds to 2 paint cans because you can't buy .1 of a paint can. You have to buy the whole can, making answer B correct.
44	B	IV	The quadrants make a C if you start at quadrant I and go around the coordinate plane in order to quadrant IV. Thus, the point is in quadrant II. The correct answer is B.

Number	Answer	Category	Answer Explanation
45	C	IV	Because a square has equal side lengths, the square with an area of 49 will have side lengths of 7 inches because $7 \times 7 = 49$ (recall the area of a square is $A = s \times s$). Thus, the perimeter of the square, $P = 4s$, is $4 \times 7 = 28$ inches.
46	D	IV	To solve composite area (area of basic figures joined together), separate the figure into two rectangles. This can be done two ways. We separate the figures horizontally, but they can also be separated vertically. Next, find the area of each rectangle. Add the two areas together to find the total area. $A = lw = 12 \times 8 = 96$ $A = lw = 11 \times 22 = 242$ $96 + 242 = 338$ square centimeters
47	D	IV	We can eliminate answer choice A because it is too light. For example, a paperclip weighs about 1 gram. We can also eliminate answer choice B because 10 grams is about 10 paperclips, which is still much lighter than a textbook. Larger textbooks can weigh about 5 pounds. One pound is a little less than one-half of a kilogram, so a 5-pound textbook would weigh a little less than 2.5 kilograms. Thus, answer choice D is the best answer choice.
48	B	IV	A school-sized milk carton is one-half pint. Thus, answer choice B is the best answer. A quart and gallon are too large, and milliliters are too small.

Number	Answer	Category	Answer Explanation
49	D	IV	For answer choice A, we are converting from grams to centigrams, so we would multiply 2.8 times 100. This conversion is correct. For answer choice B, we are again converting to a smaller unit, mg, so we multiply 400 times 1,000. This conversion is also correct. For answer choice C, we are converting to a smaller unit by one place value, so we would multiply 1.2 times 10. This conversion is correct. This leaves answer choice D as the incorrect conversion. Checking this conclusion, kg to g is moving to a smaller unit that is three place values away, so we would multiply 0.4 times 1,000. Because 0.4 times 1,000 is 400, the conversion in D is not correct.
50	B	IV	Student 2 has a misconception that multiplication always comes before division. However, sometimes division will happen before multiplication depending on where it falls in the problem.
51	D	IV	In step 1, the student used the distributive property by multiplying 3 to everything inside the parentheses. In step 2, the student used the commutative property by switching the order of 6 and $6x$. In step 3, the student did not use a property; he simply placed parentheses around the x terms. In step 4, the student used addition. The student never used the associative property, so answer choice D is the correct answer choice.
52	A	IV	For this equation use $d = r \times t$. If we substitute in the information we are given, we have the following: $650 = 75x$. Because none of the answer choices look like our equation, we have to solve it for something other than 650. If we solve for x by dividing both sides by 75. Then we get $x = \dfrac{650}{75}$. Which is answer choice D. Don't worry if you don't see your first answer choice. Test writers like to "rearrange" equations and formulas to test your knowledge of finding equivalent equations.

7814 Science

This page intentionally left blank.

About the Science CKT – 7814

The Praxis 7814 Science Content Knowledge for Teaching (CKT) test assesses knowledge and skills of aspiring educators in the field of science instruction. This test examines candidates' understanding of scientific concepts, principles, and practices across various scientific disciplines, including physical sciences, life sciences, earth and space sciences, and scientific inquiry.

Test takers are expected to demonstrate their ability to apply scientific knowledge to solve problems, analyze data, and make informed scientific decisions. The exam also assesses candidates' understanding of the nature of science, scientific inquiry processes, and the ability to effectively communicate scientific concepts. Additionally, the Praxis 7814 test focuses on pedagogical content knowledge, including instructional strategies, assessment techniques, and the ability to adapt science instruction for diverse learners.

Success on the Praxis 7814 Science test demonstrates a strong foundation in science concepts and the ability to effectively teach and engage students in scientific exploration and understanding.

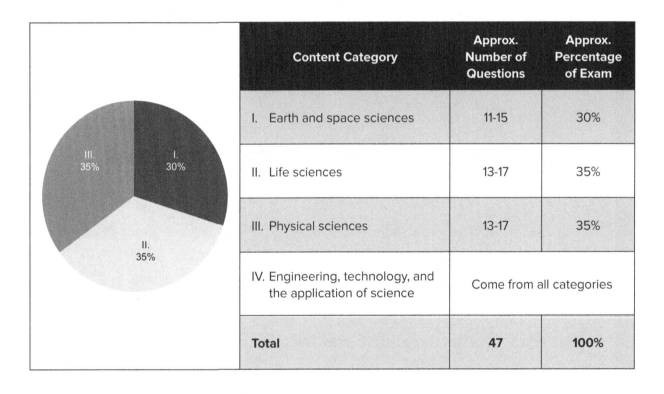

Content Category	Approx. Number of Questions	Approx. Percentage of Exam
I. Earth and space sciences	11-15	30%
II. Life sciences	13-17	35%
III. Physical sciences	13-17	35%
IV. Engineering, technology, and the application of science	Come from all categories	
Total	**47**	**100%**

This page intentionally left blank.

I. Earth and Space Sciences

The following topics are aligned with the test specifications of the Praxis 7814 exam. It is important that you examine these closely because these are the skills assessed on the exam.

A. Earth's Place in the Universe

    1.   The universe and its stars

    2.   Earth and the Solar System

    3.   The History of the Planet Earth

B. Earth's Systems

    1.   Earth's Materials and Systems

    2.   Plate Tectonics and Large-Scale System Interactions

    3.   Water in Earth's Surface Processes

    4.   Weather and Climate

    5.   Biogeology

C. Earth and Human Activity

    1.   Natural Resources

    2.   Natural Hazards

    3.   Human Impacts on Earth Systems

IMPORTANT: References for the information in the following sections can be found in the bibliography of this study guide.

A. Earth's Place in the Universe

Our solar system consists of the star known as the sun, several planets, an asteroid belt, numerous comets, and other objects. Earth is the third planet from the sun at about 93 million miles (150 million km). Earth's position in the solar system provides the opportunity and conditions for life.

Students should be able to compare and differentiate the composition and various relationships among the objects of our solar system (e.g., sun, planets, moons, asteroids, comets).

Earth is the third planet from the sun. Earth is the densest planet in the solar system, the largest of the solar system's four terrestrial planets, and the only astronomical object known to harbor life.

The sun is the star at the center of the solar system. It is the most important source of energy for life on Earth.

The moon is Earth's only natural satellite. The moon is thought to have formed approximately 4.5 billion years ago, not long after Earth.

Quick Tip

The sun is a star. The reason the sun appears so large is that it is the closest star to Earth.

Solar system

The solar system is a planetary system that orbits the sun. The solar system consists of the sun and everything that orbits around it. This includes the eight planets and their natural satellites (such as our moon), dwarf planets and their satellites, as well as asteroids, comets, and countless particles of smaller debris.

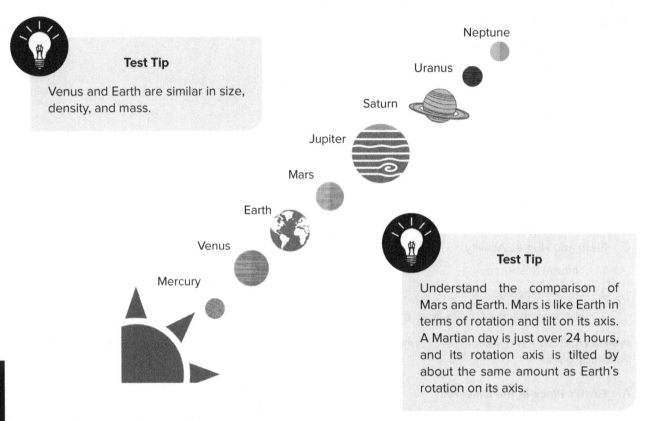

Test Tip

Venus and Earth are similar in size, density, and mass.

Test Tip

Understand the comparison of Mars and Earth. Mars is like Earth in terms of rotation and tilt on its axis. A Martian day is just over 24 hours, and its rotation axis is tilted by about the same amount as Earth's rotation on its axis.

Other Components of the Solar System

- **Comets** – A chunk of ice and rock originating outside of the solar system
- **Asteroids** – A chunk of rock and metal in orbit between Mars and Jupiter
- **Meteorite** – A small asteroid

Quick Tip

Light Year

A light year is a unit of astronomical distance equal to the distance light travels in one year. For example, if an event occurs 13 light years away, it will take 13 years to observe the event from Earth.

Speed of Light

The speed of light in a vacuum is approximately 300,000 km/sec. In a vacuum is where speed of light is fastest. When traveling through any other medium, the speed of light is slower.

Earth's tilt

Seasons are a result of Earth's **tilt on its axis.** When Earth is tilted toward the sun, it is warmer (summer). When Earth is tilted away from the sun, it is colder (winter). During spring and fall, Earth is tilted on its side. See diagram below.

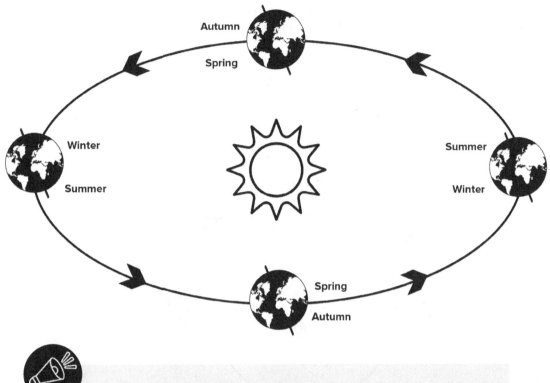

Quick Tip

The seasons in the Northern Hemisphere are the opposite of those in the Southern Hemisphere. For example, in Argentina and Australia, winter begins in June. The winter solstice in the Southern Hemisphere is June 20 or 21, while the summer solstice in the Southern Hemisphere is the longest day of the year and is on December 21 or 22.

Season	Description
Fall – Autumn Equinox	Date in the fall when Earth experiences 12 hours of daylight and 12 hours of darkness. In the Northern Hemisphere, this occurs around September 23.
Summer – Solstice	Earth's maximum tilt is toward the sun, causing the longest period of daylight. In the Northern Hemisphere, this occurs around June 22.
Spring – Vernal Equinox	Date in the spring when Earth experiences 12 hours of daylight and 12 hours of darkness. In the Northern Hemisphere, this occurs around March 21.
Winter – Solstice	The North Pole is tilted farthest away from the sun, causing the shortest period of daylight. In the Northern Hemisphere, this occurs around December 21.

Heliocentric and geocentric

The Scientific Revolution began as the Renaissance was coming to an end. The Scientific Revolution marked the emergence of modern science and the heliocentric model regarding the universe. The heliocentric theory, introduced by Nicolaus Copernicus, positioned the sun at the center of the universe. Copernicus also asserted that Earth rotates on its axis while revolving around the sun. Up until that point, it was believed that Earth sat stationary at the center of the universe (the geocentric theory). In his book, *On the Revolutions of Heavenly Spheres*, Copernicus' heliocentric model replaced the geocentric model.

The Moon

The moon affects the tides. When the part of the moon that is illuminated is increasing, the moon phase is waxing. When the part of the moon that is illuminated is decreasing, the moon phase is waning. A waxing moon is illuminated on the right side; a waning moon is illuminated on the left side.

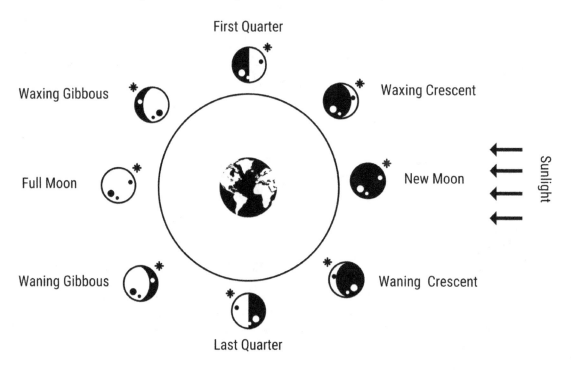

Stars

A star is a luminous ball of gas, mostly hydrogen and helium, held together by its own gravity. A star's color relies on its temperature—hotter stars emit bluer light, and cooler stars emit redder light.

Type	Color	Temperature
O	Blue	Over 25,000 Kelvin
B	Blue	11,000–20,000 Kelvin
A	Blue	7,500–11,000 Kelvin
F	Blue to White	6,000–7,500 Kelvin
G	White to Yellow	5,000–6,000 Kelvin
K	Orange to Red	3,500–5,000 Kelvin
M	Red	Under 3,500 Kelvin

Lunar eclipse positions

A **lunar eclipse** occurs when the moon passes directly behind Earth into its umbra (shadow).

 Moon

 Earth

 Sun

Solar eclipse positions

A **solar eclipse** happens when the moon moves in front of the sun.

 Earth

 Moon

 Sun

Earth's patterns, cycles, and change

Earth goes through several patterns, cycles, and changes.

- **Patterns**. Earth spins on its axis. It makes one full rotation on its axis every 24 hours. Earth also revolves around the sun. It takes 365 days for Earth to make one full revolution around the sun.

- **Cycles**. Earth's rotation on its axis and revolution around the sun causes cycles on Earth: day, night, seasons, weather. Other cycles include the phases of the moon, water cycle, and life cycles.

- **Changes**. Earth goes through various changes. Some changes happen quickly; for example, an earthquake or a storm can change Earth rapidly. Other changes happen slowly; for example, the North American and Eurasian tectonic plates are separated by the Mid-Atlantic Ridge. The two continents are moving away from each other at the rate of about 2.5 centimeters (1 inch) per year.

Quick Tip

A major change in Earth is called continental drift, which suggests Earth's continents were all once one big landmass and over time, separated or drifted apart because of plate tectonics.

The Earth's plates are still constantly moving. Plate tectonics cause earthquakes, volcanic eruptions, and rift valleys.

Earth's magnetic poles

Earth has a magnetic field that extends from its interior to outer space. A compass is calibrated based on Earth's magnetic field. Over time, Earth's poles reverse—every 200,000 to 300,000 years. Magnetic fields morph, push, and pull at one another, with multiple poles emerging at odd latitudes throughout the process. Scientists estimate reversals have happened at least hundreds of times over the past 3 billion years.

On Earth, the magnetic field of the South Pole is near Earth's geographic North Pole. The magnetic field of the North Pole is near Earth's geographic South Pole. This makes a compass usable for navigation.

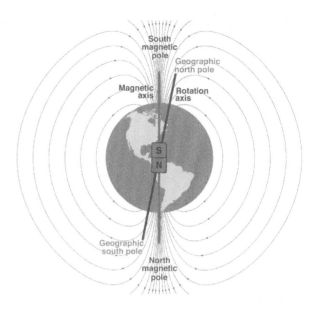

B. Earth's Systems

Earth's Materials

Solid Earth

Earth is made up of several layers: crust/lithosphere, mantle, and core.

Earth gets denser toward the center.

The temperature increases deeper into Earth. For example, the mantle is 1900°K, the outer core is 3000°K, and the inner ore is 5000–7000°K.

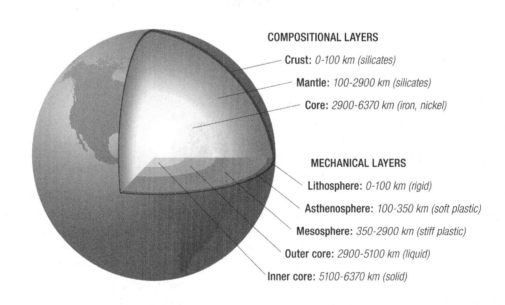

COMPOSITIONAL LAYERS

Crust: *0-100 km (silicates)*

Mantle: *100-2900 km (silicates)*

Core: *2900-6370 km (iron, nickel)*

MECHANICAL LAYERS

Lithosphere: *0-100 km (rigid)*

Asthenosphere: *100-350 km (soft plastic)*

Mesosphere: *350-2900 km (stiff plastic)*

Outer core: *2900-5100 km (liquid)*

Inner core: *5100-6370 km (solid)*

Composition Layers		
Layer	Definition	Depth
Crust	The outermost solid layer of Earth.	0–100 km
Mantle	The mantle is not liquid; it is ductile or plastic, which means that some parts of the mantle can flow under certain conditions and changes in pressure. The mantle is mainly composed of aluminum and silicates.	100–2900 km
Core	The innermost layers of Earth. Earth has an outer core (liquid) and an inner core (solid). The core is mainly composed of nickel and iron.	2900–6370 km

Mechanical Layers		
Layer	Definition	Depth
Litho-sphere	The outermost and most rigid mechanical layer of Earth. The lithosphere includes the crust and the top of the mantle.	0–100 km
Astheno-sphere	Underneath the lithosphere. It is about 100km thick. This region of the mantle flows relatively easily. The mantle is NOT liquid.	100–350 km
Meso-sphere	Beneath the asthenosphere. It encompasses the lower mantle, where material still flows but at a much slower rate than in the asthenosphere.	350–2900 km
Outer Core	A layer of liquid iron and nickel (and other elements) beneath the mesosphere. This is the only layer of Earth that is a true liquid.	5100–6370 km

Earth's atmosphere is a layer of gases surrounding the planet. The gases present in Earth's atmosphere are:

- **Nitrogen**: 78%
- **Oxygen**: 21%
- **Argon**: 0.09%
- **Carbon dioxide**: 0.01%
- **Helium**: small traces
- **Neon**: small traces
- **Other gases**: small traces

Quick Tip

Nitrogen and oxygen make up 99% of the gases in Earth's atmosphere, with nitrogen being the most prevalent.

Researchers assert Earth's atmosphere was formed from volcanic eruptions that happened early in Earth's history.

Earth's atmosphere also contains multiple layers:

- **Troposphere**: 0–12 km above Earth. *Most of Earth's weather occurs here.

- **Stratosphere**: 12–50 km above Earth. *Contains the ozone layer.

- **Mesosphere**: 50–80 km above Earth.

- **Thermosphere**: 80–700 km above Earth.

- **Exosphere:** 700–1000 km above Earth.

The ozone layer absorbs 97–99% of the sun's ultraviolet light and is contained in the stratosphere. This layer contains high levels of ozone (O_3). Two decades of scientific research has shown that human-produced chemicals are responsible for the observed depletion of the ozone layer.

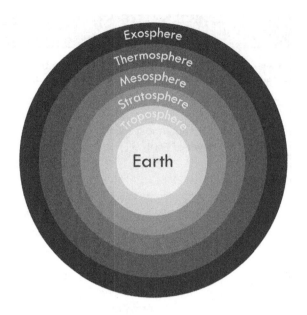

Quick Tip

When we drive cars, carbon dioxide (CO_2) is released into the atmosphere. The CO_2 is trapped inside the ozone layer and prevents the sun's rays from escaping, which contributes to Earth's increase in temperature.

Processes of the lithosphere (crust)

Geologic formations are formations made from rocks that exist on the lithosphere. Examples include volcanoes, mountains, and canyons.

Mountains are formed because of Earth's tectonic plates smashing together.

Volcanoes are formed when magma from within Earth's upper mantle erupts through the surface.

Canyons are formed by weathering and erosion caused by the movement of rivers. Canyons are also formed by tectonic activity.

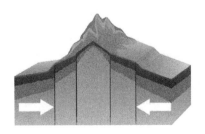

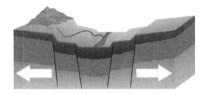

Earthquakes

Earthquakes are usually caused when plates rub against each other in an opposite motion, and rock underground suddenly breaks along a fault. This sudden release of energy causes seismic waves that make the ground shake.

Scientists assign a magnitude rating to earthquakes based on the strength and duration of their seismic waves. A quake measuring 3 to 4.9 is considered minor or light; 5 to 6.9 is moderate to strong; 7 to 7.9 is major; and 8 or more is great.

Seismic waves

A seismic wave is an elastic wave caused by an earthquake. There are three types of seismic waves:

1. **Primary (P waves).** These are the fastest waves (5 kilometers per second or approximately 3 miles per second) and can travel through solid, liquids, and gases.

2. **Secondary (S waves).** Secondary waves travel through Earth's interior at about half the speed of primary waves. Secondary waves can travel through rock, but unlike primary waves, they cannot travel through liquids or gases.

3. **Surface.** Surface waves are seismic waves that move along Earth's surface, not through its interior. Surface waves are the slowest of the three seismic waves.

Tsunamis

Tsunamis are giant waves caused by earthquakes or volcanic eruptions under the sea. Out in the depths of the ocean, tsunami waves do not dramatically increase in height. However, as the waves travel inland, they build up to higher and higher heights as the depth of the ocean decreases. The speed of tsunami waves depends on ocean depth. Tsunamis may travel as fast as jet planes over deep waters, only slowing down when they reach shallow waters.

Plate tectonics is the theory that Earth's outer shell is divided into several plates that glide over the mantle or the rocky inner layer above the core. The plates move and separate, causing Earth to separate and change.

Divergent – Pulling apart   **Convergent** – Coming together   **Subduction** – Sideways and downward movement of the edge of a plate into the mantle beneath another plate

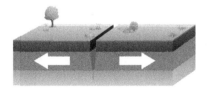  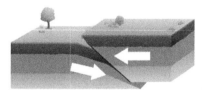

Quick Tip

Most earthquakes occur in a region known as the Ring of Fire. The Ring of Fire is a ring of volcanoes around the outer edge of the Pacific Ocean.

Rocks

A rock is any naturally occurring solid mass or aggregate of minerals or mineraloid matter. Rocks are categorized by the minerals they include, their chemical composition, and their formation (origin). Rocks are usually grouped into three main categories: igneous, metamorphic, and sedimentary. Rocks form the Earth's outer solid layer: the lithosphere.

Type	Igneous	Metamorphic	Sedimentary
Made from...	lava, magma	heat pressure	deposition, cementation
Looks like...	glassy, smooth surface, gas bubble holes, random arrangement of minerals	sparkly crystals, ribbon-like layers	sand grains or visible pebbles; fossils may be visible
Examples	granite, pumice, obsidian	marble, slate, gneiss	conglomerate, sandstone, limestone, shale

Soil

Soil is a mixture of minerals, organic matter, gases, liquids, and many organisms that together support life on Earth.

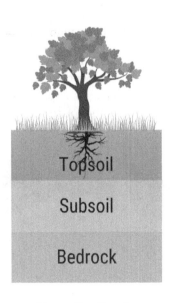

Quick Tip

Aquifers are bodies of permeable rock which can contain or transmit ground water. Aquifers are located just above the bedrock.

Earth's Spheres – Above the Crust

Earth is made up of different types of spheres.

- **Lithosphere** – The outermost shell of Earth. Earth's crust is the lithosphere.
- **Hydrosphere** – All the water on Earth in liquid form. For example, lakes, rivers, and oceans are all part of the hydrosphere.
- **Biosphere** – The global sum of all ecosystems and living organisms.

- **Cryosphere** – The masses of frozen water. For example, frozen lakes, frozen rivers, frozen oceans, and glaciers are part of the cryosphere.
- **Atmosphere** – The layer of gases that surround the planet.

The Water Cycle

The water cycle, also called the hydrologic cycle, is a continuous circulation of water throughout Earth and Earth's atmosphere.

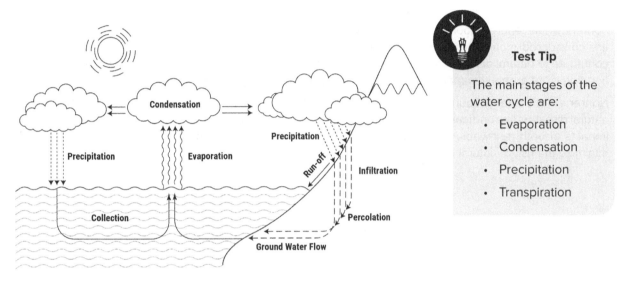

- **Precipitation** is rain and snow.
- **Evaporation** is when water turns from a liquid to a gas (water vapor).
- **Condensation** is when water vapor turns back into liquid—water collects as droplets on a cold surface when humid air is in contact with it, forming clouds.
- **Transpiration** is when plants suck water from roots to the small pores in leaves, releasing the water vapor into the atmosphere.

C. Earth and Human Activity

Energy resources play a critical role in everyday human life. We use energy to power everything from a coffee machine to the space shuttle. Our energy resources come from the Earth in a variety of forms. Some energy resources cannot be renewed as quickly as they are being consumed (nonrenewable); some energy resources can be renewed quickly by the Earth's physical processes (renewable).

- **Clean energy**. Energy from wind, solar, water, geothermal, biomass, and nuclear
- **Fossil energy**. Energy from coal, oil, and natural gas
- **Electric power**. Energy from charged particles

Renewable and Nonrenewable Resources

Renewable	Nonrenewable
Solar	Fossil fuels
Wind	Coal
Hydro power	Natural gas

Human activities have had a significant impact on the environment, including the use of renewable and nonrenewable energy sources. While renewable energy sources such as solar, wind, and hydropower are considered more environmentally friendly than nonrenewable sources like fossil fuels, they can still contribute to natural disasters such as flooding, earthquakes, and fires. For example, hydropower can cause flooding if not properly managed, and geothermal energy can trigger earthquakes.

Nonrenewable energy sources like coal and oil have been linked to climate change, which can exacerbate natural disasters like hurricanes and wildfires. Therefore, it is important to carefully consider the environmental impacts of both renewable and nonrenewable energy sources and to promote sustainable practices that minimize the risk of natural disasters.

Earth and Space Science Practice Questions

1. Where are aquifers located?

    A. beneath Earth's crust

    B. beneath the bedrock

    C. in Earth's mantle

    D. in Earth's core

2. What happens during a solar eclipse?

    A. Earth casts a shadow on the moon.

    B. Earth and the moon are on opposite sides of the sun.

    C. The moon moves in front of the sun relative to Earth.

    D. Earth and the sun align.

3. Which planet is closest in size and density to Earth?

    A. Venus

    B. Uranus

    C. Saturn

    D. Mercury

4. Gravity is responsible for:

    A. rotation of Earth on its axis.

    B. phases of the moon.

    C. Earth's orbit.

    D. Earth's seasons.

5. This type of rock was originally liquid below Earth's crust and is formed by lava and magma:

    A. sedimentary

    B. igneous

    C. metamorphic

    D. fossils

7814
Science

6. The picture below is an example of the:

Water cycle

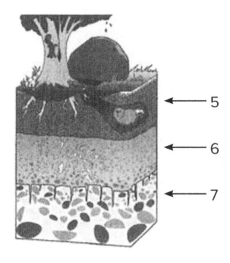

A. geosphere

B. cryosphere

C. biosphere

D. hydrosphere

7. In the diagram below, number 6 is:

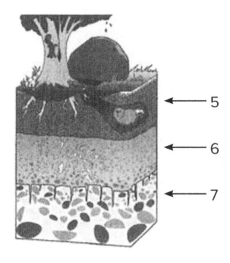

A. topsoil

B. subsoil

C. bedrock

D. mantle

8. This area is located around the outer edge of the Pacific Ocean and is where most volcanic activity occurs.

    A. Ring of Fire

    B. Horn of Africa

    C. San Francisco Bay

    D. Arctic Circle

9. Which of the following human uses of renewable energy can trigger earthquakes?

    A. Recycling

    B. Hydropower

    C. Coal

    D. Geothermal energy

10. Which of the following is the densest part of Earth?

    A. stratosphere

    B. lithosphere

    C. mantle

    D. core

This page intentionally left blank.

Number	Answer	Explanation
1.	A	Aquifers are below Earth's crust, below the water table, and above the bedrock. The mantle and the core are very deep below Earth's crust.
2.	C	A solar eclipse happens when the moon moves in front of the sun.
3.	A	Venus and Earth are similar in size, density, and mass.
4.	C	Earth remains in an orbit around the sun because of the gravitational pull of the sun and the other planets.
5.	B	Igneous rocks are formed from magma or lava.
6.	D	Hydro means water. The picture is of the water cycle; therefore, it is the hydrosphere.
7.	B	The top layer of soil is called topsoil. The layer under topsoil is subsoil (*sub* means *under*). The rock below the subsoil is bedrock. The mantle is not pictured here.
8.	A	The Ring of Fire is a ring of volcanoes around the outer edge of the Pacific Ocean. These volcanoes are a result of subduction of oceanic plates beneath lighter continental plates. Most of Earth's volcanoes are in the Ring of Fire.
9.	D	Geothermal energy is a type of renewable energy that comes from the natural heat of the Earth's core. The Earth's core is extremely hot, and this heat is constantly being generated by the decay of radioactive elements such as uranium and thorium. Geothermal energy is generated by harnessing this heat and converting it into usable energy. If not managed properly, it can cause earthquakes.
10.	D	The center of Earth is also the densest part of Earth. Therefore, Earth's core is the answer.

This page intentionally left blank.

II. Life Sciences

The following topics are aligned with the test specifications of the Praxis 7814 exam. It is important that you examine these closely because these are the skills assessed on the exam.

A. Organisms

    1.   Structure and Function

    2.   Growth and Development of Organisms

    3.   Organization for Matter and Energy Flow in Organisms

    4.   Information Processing

B. Ecosystems: Interactions, Energy, and Dynamics

    1.   Interdependent Relationships in Ecosystems

    2.   Cycles of Matter and Energy Transfer in Ecosystems

    3.   Ecosystem Dynamics, Functioning, and Resilience

C. Heredity: Inheritance and Variation of Traits

    1.   Inheritance of Traits and Variation of Traits

D. Biological Evolution: Unity and Diversity

    1.   Evidence of Common Ancestry and Diversity

    2.   Natural Selection

    3.   Adaptation

    4.   Biodiversity and Humans

IMPORTANT: References for the information in the following sections can be found in the bibliography of this study guide.

A. Organisms

To study life science, students should understand cell theory and how living organisms are made up of cells.

Structures and Processes

Cell theory is made up of three components:

1. All living things are composed of cells.

2. The cell is the smallest unit of life.

3. All cells come from pre-existing cells.

The structural hierarchy of life is as follows:

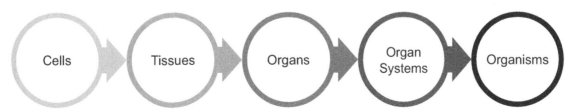

Cells → Tissues → Organs → Organ Systems → Organisms

Prokaryote and eukaryote

A **prokaryote** is a unicellular organism that lacks a nucleus, mitochondria, or any other membrane-bound organelle. In a prokaryotic cell, the deoxyribonucleic acid (DNA) floats freely throughout the cell. Prokaryotes are divided into two domains: **archaea** and **bacteria**.

A **eukaryote** is a multicellular organism that contains a nucleus, mitochondria, and membrane-bound organelles.

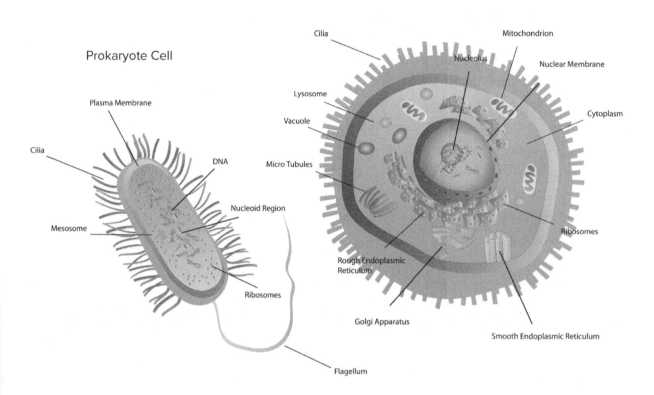

The structures within the cell membrane or cell wall are called **organelles**. The main structures of the cell are designed to perform certain functions.

- **Cellular membrane**. Fluid, permeable outside covering of the cell. In a plant cell, this is a cell wall, and it is rigid.

- **Nucleus**. Command center of the cell. The nucleus controls the rest of the cell. This is where the DNA lives in eukaryotic cells.

- **Mitochondria**. Powerhouse (energy source) of the cell.

- **Cytoplasm**. Water-like substance in the cell.

Plant vs. Animal Cells.

On the exam, you will need to be able to identify the unique components of plant and animal cells.

Animal and plant cell structures

Animal and plant cells are both eukaryotic in structure. However, there are functional differences between an animal cell and a plant cell.

Animal cell

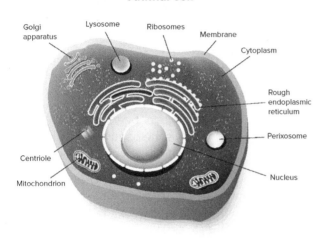

> ### Cellular Respiration
> Animal cells go through a process of cellular respiration. This is the process of taking in food in the form of carbohydrates, making energy in the form of ATP, and removing waste. The equation for this process is:
>
> **glucose (sugar) + oxygen →**
>
> **carbon dioxide + water + energy (as ATP)**

Plant cell

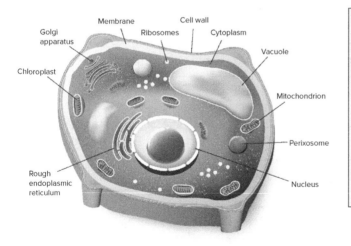

> ### Photosynthesis
> Plant cells make their own food through photosynthesis. This is the process of using carbon dioxide, water, and sunlight, and turning them into carbohydrates. The equation for this process is:
>
> **carbon dioxide + water + sunlight →**
>
> **glucose (sugar) + oxygen**

Notice the waste of animal cells becomes the nutrients plants use to go through photosynthesis, and the waste of plant cells becomes the nutrients animals use to go through cellular respiration. It is a symbiotic relationship.

Plant Cells	Animal Cells
Cell wall	Plasma membrane
Chloroplast	No chloroplast
Photosynthesis (CO_2 + H_2O + light = Carbohydrates)	Cellular respiration (Carbohydrates + O_2 = CO_2 and H_2O

B. Ecosystems: Interactions, Energy, and Dynamics

Interdependence of organisms

The continuation of life depends on how organisms interact with each other and their environment. Life can be organized into several different levels of function and complexity. These functional levels are species, populations, communities, and ecosystems.

Level	Description	Examples
Species	A group of interbreeding organisms that do not ordinarily breed with members of other groups.	The polar bear (Ursus maritimus) is a hyper carnivorous bear whose native range lies largely within the Arctic Circle.
Populations	Comprises all the individuals of a given species in a specific area or region at a certain time. Populations can evolve over time because of genetic variation.	All the polar bears in the Arctic Circle is the population. Within the population, polar bears contain genetic variance within the species.
Communities	All the populations in a specific area or region at a certain time. There are many interactions among species in a community (food webs).	The polar bears, the penguins, the fish, and the plants make up the community. These all interact when it comes to food and survival.
Ecosystems	The dynamic entities composed of the biological (living) community and the abiotic (nonliving) environment.	The Arctic ecosystem is made up of the water/ice, the animals, and the atmosphere in that area.

Energy pyramids and food webs

Within ecosystems, there is an interdependence among organisms of the same or different species. There is also interdependence between living and nonliving elements in the environment. For example, organisms in an ecosystem interact with one another in complex feeding hierarchies, which together represent a food web. A **food web** is when multiple food chains are interacting simultaneously. See picture below.

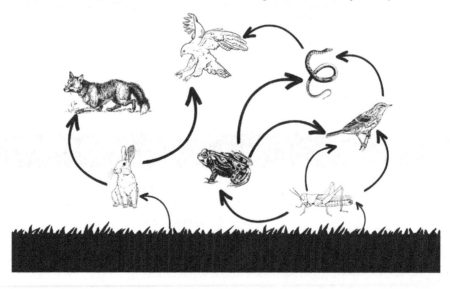

Energy pyramids (or trophic pyramids) show the transfer of energy from one stage of a food chain to another. A **food chain** is a hierarchical structure of organisms that are dependent on each other for food.

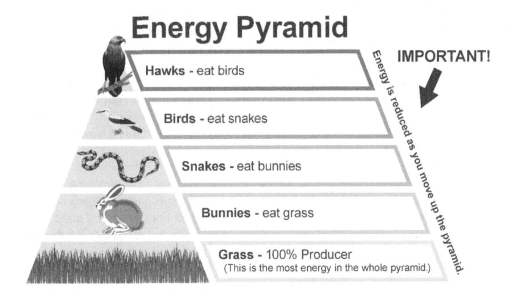

Producers (plants) produce their own food from sunlight, carbon dioxide, and water. These are usually the bottom tier of the food web or energy pyramid.

Consumers eat their food and are categorized into four main groups:

1. **Primary** consumers are herbivores; they eat plants. In the energy pyramid, the bunny is the primary consumer.

2. **Secondary** consumers eat the primary consumer. In the energy pyramid, the snake is the secondary consumer.

3. **Tertiary** consumers eat the secondary consumers and are usually carnivores (meat-eaters). In the energy pyramid, the bird is the tertiary consumer.

4. **Quaternary** consumers eat the tertiary consumers and are carnivores. In the energy pyramid, the quaternary consumer is the hawk. This food chain ends with the hawk, which would be considered the top carnivore.

Decomposers are organisms that turn dead material, such as an animal carcass or a dead tree, into soil by recycling nutrients as food. Decomposers include earthworms, small soil beetles, fungi, and bacteria.

Carrying capacity is the maximum population of a particular organism that a given environment can support without detrimental effects. Individual survival and population sizes depend on such factors as predation, disease, availability of resources, and parameters of the physical environment. Earth's varied combinations of these factors provide the physical environments in which its ecosystems (e.g., deserts, grasslands, rain forests, and coral reefs) develop and in which the diverse species of the planet live.

Interaction of organisms

Interactions among organisms may be predatory, competitive, or mutually beneficial. These are referred to as ecological relationships.

Relationship	Definition	Example
Competition	When two or more organisms rely on the same environmental resource	Because they eat the same type of food, cheetahs and lions compete within their ecosystem.
Predation	Behavior of one animal feeding on another	The lion eats the zebra. The lion is the predator; the zebra is the prey.
Symbiosis	The close relationship of two dissimilar organisms	There are three type of symbiosis: mutualism, commensalism, and parasitism.
Mutualism	A symbiotic relationship where both organisms benefit	Humans have a mutualistic relationship with micro-organisms. Bacteria in the digestive tract keeps humans healthy while the bacteria are fed by what the human eats.
Commensalism	A symbiotic relationship where one organism benefits and one does not benefit but is unharmed	The cattle egret sits on top of the cattle and eats the bugs that land on the cattle.
Parasitism	A symbiotic relationship where one organism benefits and one is harmed	A tick living on a dog benefits while the dog is harmed.

When put together, all the above processes comprise an ecosystem, which is a biological community of organisms interacting with their environment and each other.

Pollution can impact an environment in several ways. It can directly kill organisms, such as an oil spill that prevents water from being reoxygenated and starving waterborne organisms of air. Pollution can also interrupt any of the above interactions, negatively impacting life throughout the ecosystem in a ripple effect.

Plant structures consist of a root system and a shoot system. The root system is all parts of the plant below ground; the shoot system is all parts of the plant above ground. The shoot system usually involves a trunk or stem structure, branches, leaves, and reproductive organisms such as flowers, seeds, or cones.

Photosynthesis is a process used in plants to convert light energy from the sun into chemical energy that can be later released as fuel in the form of carbohydrates for other organisms.

Transpiration is when plants suck water from roots to the small pores in leaves, releasing the water vapor into the atmosphere. This is part of the water cycle, also referred to as the hydrologic cycle.

Reproduction

There are two main types of reproduction in living things: **sexual** and **asexual**.

Sexual reproduction. Involves two parents. Each parent contributes a gamete to the process of reproduction. Gametes are sex cells. In males, the gametes are sperm. In females, the gametes are ova (or eggs). Sexual reproduction occurs in plant and animal cells.

Asexual reproduction. Involves only one parent. There are four main types of asexual reproduction.

1. **Binary fission** is when a single parent cell doubles its DNA, then divides into two cells. This usually occurs in bacteria.

2. **Budding** is when a small growth on the surface of parent breaks off to continue growing into adulthood. This typically occurs in yeast and some animals.

3. **Fragmentation** is when a piece of an organism breaks off, and those pieces develop into a new organism. This happens with starfish. If a piece of a starfish leg breaks off, the fragment will form a new starfish.

4. **Parthenogenesis** is when an embryo develops from an unfertilized cell. This occurs in invertebrates as well as in some fish, amphibians, and reptiles.

Example question

Which of the following processes is used by plants to create energy?

    A. Reproduction

    B. Transpiration

    C. Expiration

    D. Photosynthesis

Correct answer: D

Reproduction is how a plant creates seeds; transpiration is how a plant obtains water; and photosynthesis is how a plant converts light energy to chemical energy. Expiration is another term for dying.

Responses to Stimuli (e.g., heat, light, gravity).

Plants are unique living organisms in that they cannot move like humans, bugs, birds, and reptiles can, but plants do respond to stimuli, especially as they grow and survive. A plant's primary response to stimuli is how it grows. These responses are governed by hormones or signal molecules.

Tropisms

A tropism is a turning toward or away from something in the environment. Tropisms are how plants grow and survive.

Geotropism is when the roots of the plant grow downward, and the stalk or leaves of the plant grow upward. Growing with gravity, as in the roots growing downward, is called positive geotropism. Growing against gravity, as in stalks growing upward, is called negative tropism.

Phototropism is when the plant grows toward the light. The word photo means light. Growth toward a light source is called positive phototropism. Growth away from the light is called negative phototropism.

Example question:

The picture below is an example of:

    A. Phototropism

    B. Photosynthesis

    C. Chloroplasts

    D. Geotropism

Correct answer: A

Phototropism is when a plant grows toward a light source. Photo means light, and tropism means response. Photosynthesis is the process by which plants make carbohydrates from light, water, and CO_2. Chloroplasts are small disks inside of a plant cell that aid in photosynthesis. Finally, geotropism is the way in which a plant grows in terms of gravity—roots grow downward, stalk grows upward.

Life cycle of plants

- **Seed.** The next generation of plants is dispersed via environmental methods (like wind or water) or interaction with other organisms (spreading through animal or human actions).

- **Germination.** When soil and temperature conditions are right, the seed will germinate. This involves breaking through its outer shell and growing root and shoot systems. When life first begins to show in a germinated seed, it is called a seedling.

- **Growth.** The plant will continue to grow until it reaches maturation. This can be as short as a single season for many plants, or it can take up to 100 years for some trees.

- **Reproduction.** When a plant reaches maturity, it will produce flowers or seeds. Pollination is an important part of this process for many plant species. These seeds begin the life cycle all over again.

Life cycle of animals

Animal life cycles vary widely. Insects most frequently have four stages: **egg, larva, pupa,** and **adult**. Less commonly, insects such as cockroaches, grasshoppers, and dragonflies will go through multiple **molting** stages to shed an exoskeleton and grow larger.

Vertebrates (including mammals, reptiles, birds, and fish) typically have three stages: **birth** (either live or via hatching from an egg), **young,** and **adult**. The middle stage consists of a period of growth before sexual maturity is reached.

Amphibians are also born live or from eggs but spend the early part of their life in water and breathe through gills. As they grow older, they develop lungs and various appendages (such as legs) and move onto land.

Example question

"Pupa" is a life stage in which of the following organisms?

    A. Fish

    B. Amphibians

    C. Insects

    D. Reptiles

Correct answer: C

Although not present in all insects, pupa is a life stage in many different insect species. It does not appear as a life stage in fish, amphibians, or reptiles.

C. Heredity: Inheritance and Variation of Traits

Heredity is the passing on of physical or mental characteristics genetically from one generation to another.

A gene is the basic physical and functional unit of heredity. Genes are made up of deoxyribonucleic acid or **DNA**. Genes act as instructions to make molecules called **proteins**. These proteins make cells, which make tissues, which make organs, which make organ systems.

Living things have two copies of each gene, one inherited from each parent. Most genes are the same in all people, but a small number of genes (less than 1 percent of the total) are slightly different among people. These small differences contribute to each person's unique physical features.

Alleles are forms of the same gene with slight differences in their sequence of DNA bases. **Dominance** is when the effect of one phenotype of one allele masks the contribution of a second allele at the same locus. The first allele is dominant, and the second allele is recessive. For example, in humans, brown eye color is dominant over blue eye color. For a person to display blue eyes, she must have both recessive alleles.

Gregor Mendel

Gregor Mendel is known as the Father of Genetics for his work with pea plants in the 1850s and 1860s. Mendel showed that when a true-breeding yellow pea (YY) and a true-breeding green pea (yy) were cross-bred, their offspring always produced yellow seeds. However, in the next generation, the green peas reappeared. To explain this phenomenon, Mendel coined the terms recessive and dominant in reference to certain traits.

Reginald Punnett

Reginald Punnett was a British geneticist and mathematician known for his contributions to the field of genetics. He developed the Punnett square, which is a visual representation used to predict the outcomes of genetic crosses. The Punnett square is a simple diagram used to determine the probability of specific traits being passed on to offspring. It is a valuable tool to use in the life science classroom to show students that offspring inherit half of their genes from one parent, and half of their genes from another.

Punnett Square

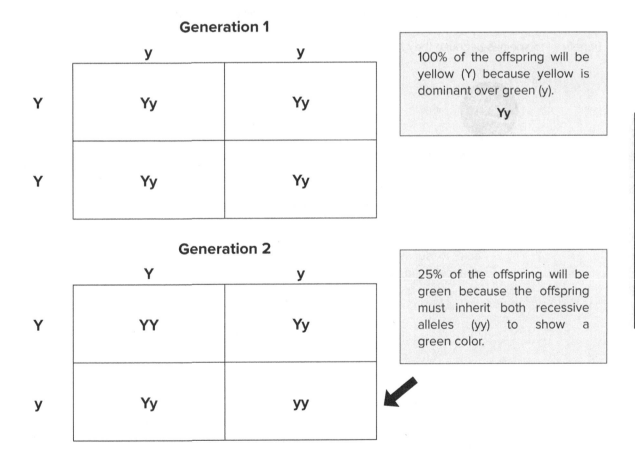

D. Biological Evolution: Unity and Diversity

Natural Selection

Charles Darwin and Alfred Russel Wallace developed the theory of evolution: Traits can be passed down to offspring that allow organisms to adapt to the environment better than other organisms of the same species. This enables better survival and reproduction compared with other members of the species, leading to evolution.

Evolution is a type of change that happens over thousands of years. It is important to note that organisms do not evolve; populations evolve. For example, a bird will not suddenly go through evolution during its lifetime. However, through genetic mutations over long periods of time, populations of birds will evolve and change to adapt to their environment.

Adaptation is the distribution of traits in the population that are matched to and can change with environmental conditions. For example, over time, frogs inherited genetic variations that resulted in camouflage—the ability to blend in with their surroundings. This allowed the frog to survive and reproduce.

Variations of genetically determined traits in a population may give some members a reproductive advantage in each environment. This is often random and a result of a mutation in the DNA molecule. This natural selection can lead to adaptation. Such adaptations can eventually lead to the development of separate species in separated populations.

Mutations are changes in the DNA molecule caused by mistakes during cell division or exposure to environmental factors (such as ultraviolet [UV] light and cigarette smoke). Sometimes these mutations are beneficial to species because they help species evolve.

Quick Tip

In the 19th century, smog from the factories in England turned many trees in the area black. This made the white moths living in the area easily seen by predators. The white moths were picked off as food. The black moths, that had inherited a certain gene sequence to make them black, were camouflaged against the black trees. Because of the mutation, more black moths were able to survive and reproduce. The black moths ended up dominating in the area.

7814
Science

1. Red plants have the dominant trait for color (R), while white plants have the recessive trait for color (r). How many red plants and white plants are produced when Rr x Rr are crossed?

    A. 3 red plants; 1 one white plant

    B. 1 red plant; 3 white plants

    C. 2 red plants; 2 white plants

    D. All red plants

2. Which of the following is a producer?

    A. hawk

    B. snake

    C. bunny

    D. grass

3. A symbiotic relationship where both organisms benefit is called:

    A. competition

    B. predation

    C. commensalism

    D. mutualism

4. What is the term called for a plant in a room growing toward the light coming from a window?

    A. photosynthesis

    B. phototropism

    C. cellular respiration

    D. angiosperm

5. A teacher shows students two pictures. One picture is of a penguin on a tropical island, and the other is of a lizard in a snowstorm. The teacher then leads a discussion on how these animals might adapt over time. Which of the following would be most appropriate to include in this discussion?

    A. A Punnett square to show the variation of gene inheritance

    B. A diagram showing the internal structures animals need to reproduce

    C. A video on the role different ecosystems play in species' survival

    D. An explanation of trait variations different species experience to survive

7814
Science

6. A teacher is showing students that plants need the assistance of other species to aid in pollination. Which of the following THREE student responses indicate that the students understand this concept?

    ☐ A. Pollen can get stuck on the fur of a bear. As the bear moves around the environment, the pollen rubs up against other plants so they can get pollinated.

    ☐ B. Pollen gets attached to bees' legs. As the bee flies from one plant to another, the pollen is transferred to different plants, which helps them get pollinated.

    ☐ C. Lizards can change their color based on what plants they are standing next to, which allows them to stay camouflaged and ward off predators.

    ☐ D. Bugs recognize flowers by color and smell, which helps the bugs move from one plant to another.

    ☐ E. Plants are at the bottom of the energy pyramid and 100% producers.

7. Which of the following would be most effective in showing students that energy is lost as it is transferred from one trophic system to another?

    A. Energy pyramid

    B. Food web

    C. Food chain

    D. Family Taxonomy

8. A teacher explains that all cells must reproduce to make new cells. Which of the following concepts is the teacher going over?

    A. Cell structures

    B. Cell membrane

    C. Cell Theory

    D. Sexual reproduction

9. A teacher is helping students understand that when two organisms reproduce, the offspring receives half of its genes from one parent and half of its genes from another parent. Which of the following would be most helpful in explaining this?

    A. A diagram of the sexual reproductive organs of a plant

    B. A video on DNA transcription

    C. A Punnett square activity

    D. A picture of an albino squirrel, which has inherited all recessive alleles.

10. Which of the following statements indicates that students understand how traits in a population may give some members a reproductive advantage in each environment?

    A. Evolution is a type of change that happens over thousands of years.

    B. Some species reproduce sexually, and some reproduce asexually.

    C. Trait variation can lead to natural selection and adaptation.

    D. Mutations are changes in the DNA molecule caused by mistakes during cell division or exposure to environmental factors.

Number	Answer	Explanation
1.	A	When Rr and Rr are crossed, it results in 1 RR, 2 Rr, and 1 rr. RR and Rr show red. The only way to show white (recessive) is if the offspring inherit rr. |	R	r
R	RR	Rr
r	Rr	rr	
2.	D	Grasses go through photosynthesis; therefore, they are producers. They produce their own food and are at the bottom of the energy pyramid. Bunnies eat the grass; snakes eat the bunnies; and hawks eat the snakes.
3.	D	A symbiotic relationship where both organisms benefit is called mutualism. Predation and competition benefit only one organism. Commensalism is a symbiotic relationship where one organism benefits and one does not benefit but is unharmed.
4.	B	Plants growing toward a window in response to the light coming through the window is an example of phototropism.
5.	D	Species will adapt to their environments through evolution. In this activity, the teacher needs to explain how the penguin and lizard species will adapt over time due to the environment.
6.	A, B & D	All three of these answer choices explain how pollination occurs. Answer C is not related to pollination.
7.	A	An energy pyramid shows students that the energy stored in plants is the highest in the pyramid. As you move up the pyramid, energy is lost.
8.	C	There are three parts to cell theory: 1. All living things are composed of cells. 2. The cell is the smallest unit of life. 3. All cells come from pre-existing cells. The teacher is going over the third part of cell theory.
9.	C	A Punnett square is a valuable tool to use in the life science classroom to show students that offspring inherit half of their genes from one parent and half of their genes from another.
10.	C	Variations of genetically determined traits in a population may give some members a reproductive advantage in each environment, making answer C the best answer.

This page intentionally left blank.

III. Physical Sciences

The following topics are aligned with the test specification of the Praxis 7814 exam. It is important that you examine these closely because these are the skills assessed on the exam.

A. Matter and Interactions
   1. Structure and Properties of Matter
   2. Chemical Reactions

B. Motion and Stability: Forces and Interactions
   1. Forces and Motion
   2. Types of Interactions

C. Energy
   1. Definition of Energy, Conservation of Energy, and Energy Transfer
   2. Relationship between Energy and Forces
   3. Energy In Chemical Processes and Everyday Life

D. Waves and Their Application in Technologies for Information Transfer
   1. Wave Properties
   2. Electromagnetic Radiation
   3. Information Technologies and Instrumentation

IMPORTANT: References for the information in the following sections can be found in the bibliography of this study guide.

A. Matter and Interactions

Physical and chemical properties and structure of matter

- **Solid.** Particles are very close together.
- **Liquid.** Particles are closer together than a gas but farther apart than a solid.
- **Gas.** Particles are very far apart.
- **Texture**. Characteristics and appearance of an object given by the size, shape, density, arrangement, proportion of its elementary parts. Examples of texture include hard, soft, rough, smooth, coarse, fine, matt, glossy.
- **Hardness**. A measure of how much a material resists changes in shape. For example, hard things resist pressure. Some examples of hard materials are diamond, steel, ice, granite, concrete.
- **Freezing point.** The temperature at which a liquid changes to a solid
- **Melting point**. The temperature at which a solid changes to a liquid
- **Boiling Point.** The temperature at which a liquid changes into a gas

Atoms

- **Atoms.** The smallest part of an element that retains its chemical properties. More than 99.94% of an atom's mass is in the nucleus.

- **Electrons.** Negatively charged subatomic particles that circle around the atom's nucleus.

- **Neutrons.** Neutrally charged subatomic particles that are located in the atom's nucleus.

- **Protons.** Positively charged subatomic particles that are located in the atom's nucleus.

Mass

Mass is how much matter there is in an object. Mass does not equal weight. For example, Jupiter, a planet made of gas, is much denser than Earth, a planet made of rock.

$$mass = density \times volume$$

Volume

Volume is the amount of space an object takes up.

$$volume = \frac{mass}{density}$$

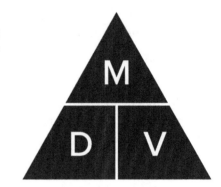

Please note that density is represented by the variable p. For the sake of clarity above, we used D. However, in the real world, density is represented as p.

- Mass = m

- Density = p

- Volume = V (capital letter)

Density

Density is the amount of matter an object has to its volume. An object with a lot of matter in a certain volume has high density. An object with little matter in the same amount of volume has a low density.

$$density = \frac{mass}{volume}$$

Physical vs. Chemical Changes

Physical changes result in a change in shape and size. Chemical changes result in a change that forms a new substance at the molecular level.

Changes in Matter

Physical	Chemical
Tearing	Rotting
Folding	Burning
Melting	Cooking
Freezing	Rusting
Evaporating	
Cutting	

Heat transfer

Heat transfer is the exchange of thermal energy between physical systems.

- **Convection.** The transfer of heat by the actual movement of the warmed matter. For example, in a convection oven, air is moved by a fan around the food.

- **Conduction.** The transfer of heat from particle to particle. For example, if a cold spoon is placed in hot soup, the spoon will get hotter until the soup and the spoon become the same temperature.

- **Radiation.** The transfer of heat from electromagnetic waves through space. Sunlight is a form of radiation.

Convection

In a convection oven, a fan swirls heat around the food.

Conduction

The spoon handle will get hot because it is touching the hot water

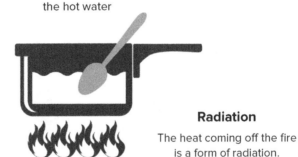

Radiation

The heat coming off the fire is a form of radiation.

Quick Tip

We use wooden spoons when cooking because wood is a bad conductor of heat. The handle of a wooden spoon stays cool even when submerged in hot water. A metal spoon will eventually become as hot as the water because metal is a good conductor of heat.

Mixtures

A mixture is a material system made up of two or more different substances that are mixed but are not combined chemically. The identities of the mixed elements are retained in a mixture. There are two types of mixtures: **homogeneous** and **heterogeneous**.

Homogeneous Mixture	Heterogeneous Mixture	Colloid	Suspension	Solutions
homo = same	hetero = different	homogeneous mixture	heterogeneous mixture	homogeneous mixture
You cannot see different parts of the mixture.	You can see different parts of the mixture.	One substance of microscopically dispersed insoluble particles is suspended throughout another substance. Particles do not settle and cannot be separated out by ordinary filtering.	Contains solid particles that are sufficiently large for sedimentation.	The dissolving agent is the solvent.
coffee, creamy peanut butter, Kool-Aid	chicken noodle soup, cereal	gels, emulsions	orange juice, salad dressing	salt water, sugar water

Electricity

Electricity can be defined as the flow of an electric charge. The most familiar electricity is the type used in homes and businesses to power lights and appliances. Electrical circuits allow electricity to flow in a loop and power different things.

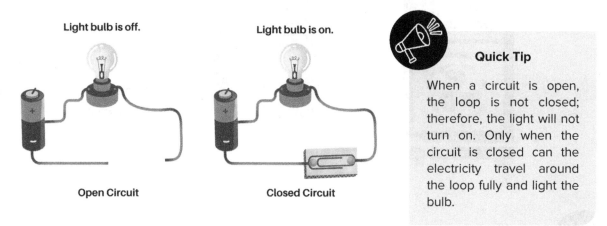

Light bulb is off.

Light bulb is on.

Open Circuit

Closed Circuit

Quick Tip

When a circuit is open, the loop is not closed; therefore, the light will not turn on. Only when the circuit is closed can the electricity travel around the loop fully and light the bulb.

Series circuits. The components are arranged end to end. The electric current flows through the first component, then through the next component, and so on until it reaches the battery again.

Parallel circuits. A circuit with branches that allow multiple applications to happen at once.

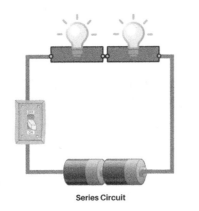

Series Circuit

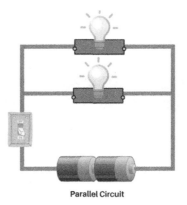

Parallel Circuit

Conductors and Insulators

Conductors (good for electricity)	Insulators (bad for electricity)
Wire	Rubber
Metal	Cloth
Water	Polystyrene (Styrofoam)

Lightning

Lightning is a giant spark of electricity in the atmosphere between clouds, the air, or the ground. As lightning starts, air acts as an insulator between the positive and negative charges in the cloud and between the cloud and the ground. When the opposite charges build up enough, this insulating capacity of the air breaks down, and there is a rapid discharge of electricity.

Cloud-to-ground lightning occurs between opposite charges within the thunderstorm cloud (intra-cloud lightning) or between opposite charges in the cloud and on the ground (cloud-to-ground lightning).

Quick Tip

Right before cloud-to-ground lightning occurs, the ground becomes positively charged because negative charges seep into the earth leaving fewer electrons on the earth's surface. The negative charges in the cloud are attracted to the positive charges on the earth's surface. Therefore, the negative charges move down the cloud close to the earth's surface. When the attraction is strong enough, lightning occurs.

B. Motion and Stability: Forces and Interactions

A **force** is any interaction that, when unopposed, will change the motion of an object. A force can cause an object with mass to change its velocity (including beginning motion from a state of rest).

Friction is the force resisting the relative motion of solid surfaces, fluid layers, and material elements sliding against each other.

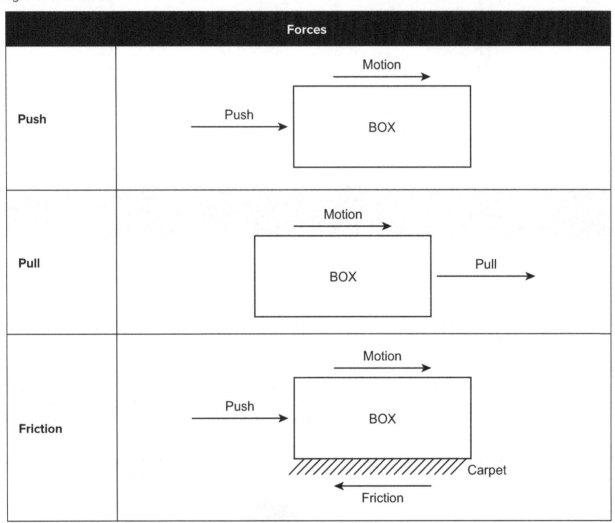

Newton's Laws of Motion

1. An object either remains at rest or continues to move at a constant velocity unless acted upon by a force.

2. Force is equal to the change in motion (mV) per change in time. For a constant mass, force equals mass times acceleration .

3. For every action, there is an equal and opposite reaction.

Equilibrium. A state in which opposing forces or influences are balanced.

C. Energy

On this exam, you will be required to differentiate among different forms of energy when answering questions.

Forms of Energy

Form	What It Does...	Examples
Mechanical	Objects in motion	Swing
Electrical	The movement of electrons through a wire	Light bulb
Chemical	Rearrangement of molecular structure	Photosynthesis, lighting a match, rusting
Thermal/heat	The movement of particles because of heat and friction.	Boiling water
Sound	The movement of energy through a substance, such as air or water, in the form of waves.	Sonic boom
Light	Electromagnetic radiation where photons are produced when an object's atoms heat up.	Fire

Energy is a property that can be transferred between and among objects. Energy can also be converted into different forms.

Speed and Energy

An object's speed affects the object's energy. The higher the speed, the more energy it has. Higher amounts of energy will result in a more significant change of motion for the object it is acting on. When the speed decreases, the energy also decreases.

Kinetic energy. The object is in motion. Kinetic energy is the actual movement of an object. For example, a rock rolling down a hill or a swing swinging in the air both have kinetic energy. Because the objects are in motion, they have kinetic energy.

Potential energy. The object is at rest but has potential to move. Energy possessed by an object or individual by virtue of its position relative to others, stresses within itself, electric charge, and other factors is its potential energy. For example, a rock on the top of the hill has potential to roll down; therefore, the rock has potential energy. A swing being pulled to the top before it is released has potential energy.

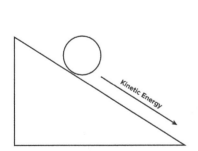

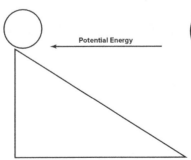

Quick Tip

A fundamental law of nature states that the total amount of energy in a system never changes. Energy is neither created nor destroyed. This is the law of conservation energy.

D. Waves and Their Application in Technologies for Information Transfer

A wave is a disturbance that travels through a medium from one location to another location.

Mechanical waves travel through a medium, which serve as the "mechanism" for the transfer of energy across the medium. There are three types of mechanical waves:

1. **Longitudinal waves.** In this type of wave, the movement of the particles is parallel to the motion of the energy, i.e. the displacement of the medium is in the same direction in which the wave is moving. Example – sound waves, pressure waves

2. **Transverse waves.** When the movement of the particles is at right angles or perpendicular to the motion of the energy, then this type of wave is known as a transverse wave. Light is an example of a transverse wave.

3. **Surface Waves**. Surface waves are a combination of longitudinal and transverse waves where particles in the medium follow a circular path. They occur at the interface of two different mediums like the interface of water and air (waves in the ocean) or layers of the earth's crust (earthquake waves).

Electromagnetic waves are a form of radiation that travels though the universe. X-rays, UV light, microwaves, and radio waves are all examples of electromagnetic waves.

Quick Tip

Mechanical waves require a medium (solid, liquid, or gas) to travel. Electromagnetic waves do not need a medium to travel. They can travel through a vacuum (a space devoid of matter).

For this exam, you should know the basic components of a wave: amplitude, wavelength, frequency, and speed.

- **Amplitude** – the distance between the resting position and the maximum displacement of the wave

- **Wavelength** – the distance between two crests of a wave

- **Crest** – the highest part of a wave

- **Frequency** – the measurement of how often a recurring event such as a wave occurs in a measured amount of time

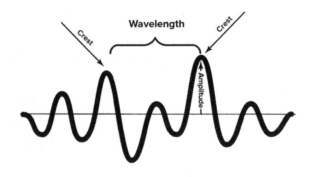

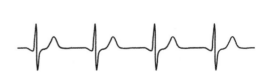

Physical Sciences Practice Questions

1. Which of the following is considered the least resistant to electricity and the best conductor of electricity?

    A. Wood

    B. Copper

    C. Rubber

    D. Plastic

2. Which **TWO** of the following is a chemical reaction?

    ☐ A. Rust forming on a bike left out in the rain

    ☐ B. Plants going through photosynthesis

    ☐ C. Water boiling on the stove

    ☐ D. A pendulum swinging back and forth

    ☐ E. A rock crumbling under pressure

3. At what point on the graphic below is kinetic energy the highest?

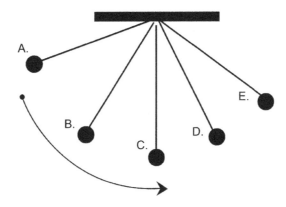

4. At what point on the graphic below is potential energy the highest?

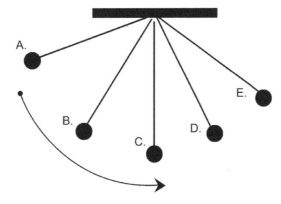

5. In a glass of water, ice floats to the surface of the water. Why does this happen?

   A. The water weighs more than the ice.

   B. The ice weighs more than the water.

   C. The ice is less dense than the water.

   D. The water is less dense than the ice.

6. Why is it easier to compress a gas rather than a solid?

   A. The particles in a gas are further apart than they are in a solid.

   B. The particles in a gas are closer together than they are in a solid.

   C. The particles in a solid are moving faster than they are in a gas.

   D. The particles in a solid are moving the same speed as they are in a gas.

7. This is considered a homogenous mixture.

   A. orange juice

   B. gel

   C. salad dressing (oil and vinegar)

   D. cereal

8. Why won't the light bulb turn on the circuit below?

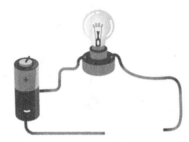

   A. The circuit is a series circuit.

   B. The circuit is a parallel circuit.

   C. The circuit is open.

   D. The circuit is closed.

9. Which of the following waves do not need a medium to travel?

   A. Light

   B. Sound

   C. Mechanical

   D. Microwaves

10. This is the highest point on a wave.

   A. Crest

   B. Amplitude

   C. Frequency

   D. Wavelength

Number	Answer	Explanation
1.	B	Copper is a type of metal and therefore the best conductor of electricity of all the choices. A good conductor of electricity resists the electricity the least.
2.	A & B	A chemical reaction is a process that involves rearrangement of the molecular structure of a substance. Rust and photosynthesis both involve the rearrangement of molecules.
3.	C	Kinetic energy is at its highest when potential energy is at its lowest. When the ball of the pendulum is at the bottom, kinetic energy is highest and potential energy is lowest.
4.	A	Potential energy is at its highest when kinetic energy is at its lowest. When the ball of the pendulum is in the top position of the graphic, potential energy is highest and kinetic energy is lowest.
5.	C	This is a density question. In this case, because the ice is floating in the water, the ice is less dense than the water.
6.	A	Particles in a gas are more spread out and move more freely than in a solid.
7.	B	A gel is a homogenous solution because the particles in a gel do not settle and cannot be separated out by ordinary filtering.
8.	C	The circuit is open, meaning the electricity is not flowing around the circuit and therefore not carrying electricity to the light bulb.
9.	D	Microwaves are electromagnetic waves and can travel in a vacuum, which is the absence of matter. They do not need a medium to travel.
10.	A	The crest of the wave is the highest point on a wave.

This page intentionally left blank.

IV. Engineering, Technology, and the Application of Science

The following are the test specifications taken directly from the ETS Study Companion for the 7814 exam. It is important that you examine these closely because these are the skills assessed on the exam. Following the specs are our detailed explanations of each specification.

Questions in this content category assess content from Earth and space, life, and physical sciences

A. Engineering

B. Developing Solutions

C. Optimizing Design

Scientific method

The scientific method is a body of techniques for investigating phenomena, acquiring new knowledge, or correcting and integrating previous knowledge. To be termed scientific, a method of inquiry is commonly based on empirical or measurable evidence subject to specific principles of reasoning.

Students in science:

- **Observe**. Employ the five senses to interact with phenomena and recording findings.

- **Classify.** Arrange living and nonliving things based on attributes.

- **Predict**. Make assumptions based on evidence.

- **Hypothesize**. State a prediction based on evidence.

- **Investigate**. Conduct experiments.

Test Tip

Steps to the scientific method

1. Make an observation.

2. Ask a question.

3. Form a hypothesis.

4. Conduct an experiment.

5. Analyze the data and draw a conclusion

Conducting Experiments

An experiment is a procedure carried out to refute or validate a hypothesis. Experiments help students understand cause-and-effect relationships by demonstrating what outcome occurs when a particular factor is manipulated.

An experiment usually has three kinds of variables: independent, dependent, and control. The independent variable is the one that is changed by the scientist.

- **Independent variable** is the element manipulated in the experiment.

- **Dependent variable** is what the scientist is measuring during the experiment.

- **Control variables** are the elements of the experiment that a scientist wants to remain constant, and she must observe them as carefully as the dependent variables.

Quick Tip

Adding a control makes experiments stronger because a **control group** gives reliable baseline data to compare results to.

Example:

- If a scientist wants to test the effectiveness of a fertilizer, she might make a hypothesis, "Because Fertilizer A has more Phosphorous than Fertilizer B, plants treated with Fertilizer A will grow 15% more than those treated with Fertilizer B."

- To test the hypothesis, she would place two plant bulbs of the same plant and same size in two different pots. The pots are the same size. She keeps everything the same: sunlight, water, and temperature. The only thing that changes is the independent variable, which is the fertilizer or the treatment.

- The scientist also adds a pot with neither Fertilizer A nor Fertilizer B. This is the control. It is used as a baseline and makes the experiment stronger.

- The scientist measures growth over time. The growth or lack of growth is the dependent variable or the result.

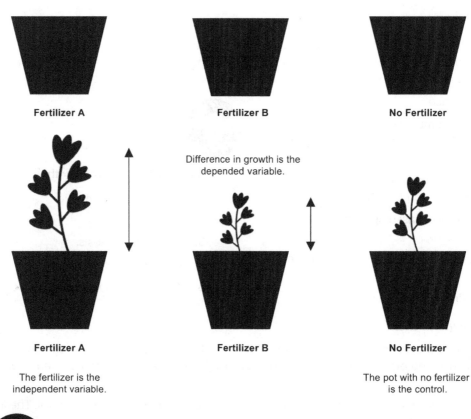

The fertilizer is the
independent variable.

Difference in growth is the
depended variable.

The pot with no fertilizer
is the control.

Quick Tip

When working with human subjects in an experiment, scientists must acquire from the participants informed consent. Informed consent is a voluntary agreement to participate in research. This includes informing participants of their rights and the risks associated with the treatment in the study or research.

While teaching methods for science are not explicitly stated in the specs, it is important to understand best practices in science. Science is inquiry-based, meaning students must be given the opportunity to interact with science. Along with this, teachers must keep students safe in the science classroom.

Safety is important when providing students with the opportunity to learn in science classrooms. Teachers must communicate procedures and guidelines repeatedly, so students understand what is expected in terms of safety and security.

Here are some do's and don'ts when it comes to science classroom safety:

Quick Tip

Developmentally appropriate practices (DAP): Match the students' age to the appropriate task. For example, 4–6 graders might have to interact with chemicals during labs, while K–3 graders probably will not.

Do	Don't
Communicate procedures repeatedly and provide plenty of practice with students to engage in procedures and emergency operations. Practice makes perfect. Send procedures home for parents to read and sign, indicating they received the procedures and understood them.	Post procedures on the wall and expect students review them on their own.
Lock up chemicals, sharp tools, and other hazardous materials used in labs.	Leave chemicals, sharp tools, and other hazardous materials near your desk.
Leave the chemical safety manual out where students can access it in case there is an emergency with chemicals.	Lock up the chemical manual with the chemicals so only the person with a key can access it.
Predetermine student lab groups to maximize time on task and minimize student misbehavior, accidents, or mishaps.	Let students get into groups on their own before the lab.
Keep your principal and administration informed when you are doing a lab or controversial science unit.	Administer complex or dangerous labs without informing administration.

Technology in the science classroom

Technology can enhance the learning environment in science class. Guidelines for using technology differ from district to district and state to state. It is important for teachers to review their own district's and school's guidelines regarding technology in the classroom.

Virtual Labs

Virtual labs are an effective way to engage students. Students can input data, gather information, and conduct an experiment in a virtual lab. Virtual labs are also helpful because they allow students the experience even if funds are not available for the physical lab.

Technology Tools

Students use a database to find other studies that relate to their topics. Students use a spreadsheet to store their data from an experiment. Students use presentation software like PowerPoint or Keynote to present their findings to the class. Teachers must know when and how to use these tools effectively.

Hands-on Tools

It's important not to over-complicate your approach in this area. Regardless of your school's budget or access to advanced technology, remember that one of your primary goals is teaching students to use tools to understand science—especially in elementary classrooms. Here are some ideas of how you can use simple resources on hand in nearly every classroom:

- Track weather trends by using a calendar to record temperature, humidity, and precipitation.

- Build interactive tools like kites, pinwheels, or parachutes, then observe and record how different shapes, sizes, and patterns are affected differently by the air.

- Use pictures to track how sunny it is each day, then record daily high and low temperatures and graph them over a set period..

1. Which of the following activities does not apply technology, science tools, and measurement units to collect data?

    A. Using a measuring cup as a rain gauge to track precipitation levels.

    B. Dropping a weight onto objects from various heights to see its effects.

    C. Using various lengths of paper streamers to measure wind strength.

    D. Evaluating a table of daily high temperatures to determine patterns.

2. A team of students wants to create a better habitat for a small school of fish in their classroom aquarium. Their current problem is the small fish are often scared away from the feeding area by larger fish. What would be the most suitable first step in developing their solution?

    A. Build a partition in the aquarium to separate the larger fish from the smaller ones.

    B. Gather information about the behaviors and feeding habits of both the small and large fish.

    C. Change the type of fish food they are currently using.

    D. Transfer the larger fish to another aquarium.

3. Susan aims to improve the design of a self-watering plant pot for desert plants, which need less water. What would be the best method to test her new prototype?

    A. Measure the amount of water her new pot uses in a week compared to a traditional pot under the same conditions.

    B. See if her pot can hold as much water as a traditional plant pot.

    C. Plant a flower in the pot and check if the flower blooms in a week.

    D. Pour water in her pot and see how long it takes to drain.

4. A science class is designing an innovative tool to streamline park cleanup processes. The class agreed on a goal: to create a device that is efficient, user friendly and environmentally helpful. The initial prototype didn't meet the efficiency expectation during preliminary field tests. Given these objectives and constraints, how should the class proceed with refining the design?

    A. Adjust individual variables in the design, one at a time, carefully documenting any changes in the tool's performance, user comfort, and environmental impact.

    B. Store the prototype in a controlled environment for a month to examine if any environmental factors could potentially enhance its performance over time.

    C. Conduct surveys among park maintenance staff and volunteers to collect feedback regarding their preferences and suggestions for a park cleanup tool.

    D. Initiate small-scale production of the tool to gather wide-ranging user feedback and adjust the design accordingly during subsequent manufacturing batches.

5. A group of students is working on the design of a compost bin that reduces smell and does not attract pests. After their initial prototype, they notice an increase in pest activity. What should be their next step in improving their compost bin design?

    A. Increase the amount of compost material to see if the pests are drawn to a specific type of compost.

    B. Research the causes behind pest attraction to compost bins and investigate pest-resistant designs and materials.

    C. Stop composting food scraps and switch to leaf and yard waste.

    D. Move the compost bin to a different location to see if fewer pests are attracted.

6. Maria wants to design a new type of pencil sharpener that collects all the shavings without any mess. Her initial prototype fails to collect shavings as she intended. What would be the most effective next step for Maria in her design process?

    A. Change the materials she used in the initial prototype, assuming they are the issue.

    B. Give the prototype to classmates to use, hoping they will come up with improvement suggestions.

    C. Identify the prototype's failure points and design controlled tests to improve its performance.

    D. Start over with a new idea for a pencil sharpener.

7. A fifth-grade class is learning about solar power. The class designed a solar oven during a lab. However, they noticed that the initial design cooks very slowly. They want to improve a solar oven design to make it cook food faster. What would be her best approach to improve her solar oven design?

    A. Cook different types of food in the oven to see if some cook faster.

    B. Place the oven in different locations to see where it works best.

    C. Discard the prototype and come up with a completely new design idea.

    D. Conduct controlled tests to refine the design.

8. Students are working on a project to improve the design of a lever that can lift heavy objects with less effort. They built a prototype, but it doesn't perform as well as they expected. What would be the most appropriate next step in their project?

    A. Redesign the lever using new materials, and then test the level with different weighted objects.

    B. Use the lever to lift a heavier object and note the outcome.

    C. Start making multiple copies of the prototype and see how they perform against one another.

    D. Plan and conduct tests, controlling for one variable at a time, to identify the aspects of the lever design that can be improved.

9. A team of students is conducting an experiment to understand the principles of buoyancy, specifically focusing on why objects of similar volumes but different materials have varying behaviors in water. Some objects float, while others sink. Given an assortment of objects made from different materials, what should be the team's FIRST step in developing a sophisticated, controlled investigation?

    A. Research the properties of each material, including but not limited to density, porosity, and rigidity. Then, hypothesize how these properties might influence an object's buoyancy.

    B. Simultaneously submerge all the objects in water and classify them into floating and sinking categories based on observations.

    C. Accurately measure and record the mass and volume of each object, then select the one with the lowest density for focused examination.

    D. Choose the object with the largest volume and conduct a detailed investigation on that particular object, disregarding the material it's made from.

10. An engineering club wants to design a suspension bridge model that can resist high-velocity winds for their science fair project. They sketched an initial design and created a prototype, but during their preliminary wind tunnel test, the bridge's deck showed excessive swaying even under a moderate wind speed. What should be their next step, considering they aim to optimize the design solution?

    A. Drop the idea of a suspension bridge and switch to an arch bridge design since they believe it may be more stable.

    B. Test the bridge prototype again in the wind tunnel but at a lower wind speed.

    C. Conduct in-depth research into the dynamics of wind flow and suspension bridge aerodynamics, then reconsider the failure points in their original design.

    D. Increase the mass of the bridge deck, assuming that a heavier deck would sway less in the wind.

Number	Answer	Explanation
1.	B	The only answer that does not use measurement is the situation in answer B. The students are experimenting with dropping objects. However, there is no tool in place to measure the differences in this experiment.
2.	B	The first step in creating a solution to a problem is to gather more information about it. Understanding the behaviors and feeding habits of both types of fish will provide useful insights into how to design a habitat that meets the needs of both.
3.	A	This answer choice aligns with the objective of planning and carrying out fair tests. By comparing the water usage of her new pot to a traditional pot under the same conditions, Susan can directly assess the efficiency of her design.
4.	A	The goal is to improve his tool's effectiveness. By adjusting one variable at a time, the class can understand the role of each element of his design and how they affect the overall performance of his tool. This strategy aligns with the objectives of controlling variables and identifying aspects of a model that can be improved.
5.	B	To solve the problem, the students first need to understand why pests are attracted to compost bins. From this understanding, they can then investigate how other designs have successfully deterred pests. This process aligns with the goals of gathering information about a problem and looking into solutions
6.	C	Maria's prototype didn't work as intended, so the next logical step would be to figure out why. By identifying where the design fails, she can create tests to specifically address these points and make improvements. This strategy aligns with the objectives of considering failure points and improving a model
7.	D	By identifying the weaknesses in the design, the class can focus on specific areas for improvement. Conducting controlled tests will allow the students to evaluate the effect of each change on the oven's performance.
8.	D	To identify the aspects of the lever that need improvement, it's best to conduct tests that isolate each variable. This way, they can see the effect of each part of the lever design on its overall performance.
9.	A	Before commencing an investigation, it's crucial to gather relevant background information. By understanding the properties of each material, the students can make informed hypotheses about how these properties may influence buoyancy. This approach aligns with the initial stages of scientific investigation, which involve making observations and forming hypotheses.
10.	C	The students need to understand why their initial design failed. This involves studying the forces and principles at play, particularly as they relate to wind dynamics and suspension bridge design. Once they gain a deeper understanding of these elements, they can reconsider the failure points in their original design and make necessary modifications.

This page intentionally left blank.

1. This type of rock is formed by heat and pressure:

    A. Fossil

    B. Sedimentary

    C. Igneous

    D. Metamorphic

2. A river flows through a canyon and picks up silt. That sediment and silt runs downstream and deposits where the river ends. When that material gets to the beach, it sits there. Over millions of years, _____ form.

    A. Fossils

    B. Sedimentary rocks

    C. Igneous rocks

    D. Metamorphic rocks

3. Mr. Lopez is teaching a unit on seasons. He explains why summer days are longer and winter days are shorter. What should Mr. Lopez emphasize regarding the Earth when explaining this phenomenon?

    A. Revolution around the sun

    B. Tilt on its axis

    C. Position in the solar system

    D. Distance away from the sun

4. The sun appears bigger than other stars because of:

    A. The size of the sun

    B. The size of the solar system

    C. The distance Earth is from the sun

    D. The distance the sun is from Mars

5. The _____ affects the ocean tides.

    A. Moon

    B. Sun

    C. Stars

    D. Solar system

6. What causes the Earth's magnetism?

    A. The Earth's rotation around the moon

    B. The moon's rotation around the Earth

    C. The inner and outer core rotation

    D. Rotation of the Earth around the sun

7. Tectonic plates slide against each other in opposite directions, causing a(n):

   A. Subduction

   B. Earthquake

   C. Mountain

   D. Volcano

8. _____ happen when warmer, lighter air at the equator moves toward the cooler air at the poles.

   A. Convection currents

   B. Conduction currents

   C. Atmospheric currents

   D. Jet streams

9. What keeps the Earth from falling into the sun?

   A. There is a fairly constant gravitational force between the sun and the Earth, keeping the Earth in its orbit.

   B. Kepler's law and Newton's laws.

   C. The Earth is not moving fast enough to "escape" the sun's gravity and leave the solar system, but it is going too fast to be pulled into the sun.

   D. All of the above.

10. In the diagram below, number 6 is:

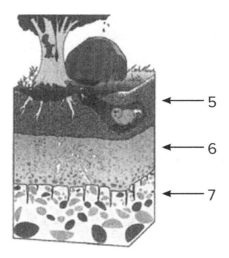

   A. Topsoil

   B. Subsoil

   C. Bedrock

   D. Lava

11. Mr. Lopez wants to conduct a DNA extraction lab but does not have the expensive materials necessary to complete the process. What can Mr. Lopez do to maximize the students' learning even though they cannot physically do the lab?

   A. Go through a lab simulation with similar items used in a DNA extraction lab.

   B. Utilize a web-based virtual lab that can be projected on a screen.

   C. Have students draw the process on a big sheet of poster paper.

   D. Have students role-play while simulating the lab.

12. A 2nd grade teacher wants students to implement the unifying processes of systems, order, and organization in a lesson on plants. Which of the following activities is the most appropriate?

   A. Completing a chart to track the growth of plants in the classroom.

   B. Creating a diagram to show how plants use energy from the sun for photosynthesis.

   C. Using a database of different plant species to compare and contrast their characteristics.

   D. Conducting an experiment to cross-pollinate pea plants and documenting results.

Use the following scenario to answer numbers 13-16

A 3rd grade class is learning about fungus and conducts an experiment on mold. The experiment is testing which type of food can grow the most mold. The class has done research on mold and the conditions in which mold grows. The students use two different types of food to test: lettuce and bread. The students predict that the bread will produce the most mold.

The students use three containers, all the same size. Container A has 1 ounce of lettuce, container B has one ounce of bread, and container C has no food in it. The students drop 5 drops of water in each container and leave the containers uncovered for 1 hour. Then they place lids on each of the containers and store them both in a dark cabinet. They check the containers every day and document what they see.

13. In this experiment, the students' prediction is called the:

   A. Control

   B. Constant

   C. Independent variable

   D. Hypothesis

14. In this experiment, the food is the:

   A. Control

   B. Constant

   C. Independent variable

   D. Hypothesis

15. In this experiment, the container with no food is the:

   A. Control

   B. Constant

   C. Independent variable

   D. Hypothesis

16. In this experiment, the difference in mold growth is the:

   A. Control

   B. Constant

   C. Independent variable

   D. Dependent variable

17. A teacher shows the students the following diagram. She asks students to explain what the diagram shows. Which of the following students provides the correct explanation?

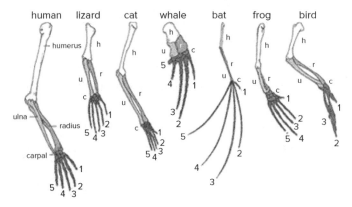

   A. The diagram is showing species that have survived over thousands of years. Therefore. The diagram is showing natural selection.

   B. The diagram is showing how different structures in different species evolve. Therefore, the diagram is showing evolution.

   C. The diagram shows different species with similar arm and hand structures. Therefore, the diagram is showing common ancestry.

   D. The diagram is showing different species within a domain. Therefore, the diagram is showing classification.

18. As **random** genetic mutations occur within an organism's genetic code, the beneficial mutations are preserved because they aid survival. This is called:

   A. Common ancestry

   B. Natural selection

   C. Dominant traits

   D. Recessive traits

19. Phototropism means plants will grow toward the:

   A. Ground

   B. Water

   C. Light

   D. Other plants

20. Students are describing the difference between plant and animal cells. Which **TWO** of the students' responses are correct?

☐ A. Animal cells have a cell wall, and plant cells have a cell membrane.

☐ B. Plant cells have a cell wall, and animal cells have a cell membrane.

☐ C. Animal cells have mitochondria, and plant cells have a nucleus.

☐ D. Plant cells go through photosynthesis while animal cells go through cellular respiration.

☐ E. Animal Cells have DNA, and plant cells do not.

21. In a third-grade class, students learn that the black moth has a genetic make-up that makes it difficult for predators to see it against the dark trees. The white moth does not have the same genetic make-up and is easily seen by predators and eaten. The students are learning about:

A. Dominance

B. Recessive

C. Natural selection

D. Classification

22. A teacher is using the following diagram to explain energy flow in an ecosystem. She asks students to identify where the most energy is and why. Which of the following would indicate the student has a misconception of this concept?

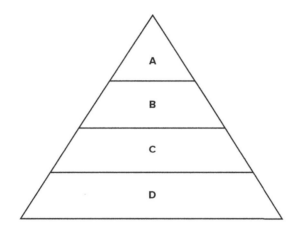

A. Section D has the most energy because plants are in section D and they get their energy directly from the sun.

B. Energy is lost as you move up the diagram from D to A.

C. The animals in section A eat the animals in section B. The animals in section B eat the animals in section C and so on.

D. Section A has the most energy because section A is closest to the sun and the sun has the most energy.

23. This is the maximum population of a particular organism that a given environment can support without detrimental effects.

A. Domain

B. Natural selection

C. Evolution

D. Carrying capacity

24. A rock sitting on top of a hill has what kind of energy?

    A. Kinetic

    B. Mechanical

    C. Chemical

    D. Potential

25. When you push a box through the doorway, you are using:

    A. Chemical energy

    B. Kinetic energy

    C. Mechanical energy

    D. Potential energy

26. Mr. Jasper wants to show students when oil and water are shaken, no matter how hard, the oil can still be seen as little oil bubbles throughout the mixture. Mr. Jasper is showing the class a:

    A. Homogeneous mixture

    B. Heterogeneous mixture

    C. Solution

    D. Colloid

27. A teacher asks students to explain the two types of circuits below. Which of the following student explanations is correct?

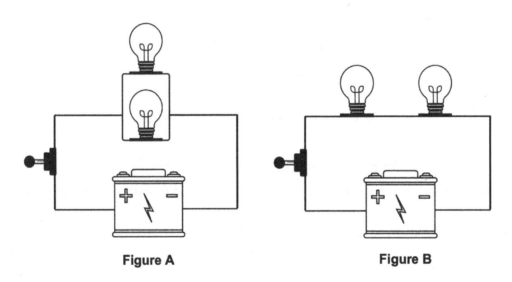

Figure A   **Figure B**

    A. Both figure A and figure B are parallel circuits.

    B. Figure A is a parallel circuit; figure B is a series circuit.

    C. Figure A is a series circuit; figure B is a parallel circuit.

    D. Both figure A and figure B are series circuits.

28. The gravitational pull of two objects depends on:

    A. The gravity of the two objects

    B. The mass of the two objects

    C. The atomic make-up of the two objects

    D. The electrons in the two objects' atoms

29. A class is investigating how friction can affect how objects move. The teacher rolls a small object down a smooth surface, and then the teacher repeats the process with a rough surface. Then the teacher rolls the ball down the ramp and increases and decreases the incline. Which of the following misconceptions might a student have with this demonstration?

    A. If the angle of the incline of the surface increases, the force of friction will increase.

    B. If the angle of the incline of the surface decreases, the force of friction will increase.

    C. The rougher a surface is, the more friction will be produced and slow down the object.

    D. The smoother the surface, the faster the object will travel.

30. A teacher is working on a unit about waves. The teacher shows students graphics of a high frequency wave and a low frequency wave. Then the teacher asks a student to explain the differences between the two. Which of the following responses indicates the student understands wave frequency?

    A. High frequency waves have crests that are far apart.

    B. Low frequency waves have higher crests than high frequency waves.

    C. High frequency waves have crests that are close together.

    D. Low frequency waves have lower amplitudes.

31. A teacher asks students to explain that the total mass of matter always stays the same when undergoing a physical or chemical change. Which of the following activity would best represent this?

    A. Melting an ice cube

    B. Separating a homogenous mixture

    C. Showing a diagram of an atom

    D. Showing the difference between an open and closed circuit

32. Mr. Jackson takes his students outside to the sidewalk and pours a bit of water on the sidewalk. He and the students wait for the water to evaporate. The area where the puddle of water was is cooler than where there was no water. The teacher is explaining what concept?

    A. Properties of water – temperature moderation

    B. Properties of atoms – molecular compound

    C. Properties of water – adhesion

    D. Properties of atoms – electrons

33. The particles in an atom that are negatively charged are:

    A. Electrons

    B. Protons

    C. Neutrons

    D. Protons and neutrons together

34. What would be the best way for a teacher to assess how students apply the scientific method during a lab on waves?

    A. Use a teacher-made multiple-choice assessment with scientific method questions.

    B. Administer a state-mandated assessment that assesses the standards for scientific method.

    C. Survey students to identify their understanding of the scientific method.

    D. Formatively assess students by walking around the lab and watch how students apply the scientific method.

35. On a field trip, a student holds a frog and reports that it has slippery skin. Which of the following is the student demonstrating?

    A. An observation

    B. A prediction

    C. An experiment

    D. An explanation

36. A teacher is showing her students how to calculate density by using displacement. What is the most appropriate tool to use in this strategy?

    A. Test tube

    B. Beaker

    C. Graduated cylinder

    D. Scale

37. A class is growing bacteria in petri dishes. There are three groups of petri dishes with the same number of bacteria in each petri dish. The students collect data regarding how many spores they see at different temperatures. What is the independent variable in this scenario?

    A. The petri dishes

    B. The bacteria

    C. The temperature

    D. The growth

38. Which of these describes water in gas state?

    A. Ice cubes in a glass

    B. Steam coming off boiling water

    C. Hail during a storm

    D. Rain falling from the clouds

39. A student riding a bicycle observes that it moves faster on a smooth road than on a rough road. This happens because the smooth road has which of the following?

    A. Less gravity

    B. More gravity

    C. Less friction

    D. More friction

40. Students are growing plants in a closed plastic container. They are observing the process of photosynthesis. They are also using a gas meter to measure gas levels within the container during photosynthesis. What gas is forming in the container?

   A. Carbon dioxide

   B. Oxygen

   C. Helium

   D. Nitrogen

41. Which of the following best explains how plant stems transport water to other areas of the plant?

   A. By using photosynthesis

   B. Through a series of tubes

   C. By making carbon dioxide

   D. Through the evaporation of water

42. Students are studying genetics using Punnet squares. They learn that in order for an offspring to display recessive traits, the offspring must inherit which of the following?

   A. Recessive and dominant alleles

   B. Only dominant alleles

   C. Only recessive alleles

   D. Mainly recessive with some dominant alleles

43. Students are testing different types of Teflon on pans to see which Teflon keeps the highest temperature. Students take 3 different pans lined with three different types of Teflon and determine which type allows water to boil the quickest. During this experiment, what should be controlled?

   A. The amount of water put in each pan

   B. The time of day the experiment was conducted

   C. The brand of stove used to head the pans

   D. The store where the pans were purchased

44. Which of the following is an example of a formative assessment in a 5th grade science class?

   A. Working on a unit for two weeks, assessing students at the end of the unit, and using those grades to communicate scores with parents.

   B. Administering a pre-test on the unit, working on a unit for two weeks, assessing students with a post-test at the end to determine gains.

   C. Administering a pre-test on the unit, making decisions on how to move forward based on the pre-test, and assessing students with a post-test at the end to determine gains.

   D. Working on a unit for two weeks, observing student engagement and understanding and assessing students along the way to drive instructional decisions.

45. What would be an appropriate activity to do when using a thematic lesson incorporating both math and science?

    A. Count how many jellybeans are in a jar.

    B. Conduct an experiment using a Bunsen burner.

    C. Categorize different seeds based on shape and color.

    D. Calculate the mass of a rock.

46. A teacher explains to students that Florida hibiscus have colorful flowers and sweet nectar to attract bees. What science standard is she covering?

    A. Earth/space science – seasons

    B. Physical science – atoms

    C. Chemistry – molecules

    D. Life science – pollination

47. The process through which photosynthesis occurs and becomes Earth's original source of food is which of the following?

    A. Chemical process

    B. Physical process

    C. Solar process

    D. Energy process

Science CKT 7814 - Practice Test Answer Explanations

Number	Answer	Category	Answer Explanation
1	D	I	Heat and pressure create metamorphic rocks.
2	B	I	Sedimentation is the process that causes mineral and/or organic particles to settle in place and become sedimentary rocks.
3	B	I	The seasons are the result of Earth tilted on its axis, traveling around the sun. Summer happens in the hemisphere tilted toward the sun, and winter happens in the hemisphere tilted away from the sun.
4	C	I	The sun is a star 93 million miles away. However, it appears bigger than other stars because Earth is closer to the sun. Other stars are 100,000 times farther away than the sun.
5	A	I	Tides rise and fall because of the gravitational forces of the moon and sun on the oceans of the Earth.
6	C	I	The Earth's outer core is made of iron. The outer core rotates around the inner core, causing magnetism on the Earth.
7	B	I	An earthquake happens when two blocks of the Earth suddenly slip past one another in opposite directions.
8	A	I	As the cold, heavy air at the poles moves toward the Equator, a constant flow of air convection currents occurs.
9	D	I	Earth is not moving fast enough to "escape" the sun's gravity and float away. Earth is also moving too fast to be pulled into the sun. Kepler's Second Law of Planetary Motion describes the speed of a planet traveling in an elliptical orbit around the sun. Newton's Law of Gravitation is also applied to planetary functions.
10	B	I	The top layer of soil is called topsoil. The layer under topsoil is subsoil (sub means under). The rock below the subsoil is bedrock.
11	B	II	Virtual labs are an effective way to provide students with lab experiences. Virtual labs are less expensive and safer than standard labs. If a teacher does not have the resources for a complete class lab, a virtual lab is an effective alternative.
12	B	Assessments	This question is asking for the most appropriate activity that focuses on systems, order, and organization for a 2nd grade class. Answer choices C and D are not grade-level appropriate. Answer choice A has to do with form and function. Answer choice B is the most age-appropriate and aligns with the unifying process of systems.

Number	Answer	Category	Answer Explanation
13	D	Assessments	A hypothesis is a prediction based on evidence. The students conducted research on mold before making the prediction. Therefore, the students made a hypothesis.
14	C	Assessments	The independent variable is the variable that is changed in the experiment. In this case, it is the food. Everything else remains the same.
15	A	Assessments	The control is kept separate from the rest of the experiment where the independent variable does influence the control. In this case, the container with no food is the control.
16	D	Assessments	The dependent variable is the thing that changes because of the experiment.
17	C	II	In biology, common ancestry refers to a group of organisms who share a most recent common ancestor. This diagram shows similar hand bones of different species, which indicates common ancestry.
18	B	II	Natural selection is the process whereby organisms better adapted to their environment tend to survive and produce more offspring.
19	C	II	Because plants need light for photosynthesis, plants engage in phototropism, which means they grow toward the light. Photo means light.
20	B & D	II	Plant cell – cell wall Animal cell – plasma membrane Plant cell – photosynthesis Animal cell – cellular respiration Plant & animal cells – have mitochondria Plant & animal cells – have a nucleus Plant & animal cells – have DNA
21	C	II	Natural selection is when species of a certain phenotype (genetic make-up) survive and pass those favorable traits to their offspring. The moths have favorable traits if they are black. They blend into the landscape, and predators cannot find them. They survive and pass on those traits.
22	D	II	Most energy is stored in plants. Plants are on the bottom of the pyramid. As you move up the pyramid, energy is lost. The student in answer choice D has the misconception that the closer to the sun the organisms are in the pyramid, the more energy they contain. Therefore, the student is misinterpreting this diagram.

Number	Answer	Category	Answer Explanation
23	D	II	Carrying capacity is the number of people, other living organisms, or crops that a region can support without environmental degradation.
24	D	III	Potential energy is the energy stored in an object as the result of its vertical position or height.
25	C	III	Mechanical energy is the sum of kinetic and potential energy on an object that is used to do work.
26	B	III	A heterogeneous mixture contains components that are not uniform, such as oil and water.
27	B	III	A series circuit connects one device to the end of the power source. A parallel circuit has multiple paths to follow. In this case, figure A is a parallel circuit; figure B is a series circuit.
28	B	III	The force of gravity depends directly upon the masses of the two objects.
29	A	III	The teacher is rolling a ball down an incline. Therefore, when the incline is increase, the friction decreases, making it easier for the ball to roll. When the incline is decreased, the friction will increase, making it difficult for the ball to roll. Therefore, answer A is a misconception.
30	C	III	Waves with a higher frequency have crests that are closer together, so higher frequency waves have shorter wavelengths. All of the other explanations are incorrect.
31	A	III	By melting an ice cube, the teacher can show how the shape of the ice cube may change, but its mass stays the same. You cannot separate a homogenous mixture. Showing a diagram of an atom does not explain that matter is neither created nor destroyed. A circuit is unrelated to this topic.
32	A	III	Water has unique properties. One of those properties is temperature moderation. When water evaporates, it leaves behind cooler temps.
33	A	III	Electrons are subatomic particles with a negative charge. Protons have a positive charge. Neutrons have a neutral charge.
34	D	III	A performance-based, formative assessment, in this case, observing students during a lab is the best way to assess the skills in applying the scientific method.

Number	Answer	Category	Answer Explanation
35	A	IV	The student is making an observation. A prediction is forecasting that something will happen based on a condition. An experiment is conducting a study or lab. An explanation is too vague here.
36	C	IV	To calculate density using a graduated cylinder, you calculate the density using the formula $D = m/v$
37	C	IV	The students are manipulating the temperature, and the independent variable is the variable the scientist changes or manipulates.
38	B	III	Water turns to vapor when it is boiled.
39	C	III	Less friction between two objects allows the objects to move freely against one another.
40	B	II	The byproduct of photosynthesis is oxygen. Animals then use that oxygen to survive. Therefore, the plant is emitting oxygen during photosynthesis, and students would be able to observe that using gas meters.
41	B	II	Stems are tubes that use the amazing property of water—adhesion—to transport water to other parts of the plant.
42	C	II	Work through the Punnet square below, and you will see that in order to display recessive alleles, you need both of them to be recessive. |	B	b
---	---	---
B	BB	Bb
b	Bb	**bb**	
43	A	IV	For the experiment to be valid, the amount of water in the pans should be the same. Otherwise, the change in temperature could be occurring because of the amount of water, not necessarily the type of Teflon used.
44	D	Assessments	Formative assessments are informal checks that help teachers make immediate and impactful decisions in the classroom. They are ongoing. Answer choice's A, C, and D are all summative assessments because they reference student outcomes—grades and gains—after a post assessment. Formative assessments are ongoing; summative assessments happen at the end of learning to determine outcomes.

Number	Answer	Category	Answer Explanation
45	C	Assessments	On questions that ask the teacher to fulfil two separate content areas or two separate activities, always make sure the answer you choose fulfills BOTH of the things being asked. Here it is asking for math and science. Categorizing in science is the Linnaean system. Using size and shape to categorize is geometry. All the other activities only fulfil one content area—either science or math, but not both.
46	D	Assessments	Bees pollinating hibiscus plants is a biological process. Biology is the study of life. Therefore, this lesson is part of the Life Sciences.
47	A	II	Occurring in the leaves of the plant, photosynthesis is the process in which plants convert CO_2, H_2O, and sunlight to make carbohydrates. It is a chemical process because molecules are changed in the process.

7814
Science

This page intentionally left blank.

7815 Social Studies

This page intentionally left blank.

About the Social Studies CKT - 7815

The Praxis 7815 Social Studies Content Knowledge for Teaching (CKT) test assesses knowledge and skills of aspiring educators in the field of social studies instruction.

Test takers are expected to demonstrate proficiency in analyzing primary and secondary sources, interpreting historical events, understanding geographic concepts, and applying economic principles. The exam also covers topics such as citizenship, government structures, cultural diversity, and global connections.

In addition to content knowledge, the Praxis 7815 test assesses candidates' pedagogical skills, including instructional strategies, assessment techniques, and the ability to engage students in critical thinking and inquiry-based learning.

Success on the Praxis 7815 Social Studies test demonstrates a strong foundation in social studies concepts and the ability to effectively teach students about the complexities of the social world.

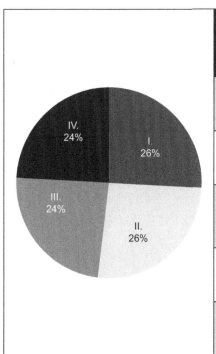

Content Category	Approx. Number of Questions	Approx. Percentage of Exam
I. History	16	26%
II. Government and citizenship	16	26%
III. Human and physical geography	14	24%
IV. Economics	14	24%
Total	**60**	**100%**

This page intentionally left blank.

I. History

The following topics are aligned with the test specifications of the Praxis 7815 exam. It is important that you examine these closely because these are the skills assessed on the exam.

A. Concept of chronology

B. Information about the past and present

C. Contributions of classical civilizations

D. Characteristics of Indigenous peoples in North America before European exploration

E. Causes and effects of European exploration and the colonization of North America

F. Conflict between the American colonies and Great Britain and American independence

G. The United States government

H. Political, economic, and social changes in the United States during the nineteenth century

I. Developments in the United States during the twentieth century

IMPORTANT: References for the information in the following sections can be found in the bibliography of this study guide.

A. Concept of chronology

A necessary skill elementary students need to understand social studies is understanding chronology. This is the act of sequencing events, stories, histories, and pictures to show how different periods evolved over time and how these events relate to one another. Effective ways to teach chronology is by using:

- Timelines
- Storyboards
- Sequential representations

Example Question

A teacher is helping students understand how ancient civilizations evolved their farming practices over several centuries. Which of the following activities would best support this lesson?

    A. Have students use a Venn diagram to compare and contrast different farming practices.

    B. Have students create a timeline to show how farming practices changed over time.

    C. Have students read about time periods in which different farming practices were used and answer questions.

    D. Have students work in groups to demonstrate different farming practices used by ancient civilizations.

Correct Answer: B

A timeline is most appropriate here because the objective of the lesson is to understand how these practices changed over time. By using the visual elements of a timeline, students can easily organize ancient civilizations' practices in a linear manner.

B. Information about the past and present

Choosing the right sources for students to reference in their learning is essential in social studies. The two main types of sources for social studies are primary sources and secondary sources.

Primary Sources

Primary sources are firsthand accounts of historical events. For example, letters, photographs, journal entries, and speeches are all considered primary sources. Using primary sources helps students relate information to their real lives. For example, students will relate more to a letter written by a student during the Holocaust than simply reading about the Holocaust in the textbook. In addition, primary sources help to provide factual evidence to what happened in history.

Secondary Sources

Secondary sources are interpretations of a historical event. For example, textbooks, newspaper articles, and political commentary are secondary sources.

It is important to understand how to select appropriate resources for social studies. The table below provides primary and secondary resources for informational text.

	Humanities	Sciences
Primary sources (original source)	<ul><li>Diaries, journals, letters</li><li>Interviews with people who lived during a particular time (e.g., survivors of genocide in Rwanda or the Holocaust)</li><li>Songs, plays, novels, stories</li><li>Paintings, drawings, sculptures</li><li>Autobiographies</li></ul>	<ul><li>Published results of research studies</li><li>Published results of scientific experiments</li><li>Published results of clinical trials</li><li>Proceedings of conferences and meetings</li></ul>
Secondary sources (interpretation of the original source)	<ul><li>Biographies</li><li>Histories</li><li>Literary criticism</li><li>Book, art, theater reviews</li><li>Newspaper articles that interpret events</li></ul>	<ul><li>Publications about the significance of research or experiments</li><li>Analysis of a clinical trial</li><li>Review of the results of several experiments or trials</li></ul>

Evaluating sources

It is important to evaluate source information for relevancy. This is especially important when using Internet sources.

Sources	Definition	Examples
Reliable sources	A trustworthy source of information.	<ul><li>Published results of research studies</li><li>Published results of scientific experiments</li><li>Published results of clinical trials</li><li>Proceedings of conferences and meetings</li></ul>
Unreliable sources	An unqualified and unreliable source to support ideas.	<ul><li>Online blogs about a particular topic</li><li>Chats or discussion forums on the Internet</li><li>Websites from private companies</li></ul>

Students are beginning a unit on the Industrial Revolution. It is important that they understand both the benefits and challenges to this time in history. Which of the following sources would be most effective in helping students evaluate the Industrial Revolution from this perspective?

    A. An informational newspaper article and an op-ed piece about the Industrial Revolution.

    B. A timecard representing the hours factory employees work and a journal entry of a factory worker during the Industrial Revolution.

    C. A newspaper article touting the advancement of machinery and a letter from a factory worker during the Industrial Revolution.

    D. A textbook passage to introduce the concepts of the Industrial Revolution and a newspaper article from that time.

Correct Answer: C

The question states that students must understand both the benefits and challenges to this time in history. Answer C provides a secondary source about the advancement of machinery, which would be considered a benefit. In addition, the letter from the factory worker would outline the challenges those who worked with the machinery faced. In addition, answer C is the only choice that provides students with a primary and secondary source, which are essential in analyzing history.

Test Tip

Most of the time, the correct answer on the exam is using both primary and secondary resources to teach history. This allows students to see many perspectives, so they can come up with their own analysis. Primary and secondary sources help students locate evidence to support their claims in their discussions of historical events.

C. Contributions of classical civilizations

The following are some of the cultural and technological contributions from ancient and modern civilizations. Many of these civilizations overlap in geography, philosophies, contributions, and time.

Please note that this timeline is very simplified and does not cover the numerous contributions of these civilizations, but it does give a general idea of the chronology and some key events. These are approximate timelines. Different reference materials define these events differently.

Contributions from Ancient Civilizations

Civilization	Dates	Major Contributions
Mesopotamia	3100 BCE – 539 BCE	• 3100 BCE: Invention of writing (cuneiform) • 3000 BCE: Invention of the wheel • 2600 BCE: Construction of the Ziggurats, early large architectural structures • 2350 BCE: Code of Ur-Nammu, one of the oldest known law codes • 1800 BCE: Hammurabi's code, one of the oldest deciphered writings of significant length in the world.

Civilization	Dates	Major Contributions
Ancient Egypt	3100 BCE – 332 BCE	<ul><li>3100 BCE: Unification of Upper and Lower Egypt under Pharaoh Narmer</li><li>2650 BCE: Construction of the first pyramids</li><li>2000 BCE: Development of hieroglyphic script</li><li>1550 BCE: The Book of the Dead, a collection of spells which enable the soul of the deceased to navigate the afterlife</li><li>700 BCE: Development of medical knowledge and techniques, as exemplified by the Edwin Smith and Ebers Papyri</li></ul>
Ancient China	2100 BCE – 220 CE	<ul><li>2100 BCE: Start of Xia dynasty, China's first dynasty according to historical records</li><li>1600 BCE: Start of Shang Dynasty, development of complex society and early forms of Chinese writing</li><li>1046 BCE: Start of Zhou Dynasty, longest lasting dynasty, creating the Mandate of Heaven concept</li><li>221 BCE: Start of Qin Dynasty, unification of China under Emperor Qin Shi Huang, beginning of the Great Wall</li><li>202 BCE: Start of Han Dynasty, invention of paper, seismograph, and the expansion of the Silk Road</li></ul>
Classical Greece	800 BCE – 146 BCE	<ul><li>776 BCE: First Olympic Games</li><li>508 BCE: Establishment of Democracy in Athens</li><li>447 BCE: Construction of the Parthenon</li><li>399 BCE: Philosophy of Socrates</li></ul>
Roman Civilization	753 BCE – 476 CE	<ul><li>53 BCE: Foundation of Rome according to legend</li><li>509 BCE: Start of Roman Republic</li><li>45 BCE: Julius Caesar becomes the first dictator of Rome</li><li>27 BCE: Start of Roman Empire under Augustus Caesar</li><li>80 CE: Construction of the Colosseum</li><li>212 CE: Edict of Caracalla extends Roman citizenship to all free men within the empire</li></ul>
Africa	2000 BCE – 350 CE	<ul><li>African Kush<ul><li>Gold</li><li>Extreme wealth</li></ul></li><li>Resources:<ul><li>Iron, incense, ivory, wheat, barley, cotton</li></ul></li><li>Trans-Sahara trade</li><li>Societies had different systems of government</li><li>Ghana, Mali, and Benin Kingdoms</li><li>Trade with Portuguese mariners</li><li>Massive stone structures and advanced urban planning.</li></ul>

D. Characteristics of Indigenous peoples in North America before European exploration

Before European exploration, Indigenous peoples in North America exhibited a rich tapestry of diverse cultures, each with distinct characteristics. One notable aspect was their deep connection to the land and the environment. Indigenous peoples had an intimate understanding of their surroundings:

- Relying on traditional ecological knowledge to sustainably manage and utilize natural resources.

- Having complex spiritual and religious beliefs that emphasized a harmonious relationship with nature, often worshipping various deities or spirits associated with specific natural elements.

- Organizing people into tribes or nations with social structures based on kinship ties and communal cooperation.

- Placing high value on oral tradition, passing down knowledge, stories, and histories through generations, thus maintaining a strong sense of cultural identity.

Indigenous peoples of North America possessed diverse languages, with over 500 distinct linguistic groups identified before European contact. These languages reflected their cultural diversity and served as vital markers of tribal identity. Art and craftsmanship were highly developed among Indigenous communities with skilled artisans creating intricate pottery, jewelry, textiles, and wood carvings. These artistic expressions often conveyed cultural symbolism and served practical functions in daily life.

The Arrival of Europeans

The arrival of European explorers in North America had a profound and devastating impact on Indigenous peoples. European exploration led to colonization, forced assimilation, displacement, and widespread violence against Indigenous communities. One of the primary consequences was the loss of land and resources. European powers claimed territories and established colonies, often through violent conflicts and treaties that were unfair and exploitative. Indigenous peoples were dispossessed of their ancestral lands, which disrupted their traditional ways of life and created immense social and economic challenges.

European explorers and settlers also brought diseases, such as smallpox, measles, and influenza, to which Indigenous peoples had little immunity. These diseases spread rapidly, resulting in devastating epidemics that decimated Indigenous populations. The loss of lives, combined with the disruption of social structures, further weakened Indigenous communities.

Additionally, European explorers and settlers frequently engaged in warfare and acts of violence against Indigenous peoples. They sought to control and dominate native populations, leading to countless conflicts, massacres, and forced displacements. Indigenous peoples were often subjected to enslavement, forced labor, and brutal treatment.

E. Causes and effects of European exploration and the colonization of North America

It is important to recognize the circumstances that led to major political, economic, social, and industrial events in history. The following section provides an overview of historical events and their cause and effect relationships to other events.

European colonization of the Americas

- Between the late 1400s and mid-1700s, European nations wanted to increase their wealth by establishing new settlements throughout the world.

- Christopher Columbus is often attributed to discovering the Americas in 1492 for Spain.

- Europeans settled the uncharted territory in pursuit of religious and economic freedom.

- The Europeans brought their food, traditions, and technology to the New World.

- The settlers also brought war and disease to the Native American population, which resulted in the decimation of an estimated 55 million people.

The exploration and colonization of the Americas by Europeans had a tremendous impact on the entire world. While the explorers discovered new land and civilizations that were previously unknown to Europeans, this movement led to the two most devastating impacts in human history: the genocide of millions of native American people and the enslavement of over 12 million African people.

Results of the Age of Exploration

- More knowledge about Americas
- Increased European wealth because of new trade in goods, spices, and precious metals
- Decline of the Ottoman Empire
- Mapping improved with the use of the first nautical maps and the invention of the compass.
- New food, plants, and animals were exchanged between the Americas and Europe.
- The Europeans decimated the Indigenous population with disease and massacres.
- The massive amount of work led to the 300-year slave trade.

Triangular Salve Trade

During the period from 1500–1900 in Africa, European mariners began capturing African people and selling them as slaves in Europe and the Americas. This had devastating effects on African civilizations.

The **Triangular Slave Trade** (or Trade Triangle) refers to the routes European Colonials used to transport slaves from Africa to the Americas and Europe. Europe brought arms, textiles, and wine to Africa, slaves from Africa to the Americas, and then sugar and coffee back to Europe.

The **Middle Passage**, or the trip from Africa to the Americas, was excruciatingly brutal for African slaves. People were shoved into impossibly tight quarters for a 20- to 90-day voyage. They were starved and tortured, and an estimated 15-20 percent did not survive.

Europeans pillaged West Africa, leaving devastation in the region. Warlords and tribes received incentives to engage in the slave trade, leading to violence and instability in the region. The loss of population and the fear of being captured made it impossible for West Africa to develop agriculture and economy.

Slaves were brought to tobacco farms in the Chesapeake area, rice and indigo farms on the southern coast, and cotton and citrus farms in the South. They were beaten, imprisoned, and malnourished. They suffered severe health disparities and high mortality rates.

The children who survived became slaves, and the cycle continued for generations. During the 1700s, between six and seven million people were taken from Africa and brought to the New World. This robbed the African continent of its most able-bodied and healthiest people.

Map of Triangular Slave Trade

(*USA.gov*)

Age of Revolution

The Age of Revolution is the period of time between 1760–1830, when significant social uprisings occurred in response to tyrannical government control. During this time, the American Revolution and the French Revolution took place, and absolute monarchies were overthrown for democracies.

F. Conflict between the American colonies and Great Britain and American independence

American Revolution

The Revolutionary War (1775–1783) was between the British and the 13 American colonies. The colonists did not like the way the British were treating them, especially when it came to taxes. Eventually, small arguments turned into larger fights, and the colonists decided to fight for their independence from Britain. In 1781, the battle of Yorktown, led by George Washington and French General Comte de Rochambeau, resulted in the final surrender of the British forces.

The American Revolution was the colonists' revolt against Great Britain from about 1765 to 1783. It began with a series of British taxes imposed on the colonists, which led to a clash of political ideologies, protests, and war. With the help of the French, the American colonists fought the British and won their independence. The 13 colonies formed the United States of America.

The following are major events during this time.

- **Stamp Act**. The Stamp Act was a tax put on the American colonies by the British in 1765.
- **Townshend Acts.** A series of laws passed by the British Parliament in 1767. The laws taxed goods (paper, paint, lead, glass, and tea) imported to the American colonies.
- **Boston Massacre**. Confrontation where a British soldier shot and killed several people in Boston. Leading patriots like Paul Revere and Samuel Adams used this as propaganda for the Revolutionary War.
- **Boston Tea Party**. A protest by the American Colonists against the British government. Occurred on December 16, 1773.
- **Sons of Liberty**. The Sons of Liberty was a secret organization created in the 13 American Colonies to advance the rights of the colonists and to fight taxation by the British government.

G. The United States government

The development of the United States government can be traced back to the founding of the nation and the adoption of its Constitution. Here is a brief overview of its key milestones:

1. **Colonial Period**: Before the United States gained independence, the American colonies were primarily governed by British rule. Each colony had its own colonial government, often with elected assemblies, but ultimate authority rested with the British monarchy.

2. **Declaration of Independence**: In 1776, the thirteen American colonies declared their independence from Britain through the signing of the Declaration of Independence. This marked the beginning of the American Revolution.

3. **Articles of Confederation**: After declaring independence, the colonies operated under the Articles of Confederation, adopted in 1781. This system established a loose alliance among the states, with a weak central government that had limited powers.

4. **Constitutional Convention**: Recognizing the need for a stronger federal government, delegates from the states convened in Philadelphia in 1787 to draft a new constitution. The result was the United States Constitution, which established the framework for the federal government and outlined the separation of powers among three branches: executive, legislative, and judicial.

7815
Social Studies

5. **Ratification and Bill of Rights**: The Constitution required ratification by the states, which was achieved in 1788. However, some states demanded the inclusion of a Bill of Rights to protect individual liberties. In 1791, the first ten amendments to the Constitution, known as the Bill of Rights, were added.

6. **Expansion and Westward Expansion**: As the United States expanded westward, new states were admitted to the union. This expansion raised debates and conflicts over issues like slavery and states' rights.

7. **Civil War and Reconstruction**: The United States faced a major crisis with the Civil War (1861-1865) fought between the northern states (Union) and the southern states (Confederacy) over issues of slavery and secession. The Union victory led to the abolition of slavery and the period of Reconstruction, during which efforts were made to rebuild the South and ensure equal rights for African Americans.

8. **Progressive Era Reforms**: In the late 19th and early 20th centuries, the Progressive Era saw significant reforms aimed at addressing social and economic issues. These included the regulation of trusts and monopolies, labor protections, women's suffrage, and initiatives for direct democracy.

9. **Expansion of Federal Government Powers**: Throughout the 20th century, the federal government's role expanded significantly, particularly during times of crisis like the Great Depression and World War II. Programs such as the New Deal and the establishment of Social Security demonstrated increased federal intervention in the economy and welfare of citizens.

10. **Civil Rights Movement**: The mid-20th century witnessed the Civil Rights Movement, a struggle for equal rights and an end to racial segregation. This led to landmark legislation such as the Civil Rights Act of 1964 and the Voting Rights Act of 1965, which aimed to eliminate discrimination.

11. **Modern Era**: The United States continues to evolve politically, with ongoing debates and reforms on issues such as healthcare, immigration, environmental policies, and national security.

It's important to note that this is a concise overview, and the development of the United States government has been a complex and ongoing process shaped by numerous factors, events, and societal changes throughout its history.

H. Political, economic, and social changes in the United States during the nineteenth century

Industrial expansion and population growth is a characteristic of the United States in the nineteenth century. America was considered a new nation. However, the Industrial Revolution radically changed the face of the nation.

Industrial Revolution (approximately 1760-1840)

The Industrial Revolution, which began in the middle of the 18th century, was the transition from an agrarian (farming) economy to an industrialized economy.

- The population shifted; people moved from rural areas and agriculture work to cities and factories.
- Goods were mass-produced.
- Increased efficiency, increased production, and lower costs.
- Wages increased.
- Technology developments increased.
- Many wealthy industrialists became philanthropists.
- Government regulations increased, leading to standards in health care and education.

While the Industrial Revolution led to numerous positive changes, such as technological advancements, increased production, job creation, and economic growth, it also had several negative impacts:

- **Poor Working Conditions**. Factories were often unsafe and unhealthy places to work. Workers were subject to long hours, low pay, and harsh conditions. Child labor was rampant and labor rights were almost non-existent initially.

- **Urbanization and Overcrowding**. As people moved from rural areas to cities in search of work, overcrowding became a serious problem. Cities expanded rapidly without sufficient infrastructure, leading to poor living conditions, such as inadequate housing and sanitation.

- **Environmental Pollution**. The Industrial Revolution marked a massive increase in pollution, contributing to air and water pollution on an unprecedented scale due to the burning of fossil fuels and disposal of waste from factories.

- **Exploitation of Natural Resources**. Rapid industrialization led to the unsustainable exploitation of natural resources. Deforestation, soil degradation, and depletion of minerals occurred because of this overconsumption.

- **Economic Inequality**. While the Industrial Revolution led to overall economic growth, it also led to significant economic inequality. The gap between the rich and the poor widened significantly, leading to social unrest and tension.

- **Health Problems**. Pollution and poor living conditions led to health problems for many people, especially the working class. Diseases such as cholera, typhoid, and tuberculosis spread in overcrowded urban areas.

- **Loss of Traditional Livelihoods**. The shift from an agrarian economy to an industrial one led to a loss of traditional ways of life. Many artisans and craftsmen found their skills obsolete in the face of machine-produced goods, leading to displacement and unemployment.

- **Imperialism and Colonialism**. The need for raw materials and new markets for goods led to an increase in imperialism and colonialism, with industrialized nations often exploiting less developed nations. This led to numerous political, social, and cultural problems, the effects of which are still evident in many parts of the world today.

War of 1812

- A series of trade restrictions introduced by Britain to impede American trade with France.

- The British support for Native Americans, who were offering armed resistance to the expansion of the American frontier to the Northwest.

- The British refused to give up lands in the western part of America and seized American ships.

- During the War of 1812, several Native American tribes fought for the British to stop the westward expansion into their homeland.

- Neither the British nor the United States had a substantial victory in the War of 1812. Both sides wanted the war to end and agreed to restore the status quo antebellum (before the war) with the Treaty of Ghent.

Antebellum period (approximately 1812-1861)

- The period after the War of 1812 and before the Civil War.

- It was characterized by an unstable political environment, including the rise of abolition and the gradual polarization of the country between abolitionists and supporters of slavery.

- This eventually led to the Civil War.

Civil War (1861-1865)

The Civil War was fought over the moral issue of slavery. In fact, it was the economics of slavery and political control of that system that was central to the conflict. Another key issue was states' rights.

- As the United States moved closer to a civil war, sectionalism became a problem as the country became increasingly divided.

- People no longer had loyalty to the entire nation. Rather, their loyalty was only to a part of the nation.

- The Civil War was the war between the Union (north) and the Confederacy (south), and it resulted in roughly 700,000 deaths.

Reconstruction (1865-1877)

The goal of this period was to rebuild the Southern states that had seceded from the Union, bring them back into the country, and integrate millions of freed Black slaves into society.

Key aspects of the Reconstruction period include:

- **Rebuilding the South.** Much of the South was devastated after the war. Reconstruction efforts focused on rebuilding infrastructure, economy, and social systems.
- **Reintegrating Southern States.** Each state had to draft a new constitution, ratify the 13th Amendment (which abolished slavery), and provide equal rights to all citizens to be readmitted to the Union.
- **Black Suffrage and Civil Rights.** The 14th Amendment (granted citizenship to all persons born or naturalized in the United States, including former slaves) and the 15th Amendment (prohibited the federal government and each state from denying a citizen the right to vote based on that citizen's "race, color, or previous condition of servitude") were significant parts of Reconstruction policy, intended to guarantee civil rights to the newly freed slaves.
- **Rise of Southern Resistance and the Ku Klux Klan.** Southern resistance to the changes of Reconstruction was significant. The Ku Klux Klan and other white supremacist groups committed acts of violence and terror against Black citizens and white Republican supporters to restore white supremacy.
- **End of Reconstruction.** The disputed 1876 presidential election, where Rutherford B. Hayes (Republican) was given the presidency in exchange for the end of federal intervention in the South, effectively ended the Reconstruction era. This led to the withdrawal of federal troops and allowed the Southern states to enact laws that severely limited the rights of Black citizens, leading to the era of Jim Crow segregation.

Jim Crow (End of Reconstruction until the Civil Rights act of 1964)

These laws were designed to marginalize African Americans by denying them the right to vote, hold jobs, get an education, and other opportunities. They established and enforced severe racial segregation in the South and were a legal means to oppress Black Americans for almost a century.

- Racial segregation in public areas and facilities and maintain a harsh system of oppression of Black Americans by whites.
- Beginning in the 1870s and 1880s, Jim Crow laws were upheld by the Supreme Court under the separate but equal legal doctrine, established with the court case Plessy v. Ferguson.
- These laws were enforced until 1965.

Abolitionist Movement (Late 18th century – Late 19th century)

The abolitionist movement in the United States began in earnest in the late 18th century and gained significant momentum in the 19th century, culminating with the Emancipation Proclamation in 1862 and the ratification of the Thirteenth Amendment in 1865.

- **Late 1700s**: The first American abolition society, the Pennsylvania Abolition Society, was founded in 1775. At this time, several states in the North began gradual emancipation programs.
- **Early to mid-1800s**: The movement gained momentum in the early 19th century with prominent figures such as Frederick Douglass, Harriet Tubman, Sojourner Truth, and William Lloyd Garrison, who launched The Liberator, a weekly abolitionist newspaper, in 1831.
- **1830s - 1860s**: The movement became increasingly active and influential, resulting in strong pro-slavery reactions in the South and escalating tensions between the North and South.
- **1850s**: The Fugitive Slave Act of 1850, which mandated that escaped slaves be returned to their owners in the South, caused outrage in the North and added fuel to the abolitionist cause.

- **1862**: President Abraham Lincoln issued the Emancipation Proclamation, declaring that all slaves in Confederate-held territory were to be set free. This shifted the Civil War's goal toward not just preserving the Union, but also ending slavery.
- **1865**: The Thirteenth Amendment, which abolished slavery throughout the United States, was ratified.

Quick Tip

Many of those who were involved in the Abolitionist Movement were also central to the women's Suffrage Movement.

I. Developments in the United States during the twentieth century

The 20th century in the United States was dominated by significant events that defined the modern era: the sixth mass extinction, Spanish flu pandemic, World War I and World War II, Jim Crow, nuclear weapons, nuclear power and space exploration, nationalism and decolonization, The Civil Rights Movement, the Cold War and post-Cold War conflicts, and technological advances.

World War I

World War I (WWI) was also known as the Great War. The assassination of Archduke Franz Ferdinand of Austria, heir to the Austro-Hungarian throne, and his wife Sophie, Duchess of Hohenberg, occurred on June 28, 1914 in Sarajevo. This was the catalyst to World War I.

The world powers aligned into two groups:

Allied Powers	Central Powers
France	Austria-Hungary
Britain	Germany
Russia	Ottoman Empire
United States	Bulgaria

Women's suffrage movement

Women's groups organized to gain political rights. Suffrage was granted in 1920 with the ratification of the 19th amendment, which granted women the right to vote.

The Great Depression (1929–1939)

The Great Depression was the worst economic downturn in the history of the industrialized world. When the Great Depression reached its lowest point, approximately 15 million Americans were unemployed, and nearly half the country's banks had failed.

- **Stock Market Crash of October 1929** – Millions of shares of stocks were traded after a wave of economic panic, causing their value to plummet.
- **The Dust Bowl 1930s** – A drought-stricken area in the Southern Plains of the United States. The Dust Bowl intensified the economic impacts of the Great Depression. Because of the Dust Bowl, many farming families set off on a migration across the United States in search of work and better living conditions.

- **New Deal (1933–1939)** – A series of programs, public work projects, financial reforms, and regulations enacted by President Franklin D. Roosevelt in the United States between 1933 and 1936. The New Deal included new constraints and safeguards on the banking industry and efforts to re-inflate the economy after prices had fallen sharply.

World War II

World War II (WWII) was a global conflict that lasted from 1939 to 1945. The conflict involved most the world's nations, including all the superpowers. Many scholars assert one of the major catalysts to World War II was the Treaty of Versailles, an agreement signed between Germany and the Allied Powers, marking the end of World War I. Germany was required to take responsibility for the war, pay retributions, and make territorial concessions to certain countries. This is often cited as the reason many Germans were bitter over the deal and why they voted for the Nazi Party.

The superpowers formed two opposing military alliances:

Allied Powers	Axis Powers
Great Britain – Winston Churchill	Germany – Adolph Hitler
Soviet Union – Joseph Stalin	Italy – Benito Mussolini
United States – Franklin Delano Roosevelt, Harry S. Truman	Japan – Emperor Hirohito
China – Chiang Kai-shek	

The Holocaust

During WWII, the Nazis killed over 6,000,000 Jewish people throughout Europe. Adolph Hitler was able to accomplish this genocide under the guise of war from 1939 to 1945. It began with the seemingly benign revoke of Jewish people's everyday rights like working for the press and ended with millions of Jewish people being killed in massive incinerators. The crimes the Nazis committed were so atrocious that Nazi symbols are still banned in many countries across Europe today.

The Cold War (1945–1990)

The Cold War was a post-World War II period of geopolitical tension between the United States and its allies and the Soviet Union and its satellite states. The conflict is referred to as a "cold war" because there was no large-scale fighting directly between the two sides; however, there were minor proxy-wars, military build-ups, and political posturing, which brought the world dangerously close to another major conflict.

The Civil Rights Movement (1940s – 1960s)

The Civil Rights Movement began in the late 1940s. The movement was initiated by African Americans as an effort to end racial discrimination created because of slavery and the Jim Crow era. Jim Crow laws enabled a caste system of oppression by White Americans on Black Americans. Not only were government and public facilities segregated, but Black Americans also experienced voter suppression, economic discrimination, mass incarceration, lack of due process, lynchings, and harassment. By the 1960s, laws were passed to help protect the civil rights of Black Americans.

- **1948**. President Truman issues an executive order to end segregation in the armed services.
- **1954**. Brown v. The Topeka Board of Education is a landmark US Supreme Court case ruling that declared racial segregation in public schools unconstitutional.

- **1955**. Rosa Parks refuses to give up her seat on a bus to a white man in Montgomery, Alabama. This incident sparks a yearlong boycott of city buses in Montgomery.

- **1957**. President Eisenhower is forced to send federal troops to Arkansas to protect nine African American students while they integrated into high school. These African American students are known as the Little Rock Nine.

- **1957**. Eisenhower signs the Civil Rights Act of 1957. The law protects voter rights.

- **1960**. A series of "sit-ins" take place around the country inspired by four Black youths refusing to leave a "whites only" lunch counter inside a Woolworth store in Greensboro, North Carolina.

- **1963**. 250,000 people march on Washington, DC for jobs and freedom. Dr. Martin Luther King Jr. gives his "I Have a Dream" speech on the steps of the Lincoln Memorial.

- **1963**. A bomb kills four young girls at the 16th Street Baptist Church in Birmingham, Alabama, sparking protests around the country.

- **1963**. President John F. Kennedy is assassinated, and Lyndon B. Johnson is sworn in as president of the United States.

- **1964**. President Johnson signs the Civil Rights Act of 1964. The law prevents employment discrimination based on race, color, creed, religion, or nationality.

- **1965**. Malcom X is assassinated.

- **1965**. March from Selma, Alabama, to Montgomery, Alabama, in protest of voter suppression.

- **1965**. President Johnson signs the Voting Rights Act of 1965. The law prevents the use of literacy tests as a voting requirement.

- **1968**. Dr. Martin Luther King Jr. is assassinated by James Earl Ray. King was shot on the balcony of his hotel room in Memphis, Tennessee.

- **1968.** President Johnson signs the Civil Rights Act of 1968, also known as the Fair Housing Act. The law requires equal housing rights for individuals regardless of race, religion, or nationality.

This page intentionally left blank.

1. Which event marked the adoption of the United States Constitution, establishing the framework for the federal government?

    A. Declaration of Independence

    B. Articles of Confederation

    C. Constitutional Convention

    D. Civil War

2. Which of the following was the central conflict of the American Civil War?

    A. Economic disparities between the North and the South

    B. Disputes over states' rights and federal power

    C. Conflicts over the expansion of slavery

    D. A desire of the South to secede from the North

3. A teacher is helping students understand the difference between the Allied and Axis Powers of World War II. Which of the following would be most effective in helping students understand these differences?

    A. A Venn diagram showing the similarities among Great Britain, the Soviet Union, China, and the US and how those countries differed from Germany, Italy, and Japan.

    B. A map of the world showing the different geographic locations of the Allied and Axis powers and their positions during battles.

    C. A timeline of the events that led to World War II and how different countries were impacted.

    D. A video about the Holocaust and how different countries reacted to the atrocities of that time.

4. A fourth-grade teacher wants to help students understand the working conditions of factory workers during the Industrial Revolution. The class has already read from the textbook and discussed working conditions. Which activity would be most effective in enhancing their understanding of this time?

    A. Reading primary source documents from factory workers during the time

    B. Watching a documentary on the technological advancements that occurred inside factories during the Industrial Revolution

    C. Creating a timeline of key events and inventions during the Industrial Revolution

    D. Participating in a debate on the social and economic impacts of industrialization and the working conditions of this time.

5. When teaching students about the population shift during the Industrial Revolution, which activity would be most effective in enhancing their understanding?

    A. Reviewing population data from different regions during the Industrial Revolution

    B. Watching a video on the technological advancements of the time

    C. Creating a visual presentation showcasing the impact of urbanization

    D. Participating in a role-play activity simulating migration and urbanization from rural areas to cities

This page intentionally left blank.

Number	Answer	Explanation
1.	C	The Constitutional Convention, held in Philadelphia in 1787, marked the event where delegates from the states convened to draft a new constitution. The resulting document, the United States Constitution, established the framework for the federal government, outlining the separation of powers among the three branches (executive, legislative, and judicial) and defining the rights and responsibilities of the federal government and the states. The Constitutional Convention played a pivotal role in shaping the development of the United States government.
2.	C	While all the issues listed in the answer choices were conflicts that contributed to the Civil War, the central conflict was the issue of slavery.
3.	A	The Allied Powers were Great Britain, The Soviet Union, China and the US, and the Axis Powers were Germany, Italy, and Japan. Therefore, answer A is correct. Answer B does little to explain the difference between Allied and Axis Powers. Answer C is helpful but not specific to the Allied and Axis Powers. Finally, answer D is later in the war and does not specifically address the Allied and Axis Powers.
4.	A	While all the options can contribute to understanding the Industrial Revolution and factory conditions, answer A provides a direct and authentic connection to the lived experiences of individuals during that time. By reading primary source documents from factory workers, students can gain insights into the harsh working conditions, the impact on individuals and families, and the societal changes brought about by industrialization. This activity promotes empathy, critical analysis, and a deeper understanding of the human aspect of the Industrial Revolution. You may be tempted to choose answer D, and while participating in a debate can foster critical thinking and analysis of the social and economic impacts, it lacks the direct connection to the experiences of individuals that primary source documents offer.
5.	D	While all the options can contribute to understanding the population shift during the Industrial Revolution, option D provides an engaging and immersive experience for students. By participating in a role-play activity simulating migration and urbanization, students can experience firsthand the challenges and opportunities faced by individuals during that time. This activity encourages empathy, critical thinking, and a deeper understanding of the social and economic factors that led to population shifts and urbanization during the Industrial Revolution. Answer D also mentions the migration from rural areas to cities, which is a main concept of the population shift during the Industrial Revolution.

This page intentionally left blank.

II. Government and Citizenship

The following topics are aligned with the test specifications of the Praxis 7815 exam. It is important that you examine these closely because these are the skills assessed on the exam.

A.   Family and community

B.   Functions of government

C.   Levels of government

D.   Forms of government

E.   The Declaration of Independence, the Constitution, and the Bill of Rights

F.   Citizenship

IMPORTANT: References for the information in the following sections can be found in the bibliography of this study guide.

A.   Family and community

Family units, as the fundamental building blocks of society, play a vital role in shaping the values, attitudes, and behaviors of individuals. Families instill a sense of identity, belonging, and socialization. These early lessons often form the foundation for individuals' understanding of their roles as citizens within a larger community.

Communities, on the other hand, encompass a broader network of individuals sharing common interests, values, or geographic locations. Communities provide a sense of belonging, social cohesion, and support systems beyond the immediate family. They foster connections and relationships that can strengthen social bonds and promote collective action for the betterment of society.

Quick Tip

Notice that family and community are the building blocks to government and citizenship. Each unit builds on the next for a well-functioning society.

Government and citizenship relate to the systems and structures that organize and govern society. Governments are responsible for establishing and enforcing laws, maintaining order, and providing public services. Citizenship refers to the legal and social status of individuals as members of a particular country or community, with associated rights, duties, and responsibilities.

B.   Functions of government

The purpose of government is to provide a framework for the organization and management of a society or nation. It serves to establish order, maintain stability, and promote the general welfare of the citizens within its jurisdiction. Government provides a system of laws, regulations, and policies that dictate how individuals and groups should behave and interact with one another, ensuring that basic human rights are protected and that societal needs are met.

The functions of government can be broadly categorized into three main areas:

I.   **The legislative function** of government involves the making of laws and policies that guide the behavior of citizens and organizations.

II.   **The executive function** of government involves the enforcement of laws and policies, including the management of public institutions and services.

III. **The judicial function** of government involves the interpretation of laws and policies and the resolution of disputes through the court system.

Ultimately, the purpose of government is to ensure that the needs and interests of the people are being met and that society can function in an orderly and equitable manner.

C. Levels of government

Federalism. Federalism refers to a type of government where powers are divided between the federal government (national) and state governments.

State government. State government is modeled after the federal government's three branches: executive, legislative, and judicial. Each state has its own constitution. State constitutions are much more detailed than their federal counterpart. State and local governments are required to uphold a republican form of government, although the three-branch structure is not a requirement (The White House, n.d.).

States' rights. Political powers held for state governments rather than the federal government. The following fall under the umbrella of state powers:

- Issue licenses (e.g., marriage, drivers, business)
- Create local governments
- Regulate industry
- Ratify amendments to the State Constitution
- Regulate commerce within state lines

Local government. Local government is the public administration of towns, cities, counties, and districts. This type of government includes both county and municipal government structures. Citizens have much more contact with local governments than they do with the federal government.

Quick Tip

Local, state, and federal government have the same structure. For example, the mayor of a city, the governor of a state, and the president of the country are all part of the executive branch of the federal government.

D. Forms of government

The United States is a republic, which means it is governed by elected representatives and an elected leader (such as a president) rather than by a king or queen. The structure of the government and division of its power and the laws by which the nation is governed are outlined in the United States Constitution.

In addition to the different levels of government in the US, powers and responsibilities are shared among the different branches of government. This is often referred as the separation of power so that no one branch is more powerful than the others.

Separation of power. Separation of power is outlined in the United States Constitution, where the government is divided into the three branches:

- Legislative Branch (House of Representatives and the Senate)
- Executive Branch (the President)
- Judicial Branch (the Supreme Court)

Checks and balances. The term *checks and balances* refers to a system that ensures that one branch does not exceed its bounds. It is a system that allows each branch of a government to amend or veto acts of another branch to prevent any one branch from exerting too much power.

Examples:

- The legislative branch can pass a law. The executive branch can check that power by either agreeing or vetoing the law (rejecting it back to the legislative branch).
- The judicial branch upholds the laws. The executive branch checks that power by appointing justices to the court.
- The executive branch can veto a bill. The legislative branch checks that power by evaluating the law again and possibly overriding the veto by a two-thirds vote in the Senate and House of Representatives.

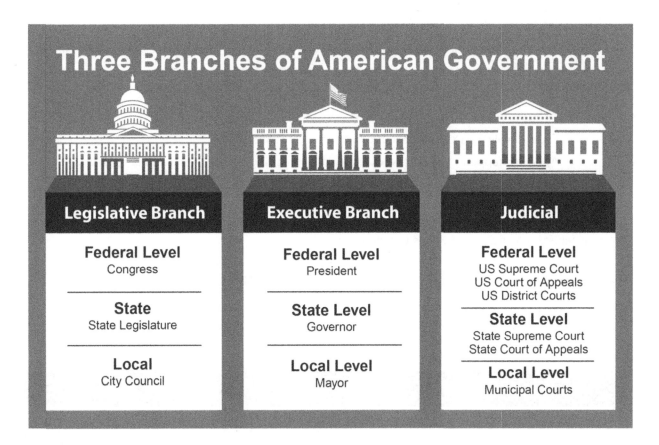

Three Branches of American Government

Legislative Branch	Executive Branch	Judicial
Federal Level Congress	**Federal Level** President	**Federal Level** US Supreme Court US Court of Appeals US District Courts
State State Legislature	**State Level** Governor	**State Level** State Supreme Court State Court of Appeals
Local City Council	**Local Level** Mayor	**Local Level** Municipal Courts

Branches of US Government (Article I, II, III)

Article I Legislative Branch. The legislative branch is responsible for **making laws**. The legislative branch includes the two chambers of Congress: House of Representatives and Senate.

1. **The House of Representatives** is responsible for making and passing federal laws. There is a fixed number of voting representatives, which is no more than 435. The number of representatives is set by law and proportionate to the population of the 50 states. Elections are held every two years.

2. **The Senate** includes 100 members, two from each state, who are elected for a six-year term in dual-seat constituencies. One-third of the total number of seats are up for reelection every two years.

Legislation cannot be enacted without the consent of both the House of Representatives and the Senate. Although there is a common misconception that the President has the power to declare war, this responsibility belongs to Congress.

Article II Executive Branch. The Executive branch is responsible for **enforcing laws**. The President of the United States is the head of state of the US, the chief executive of the federal government, and commander-in-chief of the armed forces. According to Article II of the United States Constitution, the President must be a natural-born citizen of the United States, be at least 35 years old, and must have been a resident of the United States for 14 years.

Article III Judicial Branch. The judicial branch is responsible for **interpreting laws**. The Supreme Court of the United States is the highest federal court in the country and the head of the judicial branch of government. The court has the ultimate jurisdiction over all laws and is also responsible for evaluating those laws. Supreme Court justices are nominated by the President of the United States and confirmed (or denied) by the United States Senate.

Supreme Court powers and structure:

- The Supreme Court is made up of nine justices (judges): one chief justice and eight associate justices.

- A Supreme Court appointment is a lifelong position held until death or retirement.

- Article III, Section II of the Constitution outlines the Supreme Court's jurisdiction:

    - Lawsuits between/among two or more states

    - Cases involving ambassadors or other public ministers

    - Appellate (appeals) jurisdiction over any case involving constitutional and/or federal law

    - Cases involving treaties or maritime law—navigable international and domestic waterways

- Judicial Review is the best-known Supreme Court power. Judicial Review is the Supreme Court's ability to declare a legislative (House of Representatives or Senate) or executive (President) act to be in violation of the United States Constitution.

E. The Declaration of Independence, the Constitution, and the Bill of Rights

For this exam, it is important to know and understand major concepts of the US Constitution and other historical documents. The table below provides an overview of the major concepts and historical documents.

Historical Documents

Document	What it outlines	Authors
Declaration of Independence	Government is no more powerful than man. If government is tyrannical, people have the right to rebel and start over. This was the American colonists' break from Britain.	Thomas Jefferson, John Adams, Benjamin Franklin, Roger Sherman, Robert R. Livingston
Federalist Papers	Made the case for checks and balances and separation of powers.	Alexander Hamilton, James Madison, and John Jay
Articles of the Constitution	I. Legislative Branch II. Executive Branch/Electoral College III. Judicial Branch IV. States, Citizenship, New States V. Amendment Process VI. Debts, Supremacy, Oaths, Religious Tests VII. Ratification	Thomas Jefferson, John Adams, James Madison, Alexander Hamilton
The Bill of Rights	Provides unalienable rights of citizens	Thomas Jefferson, John Adams, James Madison, Alexander Hamilton

The Bill of Rights are the first ten amendments to the constitution. The founding fathers were unable to secure the votes to ratify the US Constitution without including protections for citizens from a tyrannical government. These protections are outlined in the table below.

The Bill of Rights to the US Constitution

Number	Amendment	Description
1	Freedom of Religion, Speech, and the Press	The First Amendment provides several rights protections: to express ideas through speech and the press, to assemble or gather with a group to protest or for other reasons, and to ask the government to fix problems. It also protects the right to religious beliefs and practices. It prevents the government from creating or favoring a religion.
2	The Right to Bear Arms	The right to own weapons including guns.
3	The Housing of Soldiers	The Third Amendment prevents the government from forcing homeowners to allow soldiers to use their homes. Before the Revolutionary War, laws gave British soldiers the right to take over private homes—the Quartering Act.
4	Protection from Unreasonable Searches and Seizures	The government cannot search or seize a person or their property without just cause.
5	Protection of Rights to Life, Liberty, and Property	The Fifth Amendment provides several protections for people accused of crimes. It states that serious criminal charges must be started by a grand jury. A person cannot be tried twice for the same offense (double jeopardy) or have property taken away without just compensation. People have the right against self-incrimination and cannot be imprisoned without due process of law (fair procedures and trials).
6	Rights of Accused Persons in Criminal Cases	The Sixth Amendment provides additional protections to people accused of crimes, such as the right to a speedy and public trial, trial by an impartial jury in criminal cases, and to be informed of criminal charges. Witnesses must face the accused, and the accused is allowed his or her own witnesses and to be represented by a lawyer.
7	Rights in Civil Cases	The Seventh Amendment extends the right to a jury trial in federal civil cases.
8	Excessive Bail, Fines, and Punishments	The Eighth Amendment bars excessive bail and fines and cruel and unusual punishment.
9	Other Rights Kept by the People	The Ninth Amendment states that listing specific rights in the Constitution does not mean that people do not have other rights that have not been specified in the document.
10	States' Rights	The Tenth Amendment says that the Federal Government only has those powers delegated in the Constitution. If it isn't listed, it belongs to the states or to the people.

It is also important for teachers to understand due process as it relates to issues in the school. For example, a search warrant (4th Amendment) is needed in order for law enforcement to search a hotel room, house, office, or other private domain. A search warrant is NOT needed when searching public property (like a school locker) or anything within eyeshot.

A fifth-grade teacher is having students conduct a mock debate on the protections provided in the Bill of Rights. Which of the following amendments should students reference if they are arguing the issues of search and seizure?

    A.   1st Amendment

    B.   2nd Amendment

    C.   3rd Amendment

    D.   4th Amendment

Correct answer: D

The Fourth Amendment states that government cannot search or seize a person or their property without just cause.

F.   Citizenship

It is important to remember the roles and responsibilities citizens have as members of their community, state, nation, and the world.

US Citizen Rights and Responsibilities

Rights	Responsibilities
• Freedom to express yourself • Freedom to worship as you wish • Right to a prompt, fair trial by jury • Right to vote in elections for public officials • Right to apply for federal employment requiring US citizenship • Right to run for elected office • Freedom to pursue "life, liberty, and the pursuit of happiness"	• Support and defend the Constitution • Stay informed of the issues affecting your community • Participate in the democratic process • Respect and obey federal, state, and local laws • Respect the rights, beliefs, and opinions of others • Participate in your local community • Pay income and other taxes honestly and on time to federal, state, and local authorities • Serve on a jury when called upon • Defend the country if the need should arise

In addition to the roles and responsibilities of being a US citizen, people also have responsibilities to their local and global community. These include the shared responsibilities of taking care of the Earth and its inhabitants like reducing waste, preserving natural habitats, and helping others in need.

1. When teaching students about the three branches of government, which activity would be most effective in enhancing their understanding?

    A. Writing a persuasive essay on the importance of separation of powers

    B. Participating in a mock legislative session to pass a class bill

    C. Creating a poster depicting the key responsibilities of each branch

    D. Watching a documentary about the historical development of the government

2. When teaching students about historical documents of the US government, which activity would be most effective in enhancing their understanding?

    A. Watching a video about the Founding Fathers and their role in writing the Constitution

    B. Analyzing primary source documents, such as the Constitution and the Bill of Rights

    C. Creating a visual timeline of key events in the development of the US government

    D. Participating in a class debate about the role of government in society

3. When teaching students about checks and balances in the US government, which activity would be most effective in enhancing their understanding?

    A. Watching a documentary on the history of the US government

    B. Creating a visual diagram illustrating the three branches of government and their roles

    C. Analyzing case studies that highlight times when the president vetoed a congressional bill

    D. Participating in a group discussion on the importance of the separation of powers

4. When teaching students about Article One of the US Constitution, which activity would be most effective in enhancing their understanding?

    A. Read a summary of the power of the executive branch

    B. Watch a video on the processes of the Supreme Court

    C. Create a mock legislative session to draft and pass a bill

    D. Participate in a group discussion on the separation of powers in the US

5. When teaching students about citizens' rights in the US, which activity would be most effective in enhancing their understanding of legal interpretations and protections of those rights?

    A. Watching a documentary on the history of voting in the US

    B. Creating a poster showcasing the Bill of Rights and its amendments

    C. Participating in a group debate on contemporary issues related to citizens' rights

    D. Reading and discussing landmark Supreme Court cases on civil rights

This page intentionally left blank.

Number	Answer	Explanation
1.	B	While all the options can be valuable learning activities, option B is most effective in providing hands-on engagement and experiential learning. By participating in a mock legislative session, students actively explore the legislative branch and experience the process of creating and passing laws. This activity allows them to understand the complexities of lawmaking, negotiation, and compromise. It also fosters critical thinking, collaboration, and a deeper understanding of the legislative branch's role in the separation of powers.
2.	B	While all the options can contribute to understanding historical documents of the US government, option B provides direct access to primary sources and encourages critical analysis and interpretation. By analyzing primary source documents, such as the Constitution and Bill of Rights, students can gain a deeper understanding of the principles and values that underpin the US government and the historical context in which they were written. This activity promotes critical thinking, historical literacy, and a deeper understanding of the foundations of the US government. Also, historical documents are primary sources, which makes Answer B the best answer.
3.	C	Answer C actual shows the specific process of a check and balance of power. The president serves as a check for Congress. Congress serves as a check for the President. Finally, the legislative branch also checks these powers.
4.	C	Article One outlines the powers of the legislative branch. The legislative branch is Congress, making answer C the correct answer.
5.	D	While all the options can contribute to understanding citizens' rights in the US, option A provides an in-depth exploration of the legal interpretations and protections of those rights. By reading and discussing landmark Supreme Court cases on civil rights, students can gain a deeper understanding of how constitutional principles have been applied in specific contexts. This activity promotes critical thinking, analysis, and a nuanced understanding of the evolving nature of citizens' rights.

This page intentionally left blank.

III. Human and Physical Geography

The following topics are aligned with the test specifications of the Praxis 7815 exam. It is important that you examine these closely because these are the skills assessed on the exam.

A. Location, distance, and direction

B. Physical characteristics of geography and how it affects human activities

C. Human adaptation to variations in the physical environment

D. How humans interact with one another

IMPORTANT: References for the information in the following sections can be found in the bibliography of this study guide.

A. Location, distance, and direction

Geography is the study of the physical features of the Earth's surface and atmosphere, including how humans affect the physical features of the Earth and the ways these physical features affect humans.

There are six essential elements of geography:

1. The world in spatial terms

2. Places and regions

3. Physical systems

4. Human systems

5. Environment and society

6. Uses of geography

This section focuses on world and regional geography, which includes the world in spatial terms and places and regions. The other elements are discussed in the sections that follow.

Maps

Maps provide a representation of the elements of geography. It is important to understand how information is presented about geography using different types of maps.

Political maps show locations of cities, towns, and counties and might show some physical features such as rivers, streams, and lakes.

Physical maps illustrate the physical features of an area, such as the mountains, rivers, and lakes. The water is usually shown in blue. Colors are used to show relief, i.e., differences in land elevations. Green is typically used to indicate lower elevations. Orange and brown indicate higher elevations.

Road maps show major (and some minor) highways and roads, airports, railroad tracks, cities, and other points of interest in an area. People use road maps to plan trips and for driving directions.

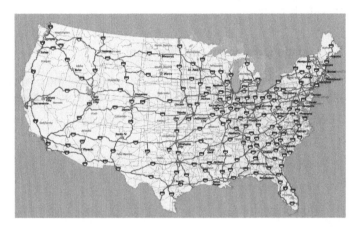

Special purpose maps focus on details such as topography, climate, or district. Special purpose maps can be useful for finding more information about population, tourism, elevation, etc.

Other Types of Maps

- **Climate maps** provide general information about the climate and precipitation (rain and snow) of a region. Climate of an area is determined by the amount of rainfall, temperature, and wind in the area. Cartographers, or mapmakers, use colors to show different climate or precipitation zones.

- **Economic or resource maps** feature the type of natural resources or economic activity that dominates an area. Cartographers use symbols to show the locations of natural resources or economic activities. For example, oranges on a map of Florida tell you that oranges are grown there.

- **Topographical maps** are like physical maps in that they show streams, valleys, rivers, mountains, hills, and more. Unlike physical maps, topographical maps use contour lines instead of colors to illustrate different features of the land. Topographical maps also display important landmarks and roads. Topographical maps can indicate how people migrated and settled the land. This type of map can also provide information about ancestral properties, buildings, local cemeteries, and other important buildings and features.

Other tools to use in the social studies classroom

For this exam, it is important to understand the different types of tools used to understand geography. You will be expected to use these tools in your classroom.

Globe. A globe is a model of the Earth. Flat maps can distort the size and shape of the Earth's features. A few things to note about a globe:

- They are tilted at a 23.5 degree angle to mimic the Earth's tilt in relation to the sun.
- Political globes highlight nation-state boundaries, whereas physical globes highlight Earth's physical features.
- There's a time dial at the north pole that that is used to compare times around the world.
- The metal ring is called a meridian and is used to show meridian degrees. The ring also holds the sphere in place on the stand.
- The figure 8 in the Pacific Ocean is called the analemma, which represents the sun's path in the sky throughout the seasons.

Global positioning system. The global positioning system (GPS) is a government service that provides positioning, navigation, and timing services. Many everyday devices use GPS for a myriad of applications including:

- Agriculture
- Aviation
- Environment
- Marine
- Public safety and disaster relief
- Railways, roads, and highways
- Recreation
- Space
- Surveying and mapping
- Timing

Quick Tip

GPS.gov provides several educational resources for students and teachers.

The world in spatial terms refers to location on the Earth.

Absolute location. Exact location of a point using latitude and longitude or an address. Example: 37N, 63W or "I live at 6570 Irish Rd."

Relative location. Location of a point in relation to another point. Example: New York City is about 90 minutes from Philadelphia.

International Date Line. The International Date Line (IDL) is an imaginary line of navigation on the surface of the Earth that runs from the north pole to the south pole and indicates the change of one calendar day to the next. It passes through the middle of the Pacific Ocean, roughly following the 180° line of longitude, but deviates to pass around some territories and island groups. The IDL detours around political boundaries.

International Date Line

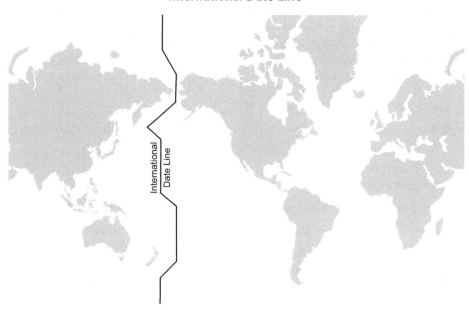

Hemispheres. The Earth is divided into four hemispheres: Northern, Southern, Eastern, and Western. The Equator (0° latitude) divides the Earth into the Northern and Southern Hemispheres. The Prime Meridian (0° longitude) and the IDL divide the Earth into the Eastern and Western Hemispheres. The Eastern Hemisphere is east of the Prime Meridian and west of the IDL. The Western Hemisphere is west of the Prime Meridian and east of the IDL.

According to an international agreement, the official Prime Meridian runs through Greenwich, England. Most of Asia and Africa are a part of the Eastern Hemisphere. The Americas and northwestern Africa are a part of the Western Hemisphere.

Equator and Prime Meridian

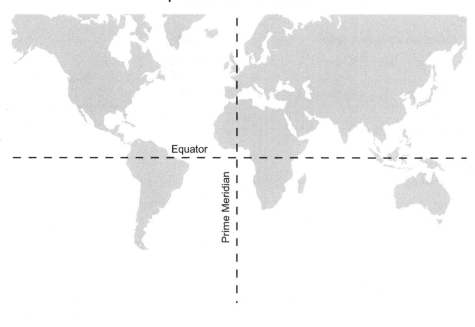

Geographic coordinate system is a series of gridlines used to describe the position on the Earth. It is made up of longitude and latitude lines.

Latitude is the angle between the equatorial plane and the straight line that passes through that point and through the center of the Earth. Latitudinal lines run horizontally across the Earth.

Longitude is the angle east or west of a reference meridian to another meridian that passes through that point. Longitudinal lines run vertically across the Earth.

B. Physical characteristics of geography and how it affects human activities

Places are defined by both physical and human characteristics, including uses of the area. Regions are areas broadly divided by physical characteristics, human impact characteristics, and the interaction of humanity and the environment. The Pacific Northwest, Southwest Florida, and the Sunbelt are all examples of regions.

- **Nation.** Nation refers to a community of people who share similar history, culture, and traditions and reside in the same area or territory.

- **Sovereign state.** A sovereign state is a self-governing geopolitical entity that has defined borders and controls its internal sovereignty over its existence and affairs.

- **Country.** A nation with its own government and economy that occupies a defined territory. A country may be an independent sovereign state or one that is occupied by another state.

- **Continent.** A continent is one of the world's seven main continuous expanses of land: Africa, Antarctica, Asia, Australia, Europe, North America, and South America.

Human Activities

According to Maslow, humans satisfy their basic needs of survival like food, shelter, and clothing before they focus on their higher-order needs. Over human history, people have migrated to new regions for food and shelter and adapted their lifestyle based on new environments.

- **Clothing**

  People adapt their clothing based on environmental factors such as temperature and precipitation. Civilizations in warmer climates wear less or lighter clothing than people in colder climates.

- **Food**

  For thousands of years, humans have adapted their methods of food production based on the environment. For example, communities in mountain regions use terrace farming to grow crops on hillsides. Communities grow crops and raise farm animals based on what works the best in their environment.

- **Shelter**

  Civilizations have adapted their dwellings based on a multitude of environmental factors including space, weather, population density, and proximity to water. Even today, housing in urban areas compared to rural areas is very different. Cities build apartment complexes within proximity to business districts, public transportation, and recreational facilities.

Population

In social studies, a population refers to a collection of humans or other entities. It's often used to refer to the total number of people living in a specific geographic area, like a city, country, or the entire planet. Demographers typically study trends within these populations, such as birth and death rates, migration patterns, and other characteristics.

7815
Social Studies

Population Density

Population density is the number of people in relation to the square miles (US Census, 2010).

$$\text{Population density} = \frac{\text{Population}}{\text{Square Miles}}$$

Technological Advancements of Humans

The technological advancements of human beings have had a tremendous impact on the environment such as urban sprawl and pollution. Having access to tools and technology greatly determines where and how people live, which directly impacts the environment.

- **Transportation.** Cars, buses, trains, airplanes
- **Communication.** Telephones, computers, Internet
- **Housing.** Single family homes, apartments, planned communities, neighborhoods
- **Utilities.** Power grid, water, sewer, waste management
- **Renewable energy.** Wind turbines, dams, solar panels
- **Manufacturing.** Industry, factories, machines, resources, and technology

The byproducts of tools and technology have negative impacts on the environment including pollution, deforestation, desertification, urban sprawl, construction, and loss of natural habitats.

C. Human adaptation to variations in the physical environment

Physical systems and processes shape the Earth's surface. This field of geography includes the study of how these systems and processes interact with plant and animal life to create, sustain, and modify ecosystems. There are four physical systems, and geographers study how the physical processes interact with the physical systems.

- **Atmosphere.** The envelop of gases surrounding the Earth or another planet.
- **Biosphere.** Includes all life on the planet.
- **Hydrosphere.** Includes all water—liquid, ice, and vapor—on the planet.
- **Lithosphere.** The outer region of the Earth. Includes the crust and upper mantle.

Geographic Features

Geographic Feature	Definition	Example
Archipelago	An archipelago is a group of islands or island chains	Hawaiian Islands
Atoll	A coral island that surrounds a lagoon	Maldives
Barrier island	A band of beach parallel to the mainland that protects the shore from the effects of the ocean	Clearwater Beach, Florida
Bays	An inlet of the sea or other body of water, usually smaller than a gulf	Chesapeake Bay, Ha Long Bay
Continent	Seven great divisions of land on the globe	Africa, North America

Geographic Feature	Definition	Example
Deciduous forest	A forest of trees that lose their leaves seasonally	Eastern Deciduous Forest, United States
Delta	A landform that forms from deposition of sediment carried by a river as the flow leaves its mouth and enters slower-moving or standing water	Mississippi Delta, Louisiana; Nile River Delta, Egypt
Desert	A barren area of landscape where little precipitation occurs and consequently, living conditions are hostile for plant and animal life; can be hot or cold	Sahara, Antarctica
Fjord	A long, narrow, deep inlet of the sea between high cliffs	Skelton Inlet, Antarctica
Forest	A dense growth of trees and underbrush covering a large tract	Tongass National Forest, Alaska
Grassland	Land on which the natural dominant plant forms are grasses and herbs	North American prairies, Argentine pampas
Ice caps	A glacier forming on an extensive area of relatively level land and flowing outward from its center	Greenland Ice Sheet
Island	A tract of land surrounded by water and smaller than a continent	Ireland, Long Island
Isthmus	Narrow strip of land connecting two large land areas otherwise separated by bodies of water	Isthmus of Panama, connecting North and South America; Isthmus of Suez, connecting Africa and Asia
Mountain	A large area of raised land formed through tectonic movement or volcanic activity	Mt. St. Helens
Mountain ranges	A series of mountains or mountain ridges closely related in position and direction	Andes, Rocky Mountains
Oceans	The whole body of saltwater that covers nearly three-fourths of the surface of Earth	Atlantic, Pacific
Peninsula	A land mass mostly surrounded by water and connected to a larger area of land	Florida
Plains	An extensive area of level or rolling treeless country	The Great Plains

Geographic Feature	Definition	Example
Plateaus	A usually extensive land area having a relatively level surface raised sharply above adjacent land on at least one side	Antarctic Plateau
Rain forest	A woodland with annual rainfall of 100 inches and heavy tree canopy	Amazon Rainforest, Daintree Rainforest
River	A large system of natural flowing water	Amazon River
Sea	A body of saltwater that is partially enclosed by land	Baltic Sea, Mediterranean Sea
Taiga	A moist, subarctic forest of conifers that begins where the tundra ends	Alaska, Canada
Tundra	A level or rolling treeless plain that is characteristic of arctic and subarctic regions, consists of black mucky soil with a permanently frozen subsoil and has a dominant vegetation of mosses, lichens, herbs, and dwarf shrubs	Arctic tundra, alpine tundra
Valleys	An elongated depression of Earth's surface usually between ranges of hills or mountains	Yosemite Valley, Grand Canyon

Uses of Geography

Geography is used in many ways to understand the Earth and its inhabitants. Geography is used to interpret the past, understand the present, and plan. Humans also use the Earth's geographical features in everyday life.

Agriculture. Agriculture is the practice of farming and has evolved since the Neolithic era. Some techniques of farming used by the ancient civilizations are still utilized today.

Energy. Energy resources play a critical role in everyday human life. We use energy to power everything from a coffee machine to the space shuttle. Our energy resources come from the Earth in a variety of forms. Some energy resources cannot be renewed as quickly as they are being consumed (nonrenewable); some energy resources can be renewed quickly by the Earth's physical processes (renewable).

- **Clean energy**. Energy from wind, solar, water, geothermal, biomass, and nuclear
- **Fossil energy**. Energy from coal, oil, and natural gas
- **Electric power**. Energy from charged particles

D. How humans interact with one another

Humans, through their daily activities, shape and reshape the Earth. This aspect of geography explores how people and the environment change each other.

Anthropology. The study of human beings, their culture, origins, environment, and social norms.

Physical anthropology. The study of physical characteristics of human groups through measurement and observation.

Cultural anthropology. The study of cognitive and social organization of human groups, including folklore, linguistics, religion, politics, and ethnology.

Assimilation. The process of individuals absorbing the dominant culture of a group different from their own heritage.

Socialization. The process of understanding oneself and societal expectations through social interactions with others.

Community. A community is an interacting population of various kinds of individuals (as species) in a common location. Generally, communities can be broken down into three types:

Urban refers to cities.

Suburban refers to residential areas surrounding urban centers.

Rural refers to areas of countryside or farmland.

Language is a method of human communication, either spoken or written, consisting of the use of words in a structured and conventional way. There are roughly 6,500 languages spoken around the world. Though English is the most widely spoken language in the United States, the United States does not have an official language.

Religion and ideologies. Religions and ideologies are both systems of belief. Religion examines the afterlife and other aspects that are not in the materialistic world, whereas ideologies focus on materiality of human nature.

Human impacts. Humans have a tremendous impact on the environment through the following:

- Settlements
- Population growth
- Technology
- Trade
- Tourism
- Agriculture and irrigation
- Production and consumption patterns
- Waste production and management
- Human-caused land degradation
- Human-induced pollution
- Anthropogenic global warming and climate change

This page intentionally left blank.

1. When teaching students about human geography and its impact on the environment, which activity would be most effective in enhancing their understanding?

    A. Conducting research to analyze the local environmental changes caused by human activities

    B. Watching a documentary on global environmental issues and their geographical implications

    C. Creating a visual presentation on the interconnectedness of human societies and the environment

    D. Participating in a class discussion on the challenges of sustainable development in different regions

2. When teaching students about the equator and prime meridian, which activity would be most effective in enhancing their understanding?

    A. Watching a video on the geographic significance of the equator and prime meridian

    B. Discussing the different temperatures of places closest to the equator

    C. Locating different places on a map using latitudinal and longitudinal coordinates.

    D. Filling out a worksheet by labeling Earth's hemispheres

3. When teaching students about geography and spatial terms, which activity would be most effective in enhancing their understanding?

    A. Watching a video on geographical terminology and concepts

    B. Engaging in a mapping and navigation activity

    C. Creating a visual poster illustrating different landforms and their characteristics

    D. Participating in a group discussion on the importance of spatial awareness in everyday life

4. A fifth-grade teacher is explaining population density to students. According to the table below, which country has the highest population density?

Country	Population	Square Miles
A	12,000	60 square miles
B	20,000	50 square miles
C	24,000	40 square miles
D	8,000	100 square miles

    A. Country A

    B. Country B

    C. Country C

    D. Country D

5. A teacher is working on a unit that is focused on human impact on the environment. Which of the following maps would be most helpful to student understanding?

    A. Political map

    B. Typographical map

    C. Population density map

    D. Special resource map

This page intentionally left blank.

Number	Answer	Explanation
1.	A	While all the options can contribute to understanding human geography and its impact on the environment, option A provides a hands-on and immersive experience that allows students to directly observe and analyze the environmental changes in their local area. By conducting field research, students can develop a deeper understanding of how human activities shape the environment and the associated consequences. This activity promotes critical thinking, data collection and analysis, and a nuanced understanding of the geographic impact of human actions. Also, answer A focuses on local environmental changes, which helps to bring an abstract concept into the real world because students can see how this directly affects them.
2.	C	Allowing students to us latitude and longitude to locate places on a map is a real-world, hands on activity, which is the best choice.
3.	B	While all the options can contribute to understanding geography and spatial terms, option B provides a practical and interactive experience that allows students to directly apply and develop their map reading and navigation skills. By engaging in a hands-on activity that involves interpreting maps and navigating through spatial information, students can gain a deeper understanding of geographic terminology and concepts. This activity promotes spatial reasoning, critical thinking, and a practical understanding of how spatial terms relate to real-world situations.
4.	C	In this example, Country C has the highest population density because it has the highest number of people per square mile.
5.	D	To show the impact humans have on the environment, a special resource map would be best because they showcase natural resources or economic activity that dominates an area. This would best explain human impact. A population density map is not as effective as a special resource map because the population density map just shows numbers of people in an area. The special resource map shows the activity of humans.

This page intentionally left blank.

IV. Economics

The following topics are aligned with the test specifications of the Praxis 7815 exam. It is important that you examine these closely because these are the skills assessed on the exam.

A. How human needs are met

B. Goods and services: producers and consumers

C. Money: earning, spending, and saving

D. Supply and demand

E. Types of economies

IMPORTANT: References for the information in the following sections can be found in the bibliography of this study guide.

A. How human needs are met

According to Maslow, humans satisfy their basic needs of survival like food, shelter, and clothing before they focus on their higher-order needs. Over human history, people have migrated to new regions for food and shelter and adapted their lifestyle based on new environments.

- **Push factors** are the circumstances that make a person want to leave. For example, lack of employment or education opportunities, a tyrannical government, famine, or war compel people to move away.

- **Pull factors** are the advantages a country has that make a person want to live there. America has pull factors for many people around the world whose native countries have unstable governments, limited job opportunities, or no reliable security.

The Great Famine of Ireland (The Potato Famine)

Beginning in 1845 and lasting for six years, the potato famine killed nearly a million men, women, and children in Ireland and caused another two million to flee the country. The crisis started with a natural event that infected potato crops. The situation was further exacerbated by the government's laissez-faire economic policies and its continuation of exporting food to Great Britain. The potato famine in Ireland resulted in Irish immigrants coming to the United States, causing a large increase in the Irish population in US cities. This is an example of push pull factors.

B. Goods and services: producers and consumers

Every day, humans make choices in how they make or acquire goods and services. People are both producers and consumers.

Producers

Producers are people who make or grow goods and provide services. Sometimes they are called workers, and they help the economy and help people get what they need. For example, a farm worker produces food, a tailor sews clothing, and a teacher educates students. These are all types of producers.

Consumers

People are also consumers, meaning they use the goods and services made by producers. When you buy something on Amazon, shop at the local grocery store, and trade items at a yard sale, you are consuming.

Resources in Economics

Resources in economics are human, natural, and capital assets used to produce goods and services.

- **Human resources.** The manpower, personnel, brainpower, and skills of humans used in a market to produce goods and services.
- **Labor.** Skilled workers who produce goods and services.
- **Management.** Managers who plan, direct, monitor, and control workers to produce goods and services.
- **Natural resources.** The Earth's natural resources or raw materials used to produce goods and services such as fossil fuels, petroleum, metals, and organic material. For example, trees are natural resources used to make lumber.
- **Capital resources.** The tools, equipment, machinery, and buildings used to make other products.
- **Factory.** Manufacturing plant or industrial site, usually consisting of buildings and machinery, where numerous workers construct goods to be sold in mass quantities.
- **Assembly Line.** A manufacturing process in which parts (usually interchangeable parts) are added in order by individuals as the semi-finished assembly moves down the line until the final product is assembled. By mechanically moving the parts down an assembly line, a finished product can be assembled faster and with less labor than by having workers carry parts to a stationary place for assembly. Also called progressive assembly.

C. Money: earning, spending, and saving

People make decisions based on the economy and other influence. These factors include:

- **Cultural.** Class, subculture, race, and religion.
- **Economic.** Income, household income, assets, expectations, consumer credit score, and savings.
- **Social.** Family, friends, reference groups, roles, and status.
- **Personal.** Age, income, occupation, and lifestyle.
- **Psychological.** Feelings, desires, motivation, perception, attitude, and beliefs.

Interest rates

Consumers must be cognizant of interest rates for both investments and loans in order to make cost-effective decisions. Interest rates impact most economic decisions like financing a new car, buying a house, and saving for retirement.

- **Investments.** Investing is the process of investing money for profit such as a retirement account. High interest rates on investments yield higher returns. This means investors receive higher profits from their investments that have higher interest rates.
- **Loans.** Loans pertain to the process of borrowing money with the expectation that the loan will be paid back over time plus interest. High interest rates on loans cost the borrower money. For example, interest rates on credit cards vary from 12 to 30 percent. This means that the borrower will pay the balance plus interest.

Example:

- 7% annual interest on $100 = $107 at the end of the year.
- 15% annual interest on $100 = $115 at the end of the year.

Consumers must also pay attention to when interest is compounded (i.e., annually, quarterly, daily).

Quick Tip

For this exam, you will have to identify ways in which teachers can help young learners understand earning, saving, and spending money. This includes helping students identify the best price for items, encouraging them to save money to buy something better later, and making good decisions around money.

D. Supply and demand

In a market economy, people buy and sell goods according to the laws of supply and demand. The value of goods and services are determined by interactions of individuals.

Supply and demand theory is one of the basic concepts of a market economy. Demand is how much product consumers want; supply is how much product the market can provide.

- **Law of supply.** When prices increase, supply increases. Supply is centered in the supplier's behavior. Suppliers want to sell at the highest price possible.

- **Law of demand.** When prices increase, demand decreases. Demand is centered on the consumer's behavior. Consumers will purchase fewer products if the price is high.

- **Equilibrium.** Supply and demand equilibrium occurs at the intersection of the demand curve and the supply curve. Equilibrium is a balance between supply and demand, also called *allocation efficiency*. This can only be reached in theory because supply and demand are constantly changing with the fluctuations of the market.

- **Price ceilings.** A mandated maximum price a seller is permitted to sell a product. An example is rent control.

- **Price floors.** A mandated minimum price a seller is required to pay. An example is minimum wage.

- **Opportunity cost**. The missed opportunity when one alternative is chosen over another. For example, a business invests in online marketing initiatives instead of building a second branch. The opportunity cost is the potential revenue that is missed by not building the second branch.

Scarcity

- Scarcity refers to a limited availability of goods and services. It occurs when people cannot obtain much of something they need. Scarcity often involves a tradeoff because people must sacrifice resources or goods to obtain more of the scarce resources they need or want.

- Scarcity also influences market prices. For example, the gasoline shortage in the 1970s resulted in soaring gas prices and long lines at the pumps.

- In some cases, governments will collaborate to increase their buying power to secure scarce resources. Consortiums and mutual aid pacts help state and local government agencies coordinate to obtain and share resources that are in short supply.

- Scarcity has an impact on immigration and where people choose to live. When resources are scarce, people will migrate toward opportunities.

Quick Tip

Think about what happens to basic supplies like water and fuel during disasters. Governments, businesses, and individuals compete for emergency supplies and equipment. Resources become limited, so prices go up.

The point where consumers are willing to pay for goods at a price that suppliers are willing to sell them is called **equilibrium**.

Supply and Demand

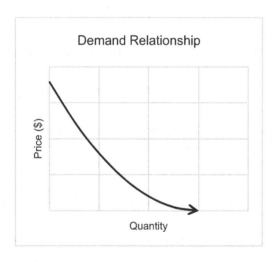

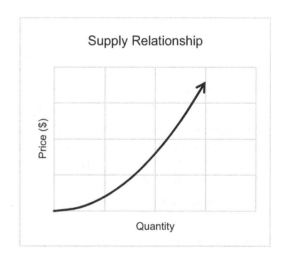

Supply and Demand Equilibrium

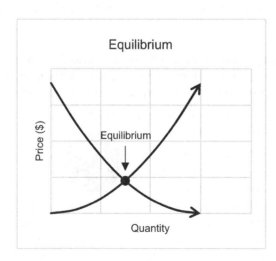

E. Types of economies

Countries use different types of economic systems depending on their leadership, customs, and values. The list below provides an overview of some of the economic systems used by nations throughout the world.

Traditional economic system. The original economic system in which traditions, customs, and beliefs shape the goods and the services the economy produces.

Command economic system. The government determines what goods should be produced, how much should be produced, and the price at which the goods are offered for sale. Also referred to as communism.

Centralized control. A feature of a command economy is that a large part of the economic system is controlled by a centralized power, most often the federal government.

Market economic system. Decisions regarding investment, production, and distribution are based on market, supply, and demand. Prices of goods and services are determined in a free price system.

Capitalism. Capitalism affords economic freedom, consumer choice, and economic growth.

Socialism. The means of production, distribution, and exchange are owned or regulated by the community.

Mixed economic system. Features characteristics of both capitalism and socialism.

Communism. An economic system where no private property exists and there is centralized production and distribution.

Monopoly. A market structure where there is only one producer/seller. The monopoly has control over the price of its goods and services. The market is restricted due to economic, political, or social barriers.

Oligopoly. A market structure where only a few producer/sellers make up the industry. An oligopoly has control over prices and maintains barriers from others entering the market.

Think About It

The US has a mixed economic system where some institutions employ capitalism, and some institutions employ socialism. For example, Medicare is a national health insurance program for seniors that is managed by the federal government. This is considered a social program.

This page intentionally left blank.

1. When teaching students about producers and consumers in an economic context, which activity would be most effective in enhancing their understanding?

    A. Watching a video on the basics of supply and demand in the market

    B. Engaging in a role-play activity simulating the interaction between a store owner and a customer

    C. Creating a poster showcasing examples of various producers and their products

    D. Participating in a group discussion on the importance of consumer choices in the economy

2. When teaching students about supply and demand, which scenario best illustrates the concept of equilibrium in the market?

    A. Scenario 1: A sudden increase in the price of smartphones leads to a decrease in the quantity demanded by consumers.

    B. Scenario 2: The price of concert tickets decreases, causing an increase in demand as more people are willing to attend the event.

    C. Scenario 3: A new technological advancement in farming techniques leads to a higher crop yield, resulting in an increase in the supply of vegetables.

    D. Scenario 4: The price of gasoline rises due to limited availability during a period of high demand, causing consumers to reduce their quantity demanded.

3. When teaching students about opportunity cost, which **TWO** scenarios best exemplify the concept?

    ☐ A. Sarah chooses to spend her money on a new video game instead of going to the movies with her friends.

    ☐ B. John decides to attend a music concert instead of studying for his upcoming exam.

    ☐ C. Lisa invests her time in learning a new language rather than playing video games.

    ☐ D. Michael purchases a new smartphone instead of going on vacation like he had planned.

    ☐ E. Rachel explores the cost of a new car at different times of the year, so she can purchase when the prices are lowest.

4. When teaching students about scarcity, which scenario best represents the concept?

    A. A local grocery store has an abundant supply of fresh fruits and vegetables available year-round.

    B. A government implements policies to ensure prices do not rise above a certain threshold.

    C. A factory produces a limited number of a popular toy, causing high demand.

    D. A community has access to an large amount of clean water from multiple sources.

5. When teaching students about push and pull factors in economics, which scenario best illustrates the concept?

    A. A company offers attractive job opportunities with competitive salaries and benefits, attracting skilled workers from other regions.

    B. A government imposes high taxes on businesses, causing many people to relocate to a different country.

    C. A decrease in the price of a popular product leads to an increase in consumer demand and sales.

    D. A natural disaster strikes a coastal town, prompting residents to move to inland areas for safety.

This page intentionally left blank.

Number	Answer	Explanation
1.	B	Answer B provides an interactive and experiential learning opportunity that allows students to directly experience the dynamics of producer-consumer interactions. By engaging in a role-play activity, students can embody the roles of both producers and consumers, understand the interdependence between them, and gain insights into supply, demand, and market exchanges. This activity promotes critical thinking, collaboration, and a deeper understanding of economic concepts in a practical context.
2.	D	Equilibrium in the market occurs when the quantity demanded by consumers matches the quantity supplied by producers at a particular price. In Scenario 4, the price of gasoline rises due to limited availability during a period of high demand. As a result, consumers reduce their quantity demanded, creating a situation where the quantity demanded and supplied reach a balance or equilibrium. This scenario exemplifies the concept of supply and demand interacting to establish an equilibrium price and quantity in the market.
3.	A & D	Opportunity cost refers to the potential benefit or value that is given up when one alternative is chosen over another. In other words, it's what you are potentially losing by choosing one option instead of the other.
4.	C	Scarcity refers to the condition of limited resources or goods relative to unlimited wants and needs. In answer C, the factory produces a limited number of a popular toy, leading to high demand in the market. This situation exemplifies scarcity because the availability of the toy is insufficient to satisfy the desires of all potential buyers, resulting in scarcity and potentially driving up prices or creating competition among consumers.
5.	B	Push/pull factors have to do with people emigrating from a country and immigrating to another country. The push factors can be economic, safety, or resource related. Answer B is the only answer choice where people leave a country for another country due to economic opportunity.

This page intentionally left blank.

V. Educational Practices for Teaching Social Studies

The questions on this exam will not just assess your knowledge of history, US government, geography, world history and economics. You will be required to apply that knowledge to teaching scenarios. Therefore, this part of the exam requires you to do two things:

1. Understand the concepts in this section

2. Use your knowledge to identify the most effective teaching practices to social studies classroom scenarios

We have added the following section, which is not included in the specifications for the exam, because to be successful on this part of the test, you'll need explicit understanding of social studies teaching applications.

Diversity in the classroom

Creating a classroom culture that supports the background of all students is essential in teaching social studies. Teachers have the power to bring multicultural texts and stories to students. This can be a daunting task for new teachers because many things should be considered when selecting multicultural texts.

Accuracy. Accuracy of cultural representation is a crucial aspect of high-quality multicultural literature, and books must contain current, correct information to avoid reinforcing stereotypes.

Authentic dialogue. The dialogue in the text should accurately represent culturally specific oral traditions.

Presentation of information or issues. The information in the text should not leave out information that is unfavorable to the dominant culture.

An important part of being a social studies teacher is evaluating and selecting resources for instructional use. The very first thing to consider when choosing materials for the classroom is whether the materials are aligned to the state adopted standards. Always consult the standards before planning instruction or choosing instructional materials. After that, there are several things to consider.

The following was taken from the Urbandale School District and is a comprehensive outline that should be considered when choosing materials for the classroom. We have found this list to be helpful when evaluating the role of the social studies educator.

- Instructional materials should support the educational philosophy, goals, and objectives of the district and the objectives of the curricular offering in which the materials will be used.

- Instructional materials should be appropriate for the age, emotional and social development, and ability level of the students for whom the materials are selected.

- Instructional materials should be diverse with respect to levels of difficulty and reader appeal and should present a variety of points of view.

- Instructional materials should meet high standards of quality in factual content and presentation.

- Instructional materials should have aesthetic, cultural, literary, or social value. The value and impact of any literary work will be judged as a whole, considering the author's intent rather than individual words, phrases, or incidents.

- Instructional materials should foster respect for men, women, the disabled, and minority groups and should portray a variety of roles and lifestyles open to people in today's world. Instructional materials should foster respect for cultural diversity.

- Instructional materials should be designed to motivate students to examine their own attitudes and behaviors and to comprehend their own duties, responsibilities, rights, and privileges as participating citizens in a pluralistic society.

- Instructional materials should encourage students to use higher-order thinking skills and to become informed decision-makers, to exercise freedom of thought and to make independent judgments through examination and evaluation of relevant information, evidence, and differing viewpoints.

Mr. Rodriguez is deciding what material he will use in a lesson over the next nine weeks. What should be the first thing he considers when choosing instructional material?

    A.   Is the material interesting and engaging?

    B.   Is the material aligned to the state adopted standards?

    C.   Is the material developmentally appropriate for students?

    D.   Is the material culturally responsive?

Correct answer: B

While all these considerations are very important, the standards should be the first thing the teacher considers. After alignment is determined, the other three questions should be considered.

Planning instruction for critical thinking

Highly effective teachers help students develop their higher-order, critical thinking skills. This way, students can move beyond simply reading aloud or memorizing information and apply their skills and knowledge to understand text. This is often referred to reading to learn rather than learning to read.

Critical thinking. This is multi-step, high-level thinking where students are stretching in their thinking to analyze, evaluate, interpret, and synthesize information to reach a conclusion or make a judgment.

Creative thinking. This requires students to create something by applying their skills. When students apply their skills, they are operating at a high cognitive level.

Reflective thinking. Students look back on and reflect upon their learning process to promote abstract thinking and to encourage the application of learning strategies to new situations.

Test Tip

There are all kinds of strategies to use to help students increase their comprehension, critical thinking, and metacognition. Be sure to choose activities that apply higher-order skills when answering questions like these on the test.

Metacognition. This is thinking about thinking. When students have metacognition, they understand the processes in their minds and can employ a variety of techniques to understand text. Strategies for boosting **comprehension**, **critical thinking**, and **metacognition** are:

Making connections and predicting. Asking students what they think will happen next.

Questioning. Having students ask questions based on what they are reading.

Read aloud/think aloud. Teacher or student reads and stops to think aloud about what the text means.

Summarizing. Asking students to summarize information they are reading about in their own words.

Question generating. Having students develop their own questions about the lesson.

Bloom's Taxonomy

Bloom's Taxonomy is a hierarchical model used to classify educational learning objectives into levels of complexity and specificity. The higher up the pyramid, the more complex the thinking skills. The skills are represented as verbs on the pyramid. When answering questions in the social studies section regarding critical thinking, reference Bloom's Taxonomy. The figure is a modified version of Bloom's Taxonomy. We have modified it to include other skills (verbs) you may see on the exam.

Apply

Create

Analyze

Evaluate

Compare & Contrast

Categorize

Understand & Identify

Remember & Memorize

Assessments

Every teacher certification exam has a component that measures your ability to select the most appropriate assessment at the appropriate time to measure the appropriate skill. You will be required to understand different assessments. Remember, assessments should always be used to make instructional decisions.

The following table provides different types of assessments teachers can use in the classroom to drive decision-making.

Assessment Type	Definition	Example
Diagnostic	A pre-assessment providing instructors with information about students' prior knowledge, preconceptions, and misconceptions before beginning a learning activity	Before starting a reading unit on Earth space science, a teacher gives a quick assessment to determine students' prior knowledge of concepts in the text. She uses this information to make instructional decisions moving forward.
Formative	A range of formal and informal assessments or checks conducted by the teacher before, during, and after the learning process to modify instruction	A teacher walks around the room checking on students as they read. She might also write anecdotal notes to review later to help her design further instruction.
Summative	An assessment that focuses on the outcomes. It is frequently used to measure the effectiveness of a program, lesson, or strategy.	A reading teacher gives a midterm exam at the end of the semester.
Performance-based	An assessment that measures students' ability to apply the skills and knowledge learned from a unit or units of study; the task challenges students to use their higher-order, critical thinking skills to create a product or complete a process.	After reading text about the Civil War, students develop stories about different historical figures in the war. Students then perform these stories in front of the class and answer questions.

Assessment Type	Definition	Example
Criterion-referenced	An assessment that measures student performance against a fixed set of predetermined criteria or learning standards	At the end of the spring semester, students take the State Standards Assessment. The state uses the scores for accountability measures.
Norm-referenced (percentile)	An assessment or evaluation that yields an estimate of the position of the tested individual in a predefined population with respect to the trait being measured	The NAEP is an exam given every few years for data purposes only to compare students' reading scores across the US.
Screening	An assessment used to place students in appropriate classrooms or grade level	Students are typically screened throughout the year to determine at what level they are reading. Placement decisions are made based on the outcomes of the screening.

Determine appropriate learning environments for social studies lessons

Effective teachers use grouping practices to achieve the objective of a lesson. For example, if you want students to evaluate text, you group students in literature circles where the focus is evaluating and discussing the story or information. When you want to employ interventions for struggling students, you group according to skill. Flexible grouping practices are essential in delivering high-quality, differentiated instruction.

The main grouping practices used in education are whole-group, small-group, peer pairing/partners, and one-to-one instruction.

Whole group. This is when teachers are in the front of the room delivering direct instruction. Teachers use whole group method for communicating explicit instructions for an activity or lesson, modeling a skill, or introducing students to a concept or lesson.

Small group. This is typically referred to as cooperative learning. Small groups are most effective when they have five or fewer members. Small-group instruction can consist of students working together in their groups to evaluate text and discuss information. It can also consist of a teacher-led session where the teacher works with a small group of students to provide specific and targeted interventions. Small groups can be divided into two categories: homogeneous and heterogenous.

Homogeneous groups. Everyone in the group has been identified as having the same learning level. The teacher targets interventions for students in this group who need the same skill. For example, for a group of all level 2 readers who struggle with fluency, the teacher uses fluency strategies during a homogeneous, small-group session.

Heterogeneous groups. Groups are formed so that there is a variety of learning levels and student interests. For example, grouping students by interest rather than scores will provide more diversity among the group members.

Quick Tip

Students should only be placed in homogenous groups when a teacher is targeting a specific skill for a selected small group of students for remediation or enrichment. Heterogeneous grouping should be used for all other classroom activities. Keeping students in homogeneous groups limits them. Research supports that heterogeneous grouping is most effective.

One-to-one instruction. The student works with the teacher individually. This approach is most effective to communicate specific and meaningful feedback on assignments. This approach is also effective for fluency interventions.

Authentic learning opportunities

Social studies content can be used to create authentic learning opportunities for students. On the exam, you may be asked about the most appropriate activity for students to learn a concept or skill. When you read the question and answer choices, consider the following:

- Is the activity aligned to the state standards?
- Is the activity appropriate for the grade level and learning level?
- Does the activity provide an authentic experience for the learner?
- Is the activity related to the lesson?

Creating an opportunity to implement the state standard in an authentic activity is always the best answer choice.

Example question

Which of the following would be the most appropriate activity for a fifth-grade class learning about aquifers?

    A. Have students read the textbook and answer the questions at the end of the unit.

    B. Have a guest speaker from the water management district come speak to the class.

    C. Have students organize a conservation campaign centered on a local town's aquifer.

    D. Take a field trip to the local spring.

Correct answer: C

All these options seem like good activities for students to learn about aquifers, but organizing a conservation campaign provides the most authentic experience for the students. Reading the textbook and answering questions is not the best answer. A guest speaker is good, but the student is sitting and listening to a lecture. Taking a field trip to the spring would be fun, but probably won't provide the same level of learning as answer choice C.

Graphic Organizers

KWL charts are used to activate or build background knowledge. KWL stands for:

- **(K)** What do you know?
- **(W)** What do you want to know?
- **(L)** What did you learn?

K Before reading	W Before and during reading	L After reading

Venn diagrams are used to compare and contrast characters, content, or events in the text.

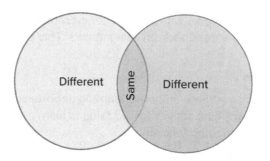

Different | Same | Different

Five "W" Questions

The five "Ws" are who, what, when, where, and why. Asking these questions can help students understand concepts at a deeper level. Also, using the five Ws helps to push students to higher complexity levels in their thinking, which is essential in social studies.

Inquiry-Base Learning

Social studies is sometimes taught in a lecture format. The teacher stands in the front of the room, maybe using a presentation or graphic. In this situation, most of the learning is passive, meaning students are sitting and watching or listening to the teacher.

However, it is important that students have an opportunity to interact with social science using inquiry-based methods. These include:

- Using maps
- Role play
- Designing their own questions
- Working with others to buy and sell goods

Test Tip

Be on the lookout for answer choices that use inquiry-based learning. They are probably the correct answers.

1. Students have been working on a social science unit for some time. The teacher wants to increase students' critical thinking about certain topics within the unit. What would be the most effective approach?

    A. Have students work in their literature circles to evaluate text, present their claims and ideas, and find areas in the text that support those claims and ideas.

    B. Have students read a piece of text, debate the sides of the topic, and determine a winner of the debate.

    C. Have students work in collaborative groups, read a selection of text, and answer comprehension questions at the end of the text.

    D. Have students pick a topic presented in the unit, use the Internet to research that topic, and write a detailed essay about the topic.

2. Which of the following would be the most appropriate desk formation for cooperative learning?

    A. Desks in rows

    B. Desks in a U-shaped pattern

    C. Desks in clusters of four or five

    D. Desks in rows of five

3. Looking over a social science text, students observe headings, charts, and graphs. They turn the headings of the text into questions. The students are engaging in:

    A. Pre-reading strategies

    B. Post-reading strategies

    C. During reading strategies

    D. Visual reading strategies

4. Which of the following should be considered first when choosing text for a unit on the Lewis and Clark Expedition?

    A. Is the text interesting?

    B. Does the text increase critical thinking?

    C. Is the text aligned to the state standards?

    D. Is the text above grade level?

5. Which of the following would be most effective in assessing students' application of knowledge of the Emancipation Proclamation?

    A. Independently read about events during this time

    B. Identify main people involved

    C. Write an essay about the event

    D. Role play the events during this time

6. What should a social studies teacher use to guide lesson planning?

    A. Textbook

    B. Standards

    C. Assessments

    D. Student surveys

7. Which of the following would be most appropriate for kindergarteners to understand social aspects of geography?

    A. Picture books, video, encyclopedias

    B. Picture books, maps, and stories

    C. Picture books, documentaries, encyclopedias

    D. Case studies, population surveys, maps

8. Which of the following is the most effective way to teach complex vocabulary in social science?

    A. Glossary

    B. Encyclopedia

    C. Highlighted words

    D. In context

9. Which of the following would be most effective in teaching students longitude and latitude?

    A. Guest speaker

    B. Role play

    C. Globe

    D. Special purpose map

10. Which of the following social science resources is considered a primary source?

    A. Ben Franklin's autobiography

    B. Textbook

    C. Newspaper

    D. Multiple-choice test

Number	Answer	Explanation
1.	A	Remember Bloom's Taxonomy when you see questions about critical thinking. All these answer choices are good activities. However, there is only one with critical thinking elements in it—evaluating text and supporting claims using evidence. Answer A is the best choice.
2.	C	Cooperative learning is small-group instruction. Therefore, arranging desks in clusters of 4-5 is most appropriate.
3.	A	This is a pre-reading strategy for tackling complex text.
4.	C	First, always align decisions to standards. Books, curriculum, and materials should all be aligned to the standards before they can even be considered for the classroom. Once alignment is established, then the teacher should consider critical thinking, interest, and grade level.
5.	D	The key word in the question stem is *apply*. Role play is the only activity where students apply their knowledge.
6.	B	The standards should always guide lesson planning and instruction.
7.	B	The key word is *kindergarten*. Choose the set of resources that is developmentally appropriate for kindergarteners—picture books, maps, and stories. Encyclopedias, documentaries, and newspapers are not choices that are developmentally appropriate.
8.	D	Always teach content area vocabulary—words you see in science, social science, math, etc.—in context.
9.	C	A globe is the best option here because it is a model of the earth that brings the abstract to the concrete.
10.	A	A primary source is a firsthand account of events. An autobiography is considered a primary source.

This page intentionally left blank.

1. A fifth-grade class is working on presentations about the American Revolution. Presentation topics include the Boston Tea Party, the Declaration of Independence, the Battle of Saratoga, and the winter at Valley Forge. Each student picks a topic and then designs a presentation around the topic using research from the Internet and other sources.

   What questions can the teacher ask individual students to encourage them to use evidence-based research methods?

   A. Will you have copyrighted images in your visual representations?

   B. Will you be acting out key events during your presentation to show authenticity?

   C. Have you written annotations on note cards to guide your presentation?

   D. Did you use a combination of primary and secondary sources to plan your presentation?

2. An elementary teacher is planning a unit on the Industrial Revolution that will include major themes during this part of U.S. history. The teacher uses the academic standards to develop lesson objectives for the unit. Identify the learning objective that best supports the teacher's content knowledge accuracy on this subject.

   A. Students will understand migration and urbanization patterns from rural to urban areas during the Industrial Revolution.

   B. Students will analyze building and construction decreases during the Industrial Revolution's peak.

   C. Students will understand migration and urbanization patterns from urban to suburban areas during the Industrial Revolution.

   D. Students will identify evidence that supports why there was a decrease in women working in factories during the Industrial Revolution.

3. Students are reading in their cooperative groups about social reform movements. While the teacher walks around the room observing students in their groups, she notices confusion regarding the separate roles and periods of the abolitionist and women's suffrage movements. Students are mixing up the contributions of activists like Sojourner Truth and Susan B. Anthony.

   Identify how the teacher can intervene and help students differentiate between the two movements accurately.

   A. Assign a compare and contrast essay where students must identify activists' actions in each movement.

   B. Organize a debate on the impacts of the 13th Amendment versus the 19th Amendment, encouraging students to explore the separate historical contexts.

   C. Encourage students to complete a timeline showing key events in both the abolitionist movement and the women's suffrage movement, highlighting the distinct periods and goals of each.

   D. Schedule a video session that features experts discussing the nuances and individual objectives of the abolitionist and women's suffrage movements.

4. A history teacher wants to use a video lesson to meet the following objective: *Students will evaluate how natural environments influence Indigenous civilizations.*

   Identify the type of video that would be most effective to achieve this objective.

   A. A narrative history of the languages used by Indigenous people in North America

   B. A documentary about European exploration and the decimation of Indigenous people

   C. A documentary about the development of agriculture in Indigenous civilizations

   D. A tutorial on how Indigenous people built tools and weapons that aided their survival

5. Which ancient civilization is credited with the invention of paper?

   A. Aztec

   B. Mesopotamian

   C. Roman

   D. Chinese

6. A fifth-grade teacher is discussing the difference in the types of weapons used by Indigenous people and European colonists in North America. Which of the following images would be most helpful to show students for this lesson?

   A. A cannon made of metal and a bayonet made of steal

   B. A trap made from steel and armor made from iron

   C. Spearheads shaped from stone and bullets made from lead

   D. Bows made from wood and atlatls made from deer antlers

7. A teacher wants to emphasize the pilgrims' quest for religious freedom in the seventeenth century and how it is applicable today. She designs the following objective for the lesson:

   Students will relate past and present events that outline people's desire for religious freedom.

   Identify the extension activity that best supports the objective.

   A. Show a movie on the harsh conditions pilgrims suffered during the voyage.

   B. Reference a current newspaper article about people in Asia fleeing their countries to avoid religious prosecution.

   C. Using a current documentary highlighting people's attitudes toward certain religious groups in the U.S.

   D. Identifying how push and pull factors impact migration in the past and present.

8. During a lesson on the American Revolution, a fourth-grade teacher develops the following objective:

   Students will compare and contrast the relationships between historical figures during the American Revolution.

   Identify the most effective activity that would best support this learning objective.

   A. Create a timeline of major events during the Revolution.

   B. Answer guiding questions about the cause of the Revolution and its effects.

   C. Create a Venn diagram to evaluate the interactions between two prominent figures in the American Revolution.

   D. Read letters from a prominent figure during the American Revolution.

9. A teacher is helping students draft essential questions while reading about the Constitution of the United States and the Bill of Rights. She calls on students to share their questions. Which student drafted the most effective question for the reading about this topic?

    A. How does democracy depend on individual citizens' rights?

    B. Who developed the U.S. Constitution and why?

    C. What symbols are most associated with America and freedom?

    D. In what ways did the colonists push back against Britain?

10. A sixth-grade class identifies connections in their own lives to the importance of the Declaration of Independence. Identify the best activity students can engage in to achieve this.

    A. Role-play the signing of the Declaration of Independence.

    B. Evaluate the school rules and discuss if they infringe on students' autonomy.

    C. Draw pictorial representations of how a bill becomes a law.

    D. Engage in a class discussion of why Britain was wrong to infringe on the rights of American colonists.

11. A teacher develops an end-of-unit activity focusing on citizenship rights and responsibilities. Identify **THREE** activities that would be most effective in engaging in this topic.

    ☐ A. Design a community-wide recycling campaign.

    ☐ B. Organize a bake sale to buy new instruments and uniforms for the school band.

    ☐ C. Speak at a city council meeting to inform council members of student issues.

    ☐ D. Volunteer in a school campus clean-up initiative.

    ☐ E. Evaluate the costs of the student government elections.

12. Before starting a unit on symbols of American patriotism, a first-grade teacher wants to identify any misconceptions students might have about the topic. Identify the most effective formative assessment the teacher can use to identify student misconceptions and design interventions accordingly.

    A. Observe students as they brainstorm project ideas for the new unit.

    B. Ask high-complexity questions to identify mastery of symbolism regarding American patriotism.

    C. Use cooperative learning to read about symbols and answer comprehension questions.

    D. Administer a pretest where students briefly explain symbols like the flag and the bald eagle.

13. A third-grade teacher is introducing a unit on the three branches of government. Before starting the assigned reading, the teacher engages in the following steps.

    1. The teacher projects a KWL chart in the front of the room.

    2. Before reading, the teacher and students discuss what they already know about the topic.

    3. The students discuss what they want to know about the current topic.

    Which of the following is the main purpose of the activity?

    A. Activate background knowledge

    B. Encourage group discussion

    C. Participate in collaborative learning

    D. Increase critical thinking

14. A second-grade teacher shows students diagrams of the different branches of government. She has students work in cooperative groups to discuss the concept of checks and balances. Which of the following group discussions indicates the students have a misconception about this concept?

    A. A student says, "Once a bill is signed into law, it is permanent."

    B. A student says, "Congress takes bills and makes the laws, and the courts determine if they are constitutional."

    C. A student says, "If people want to challenge a court decision, they can appeal their cases to the Supreme Court."

    D. A student says, "Congress can make laws, but the President can veto those laws."

15. Which of the following student activities is most likely to help students understand the roles and responsibilities of local government?

    A. Discuss a new citywide clean-up event.

    B. Explore issues currently affecting the United States.

    C. Role-play a city council meeting.

    D. Enact how a bill becomes a law.

16. Students design political cartoons in their cooperative groups and write narratives describing the cartoons. The objective of the assignment is to "Evaluate the Bill of Rights of the U.S. Constitution."

    Which of the following excerpts from the students' paragraphs meets this objective?

    A. The President and Congress are working together to pass legislation.

    B. People have assembled outside the Supreme Court to voice their objection to a current ruling.

    C. The Supreme Court is ruling on a controversial law.

    D. George Washington, James Madison, and Benjamin Franklin sign the U.S. Constitution.

17. A fifth-grade teacher develops a lesson around the following objective:

    Students will understand that societies must balance the rights and responsibilities of individuals with the common good.

    Which of the following instructional tools is the best source to support the objective?

    A. A discussion on how states disagree about the right to bear arms because of public safety.

    B. A map of the thirteen original colonies and how those transformed into the United States of America.

    C. A Venn diagram comparing the judicial branch and the executive branch of government.

    D. A KWL chart before reading a text about the Civil Rights Movement and the 14th Amendment.

18. Identify the most effective activity a fourth-grade class can engage in to meet the following objective:

    Students will understand and apply the concept of the three branches of government at the local, state, and federal levels.

    A. Students work in groups to discuss the three branches of the U.S. government.

    B. Students act out the roles of a mayor, governor, and president.

    C. Students simulate how a bill becomes a law.

    D. Students label a diagram that shows the electoral process.

19. A first-grade teacher helps students understand the world in spatial terms. Identify the lesson that would best achieve this. Choose **ALL** that apply.

  ☐   A.   Use maps and globes to show students the different continents and oceans on the planet.

  ☐   B.   Have students compare and contrast population density and climate maps.

  ☐   C.   Evaluate how people in other regions farm on the sides of mountains.

  ☐   D.   Discuss how longitude and latitude can be used to identify absolute location.

  ☐   E.   Use a map scale to estimate the distance between the United States and Japan.

20. The academic standard for a fifth-grade geography lesson states:

    Students will explain how environmental changes impact human behavior.

    The teacher decides to read a nonfiction story about natural disasters. Which of the following graphic organizers will help her students with the standard?

    A.   A diagram showing the causes and effects of hurricanes and earthquakes.

    B.   A Venn diagram comparing hurricanes and earthquakes.

    C.   A KWL chart to activate background knowledge on the topic.

    D.   A sequence map of climate events

21. A first-grade teacher begins a unit on seasonal temperature changes in the environment and how they affect agriculture practices worldwide.

    Identify the best activity to help students understand this concept.

    A.   Show a time-lapse video of seasonal changes and record student ideas and observations.

    B.   Fill out a Venn diagram to compare temperatures on land at sunrise and sunset.

    C.   Use a globe to show how seasons differ in the Northern and Southern Hemispheres.

    D.   Have students record the start of the winter solstice in the United States.

22. A third-grade teacher is planning a lesson on human-environment interaction. Which of the following would **NOT** be the best learning objective for this lesson?

    A.   Students will write an essay about the limitations of people who live in the desert.

    B.   Students will construct a diagram showing how different physical features of regions influence farming, architecture, and activities.

    C.   Students will create a cause-and-effect diagram describing how pollution affects different communities.

    D.   Students will identify immigration and emigration patterns in the United States.

23. Which assignment would be most effective for a fifth-grade social studies class focusing on push-pull factors?

    A.   Fill out a KWL chart before reading about current migration patterns in the United States.

    B.   Create a graph depicting different immigration patterns to the United States over the last 100 years.

    C.   Engage in a class discussion on why people emigrate and immigrate based on resource availability.

    D.   Draft a list describing why people want to come to the United States.

24. A first-grade geography teacher shows students how vegetation varies based on geography. She shows maps of two distinct areas: the desert and the tropics. Identify **TWO** geographic features to help emphasize this topic.

☐ A. The latitude of each region

☐ B. The amount of human pollution in each region

☐ C. The average amount of rainfall in each region

☐ D. The number of people living in the region.

☐ E. The number of cities in each region

25. A first-grade teacher is trying to clarify the differences between landforms and waterways. Students must distinguish isthmuses from straits. Which strategy best supports students' understanding and distinction between these land masses?

A. Create a list of landmasses and waterways and have students write the definitions of each.

B. Ask students to identify pictures of different land masses and waterways in the United States.

C. Provide students with brown and blue clay to create different models of landmasses and waterways.

D. Encourage the students to conduct research on the various landforms and waterways.

26. Identify the most effective way a teacher can implement inquiry-based methods to help students acquire geographical skills.

A. Watch a documentary film about different volcanic eruptions in the Ring of Fire.

B. Identify different coordinates on a map for different locations using longitude and latitude.

C. Complete a worksheet where students label geographic locations.

D. Invite a guest speaker to demonstrate latitude, longitude, the prime meridian, and the equator.

27. A fifth-grade teacher is introducing a lesson on trade practices in ancient civilizations, specifically those between the Phoenicians and Romans. Identify the most effective activity to help students understand the concept of trade between these ancient civilizations.

A. Role-play a trading system where students use items in the classroom to represent textiles and luxury goods.

B. Read from the textbook about ancient world currencies and how they were used

C. Review the type of goods ancient societies traded with each other.

D. Look over a map of the Mediterranean and identify the trade routes of the Phoenicians and Romans.

28. Students engage in a classroom discussion of supply and demand. The teacher asks a guiding question for the discussion:

How do supply and demand affect us in our everyday lives?

Identify the student response that indicates mastery of this concept. Choose **ALL** that apply.

☐ A. "Supply and demand directly influence our everyday expenses. For instance, during a product shortage, prices tend to rise because the item is harder to find, making it more valuable. On the other hand, when there's too much of an item, prices can drop since it's easier to obtain."

☐ B. "Supply and demand affect us by determining the price and availability of the goods and services we use daily. If there is a lot of something and low demand, you can typically get it for a better price."

☐ C. "Supply and demand require the consumer to make a choice. For example, if you only have enough money for a video game or a fancy dinner, you must decide which one you will buy."

☐ D. "Supply and demand matter mostly to people buying stocks or investing in the market because they set the price of goods and services."

29. As an introduction to an economics lesson, a teacher uses a real-world example of a candy manufacturer that had to change the formula of the blue dye in its candy to be safe for consumption in the US. The students also learned this policy was not enforced in a different country. Which of the following concepts does this lesson reinforce?

A. Supply and demand

B. Investment

C. Regulation

D. Corporate taxation

30. A teacher is simulating a lesson in economics. The teacher tells students they can do one of two things: buy a new bicycle or buy a new video game. The teacher emphasizes that they cannot do both; they only have enough money for one. Which of the following economic concepts does this statement best illustrate?

A. Barter

B. Opportunity cost

C. Supply and demand

D. Interest

31. A fourth-grade teacher wants to show students that comparing the costs of items is the best method to use when buying something. Identify the most effective activity students can engage in to understand this concept.

A. Have students engage in a blind taste test of an expensive brand of juice and a less expensive generic brand of juice and write down which one they liked better and look at the cost of each.

B. Ask students to examine reviews of a popular video game before deciding which one to buy.

C. Have students compare the prices of their favorite cereal from one store and another while finding coupons in the local paper to reduce the cost.

D. Show students different commercials for similar items and identify the persuasive language in each ad to entice students to buy.

32. A teacher has students choose from a list of items she displays on the board. She then has students categorize the items as "wants" and "needs." She sees that many students have items in the "needs" column that should be in the "wants" column. Identify the most effective question the teacher can ask to help students distinguish between wants and needs.

   A. "Which of these items are important to you?"

   B. "What items on this list are unsafe?"

   C. "Is this item necessary for survival?"

   D. "Where would you rank this item on your list of needs?

33. A second-grade teacher has a classroom behavior system where students are awarded blue tickets when they complete assignments, clean up without asking, and behave appropriately. Each Friday before the end of school, students can spend their tickets in the classroom store and buy stickers, pencils, and other trinkets. They can also keep collecting their weekly tickets and purchase larger things at the end of the month, like colorful notebooks or posters.

   Which **TWO** of the following economic concepts is best reinforced by the classroom store?

   ☐ A. Supply and demand

   ☐ B. Spending and saving money

   ☐ C. Equilibrium

   ☐ D. Opportunity cost

   ☐ E. Push-pull factors

34. Ms. Ramirez wants to increase critical thinking skills in her 5th grade class. She and her students are studying economics. Which activity would best cultivate critical thinking skills?

   A. While in literature circles, students are identifying common economic terms in the text before they read.

   B. Individually, students categorize attributes of macroeconomics and microeconomics using a graphic organizer.

   C. In pairs, students look at different economic systems and then evaluate how the culture of the region may or may not influence the economy.

   D. In groups, work on a poster that identifies all the different parts of a market economy.

35. After completing a unit on economics and accounting, a sixth-grade teacher wants to assess students' critical thinking about how to organize financial data. Which instructional method would be most effective?

   A. Administer a multiple-choice test at the end of the unit on accounting spreadsheets

   B. Provide a data set and have the students use the spreadsheet to analyze and evaluate the data.

   C. Assign an essay describing the benefits and challenges of using accounting spreadsheets

   D. Conduct a diagnostic to assess the students' understanding of spreadsheets before going over the material.

36. A teacher is talking to students about how, during the late 1800s, manufacturing companies grew very large and produced more and more goods. Workers in the factories decided to form labor unions. Which of the following student responses indicate that the student understands the concept of labor unions?

    A. Student 1: People joined unions to create more jobs

    B. Student 2: People joined unions to slow down production

    C. Student 3: People joined unions to increase production

    D. Student 4: People joined unions to improve working conditions

37. To assess a student's ability to analyze the development in the South and the draining of the Everglades, which of the following tasks would be most appropriate?

    A. Participate in a play about the state's agriculture.

    B. Prepare a report on early exploration in the area.

    C. Label a blank political map of the state.

    D. Write a cause-and-effect essay about the region.

38. The factors below present what type of economic system?

    • Consumers determine what will be produced.

    • Consumers determine how much will be produced.

    • Consumers determine the price of products.

    A. Communism

    B. Socialism

    C. Marxism

    D. Free Market

39. Which of the following US documents states that the purposes of government include establishing justice and securing the blessings of liberty?

    A. Articles of Confederation

    B. Constitution of the United States

    C. Declaration of Independence

    D. Bill of Rights

40. Students are reading the Bill of Rights to analyze provisions in the US Constitution. The US Constitution is considered which of the following?

    A. Scholarly source

    B. Web-based source

    C. Primary source

    D. Secondary source

41. While conducting a debate activity, the teacher notices two students not participating. When she asks them about it, they indicate they are overwhelmed by the debate process and would rather not participate. What is the most effective approach the teacher could take in this situation?

   A. Make the students participate, so they can work through their feelings.

   B. Have students use a dialogue journal where they can express their views, in private, about a topic.

   C. Have students sit out and write a paper on the topic.

   D. Have students read silently and independently on the topic.

42. If a teacher wants her students to engage in a debate about the right to peacefully assemble, which of the following is an appropriate secondary source of information for the students to reference for information?

   A. The 1st Amendment of the US Constitution

   B. Internet article about the Million Man March

   C. Online chat forum about upcoming environmental protests

   D. A documentary that includes interviews with leaders from the March on Washington

43. Which of the following best describes the purpose for having three branches of government?

   A. Passing laws

   B. Checks and balances

   C. Drafting bills

   D. Bi-partisan legislation

44. Which of the following is the state-level executive officer?

   A. President

   B. Speaker of the House

   C. Governor

   D. Chief Justice

45. Which of the following does the US Constitution mandate of state governments?

   A. Maintain a republic.

   B. Maintain bi-partisan political parties.

   C. Maintain a three-branch structure of government.

   D. Maintain an elector college for state governor elections.

46. Which article of the Constitution establishes the executive branch of the US Government?

   A. Article I

   B. Article II

   C. Article III

   D. Article IV

47. How many justices serve on the US Supreme Court?

    A. 6

    B. 10

    C. 12

    D. 9

48. How long is a US Senate term of office?

    A. 2 years

    B. 4 years

    C. 6 years

    D. Lifetime

49. A teacher is beginning a lesson involving Earth-related concepts: latitude/longitude, time zones, distance between continents. Which of the following would be the best tool to use?

    A. Time zone chart

    B. Atlas

    C. Almanac

    D. Globe

50. Which of the following tools on a map includes small representations of features using shapes and pictures?

    A. Guide

    B. Scale

    C. Legend

    D. Grid

51. Which of the following situations is a violation of the 4th Amendment in the US Constitution?

    A. Police searching a student's locker on school grounds without a warrant.

    B. Police searching a private citizen's hotel room without a warrant.

    C. Police searching bags at an airport without a warrant.

    D. Police searching the center console of a private citizen's vehicle without a warrant.

52. A teacher wants to show students a real-world example of opportunity cost. Which of the following examples would help students understand this concept?

    A. The federal government imposes a tax on imported coffee from Colombia which results in higher prices to the consumer.

    B. Receiving an income tax credit for paying worldwide taxes.

    C. A country exports a specific good that it is highly efficient at producing.

    D. A business owner shuts down for three months to build a new facility and expand operations.

53. Which of the following student explanations of a region indicates the student understands this concept?

    A. Regions are groups of cities from different areas of the US based on population.

    B. The southwest is a region because it is characterized by population, location, and climate.

    C. Regions are groups of counties based on tax revenue and government.

    D. Regions are groups of countries based on import and exports.

54. Which of the following is a criticism of socialist economic systems?

    A. Increases a sense of community rather than a sense of selfishness.

    B. Provides a social safety net for marginalized citizens.

    C. Centralized control of manufacturing creates economic shortages.

    D. Government oversight and regulation of housing market, monopolies, and environmental policy.

55. A teacher has students look over the timeline below. Which student has interpreted the timeline correctly?

1400–1430:	Portugal's Prince Henry the Navigator sponsors exploration of Africa's coast.
1450–1500:	Vasco da Gama sails around Africa and discovers sea route to India (1498).
1500–1510:	First black slaves in America brought to Spanish colony of Santo Domingo.
1510–1540:	Verrazano, sailing under the French flag, explores the New England coast and New York Bay.
1560–1570:	Publication of "On the Revolution of Heavenly Bodies" by Polish scholar Nicolaus Copernicus giving his theory that Earth revolves around the sun.
1570–1580:	Akbar the Great becomes Mogul emperor of India, conquers Afghanistan (1581), continues wars of conquest (until 1605).
1580–1600:	Francis Drake returns to England after circumnavigating the globe; knighted by Queen Elizabeth I (1581). Essays of Michel de Montaigne published.
1600–1650:	Giordano Bruno burned as a heretic. English East India Company established.
1650–1700:	Pilgrims, after three-month voyage in Mayflower, land at Plymouth Rock. Francis Bacon's Novum Organum published.

    A. Student 1: Most of the age of exploration happened in the 14th century.

    B. Student 2: Most of the age of exploration happened in the 15th century.

    C. Student 3: Most of the age of exploration happened in the 16th century.

    D. Student 4: Most of the age of exploration happened in the 17th century.

56. Which of the following would help students understand different interpretations of a law?

    A. A Supreme Court justice dissenting opinion

    B. A narrative from a state senator about a recent bill

    C. A video of a local city council meeting

    D. An interview with the president about a recent veto

57. Which of the following would help students understand retirement investment?

    A. A video on the law of supply and demand

    B. An activity on opportunity cost

    C. A graphic showing the concept of equilibrium

    D. A reading on price ceilings

58. A teacher is showing students what happens when a company has manufactured too much of a product, and there is more product than customers who will buy the product. What type of lesson is the teacher working on?

    A. Opportunity cost

    B. Surplus

    C. Regulation

    D. Push/Pull factors

59. A teacher is using a KWL chart before reading to determine what students already know about the US Constitution and other national documents. Which **TWO** of the following is the teacher assessing with this activity?

    ☐ A. Analytical skills

    ☐ B. Metacognition

    ☐ C. Background knowledge

    ☐ D. Misconceptions and preconceptions

    ☐ E. Reading fluency

60. A teacher is conducting an activity on the Bill of Rights. She decides to use the school's dress code policy as an example. Some students feel the current dress code is appropriate, while others feel it should be changed. She has students do the following:

    • Get together with other students who feel similarly about the dress code.

    • Organize an event where students with similar views will get together and discuss the dress code policy.

    • Prepare a response to be presented to the school board about the dress code.

    Which of the following amendments of the Bill of rights is the teacher working on?

    A. Amendment 1

    B. Amendment 2

    C. Amendment 3

    D. Amendment 4

7815
Social Studies

This page intentionally left blank.

Social Studies 7815 - Practice Test Answer Explanations

Number	Answer	Category	Explanation
1.	D	I	Considering the sources students use is the best way to determine if their information is factual. Students should be encouraged to use a combination of primary and secondary sources. In addition, they should consider information from scholarly, peer-reviewed, academic journals.
2.	A	I	The only objective that represents accuracy in events regarding the Industrial Revolution is choice A. During the Industrial Revolution, people seeking employment opportunities migrated from rural areas to urban areas (cities). Choices B, C, and D are not accurate depictions of what happened during that time and would indicate the teacher does not have content knowledge in this area.
3.	C	I	Providing a timeline is an effective method for clarifying chronological confusion and can visually separate the two movements, making it clear that they occurred during different times and had different objectives. The abolitionist movement, which sought to end slavery, was most active in the mid-19th century, while the women's suffrage movement, which fought for women's right to vote, gained significant momentum towards the end of the 19th century and into the 20th century. By seeing the movements laid out in a timeline, students can better grasp the sequence of events and the specific contributions of figures like Sojourner Truth, who was active in both movements at different times, and Susan B. Anthony, who was primarily associated with women's suffrage. This approach directly addresses the students' confusion and provides clear, structured information to help them differentiate between the two movements.
4.	C	I	The objective is: *Students will evaluate how natural environments influence Indigenous civilizations.* Environment affects farming; therefore, answer C is the best answer. None of the other answer choices address the environment.
5.	D	I	A major contribution of Chinese civilization was paper.
6.	C	I	Indigenous people used spearheads as weapons, while the colonists had guns and other artillery. The only answer choice that shows the two different weapons is choice B.
7.	B	I	The activity that is most closely aligned with the objective is answer B. In this case, the teacher can show the similarities in both events even though they are centuries apart. This helps to reinforce the concept that history has recurring themes. None of the other answer choices satisfies the objective fully.

Number	Answer	Category	Explanation
8.	C	I	The objective involves comparing and contrasting information. Answer C, using a Venn diagram, is the most effective graphic organizer for this purpose.
9.	A	II	The focus of instruction regarding the Constitution and Bill of Rights is individual freedom and democracy. Therefore, answer A is the most appropriate answer.
10.	B	II	The only real-world situation is in answer choice B. Students would be applying the same concepts of the Declaration of Independence to school rules and evaluating whether they infringe on their freedoms.
11.	A, C & D	II	Citizenship and responsibility go beyond the home and school and help to make the community a better place. Designing a community-wide recycling campaign is the most effective in helping students understand citizenship and responsibility. Also, speaking out at a school board meeting is part of one's civic rights to inform officials about community needs. Finally, organizing a school clean-up initiative helps the community. Choices B and E do not directly benefit the community.
12.	D	II	The teacher needs to administer a formative assessment at the beginning of the unit to determine students' current knowledge of symbolism and identify any misconceptions they have. Therefore, answer D is the most effective. You may be tempted to choose answer B. However, the question is asking about methods to use *before* the lesson takes place. Asking high-complexity questions is more appropriate after students understand the material.
13.	A	II	A KWL chart is used to activate background knowledge. Students determine what they know and do not know about the topic. Then they determine what they want to know about the topic. This helps them set the purpose for reading
14.	A	I	The student in choice A is describing absolute power, which is not part of checks and balances. People can challenge laws based on their constitutionality. In addition, the president can veto the law.
15.	C	II	The question asks specifically for local government. Therefore, answer C is the best choice. Role-playing a city council meeting is the most effective way to engage students in responsible local government and citizenship.
16.	B	II	Answer choice B shows the right to assemble, which is included in the First Amendment of the Bill of Rights. None of the other answer choices are directly related to the Bill of Rights.

Number	Answer	Category	Explanation
17.	A	II	Answer A involves the overarching idea in the objective because it focuses on citizens' Second Amendment rights and the safety of the community. Answers B, C, and D do not address the balance of the rights of citizens with the common good.
18.	B	II	The mayor, governor, and president are all part of the executive branch of government at the local, state, and federal level. Answer B meets the objective most effectively. None of the other answer choices address the local, state, and federal levels of government.
19.	A, D & E	II	To evaluate the world in spatial terms, students will use maps and other geographic representations, tools, and technologies to acquire, process, and report information. Therefore, choices A, D, and E are correct.
20.	A	III	The standard, *students will explain how environmental changes impact human behavior,* requires students to understand cause and effect. The environmental change is the cause; the effect is the impact on human behavior.
21.	C	III	Answer C directly relates to the goal of analyzing how seasons affect agriculture worldwide because when it's winter in the Northern Hemisphere, it is summer in the Southern Hemisphere. This will directly affect how different people adapt their farming practices around the world based on the seasons. None of the other choices address global seasonal changes.
22.	D	III	Geographic location influences the way people farm, build, and interact. For example, societies farm differently on the flat, dry land of the desert than they do on mountainous terrain. Architecture varies in different parts of the world because of temperature and elevation. Finally, agricultural practices differ based on location. Pollution is an environmental condition that affects populations. All the answer choices satisfy this topic except for choice D because it does not mention the environment.
23.	C	III	Push-pull factors influence people to leave their countries (emigrate) to come to another country (immigrate). Push factors include a lack of resources, and pull factors include a better life. While all the answer choices address immigration and migration, answer C is the best choice because it includes push-pull factors. .
24.	A & C	III	The latitude of each region affects its temperature and, therefore, affects the type of vegetation that grows in the area. The average rainfall also affects the vegetation.

Number	Answer	Category	Explanation
25.	C	III	Creating clay models is a hands-on, inquiry-based activity that will enhance student understanding. Defining a list of landmasses and waterways will do little to improve understanding. Asking what type of landmasses in the United States limits the lesson to just one geographical area. Finally, these are first graders, so simply telling them to conduct their own research, answer D, is insufficient.
26.	B	III	Answer B is inquiry-based because students are using latitude and longitude to plot locations. They are active in the learning which is at the heart of an inquiry-based approach. Watching a video, completing a worksheet, and inviting a guest speaker are types of passive learning.
27.	A	IV	Role play would be most appropriate because it is inquiry-based and focuses on trading and bartering, which is how ancient civilizations obtained goods and services. Also, the Phoenicians and Romans traded in textiles and luxury goods. Therefore, using items around the classroom to represent these items would be very effective. The other activities are adequate, but are not as effective as choice A.
28.	A & B	IV	The student responses in answers A and B define supply and demand correctly. The other answer choices do not. Answer C defines opportunity cost. Answer D incorrectly describes the stock market.
29.	C	IV	Regulation is when the government imposes rules on products and their ingredients to ensure the safety of those consuming the products.
30.	B	IV	Opportunity cost is the missed opportunity when one alternative is chosen over another. In this case, the students can either buy a new bike or a new video game, but they cannot by both. This is opportunity cost.
31.	C	IV	The goal of the activity is to get students to understand comparing costs of different items to choose the most economical item. Answer C is the best activity to achieve this.
32.	C	IV	Answer C is the best question to ask to help students understand that just because we love something or want something, it isn't necessarily a need.
33.	B & D	IV	Students are learning to earn money (tickets) through good behavior and helping others. They are also making choices to either spend or save money. Finally, the act of not buying smaller items and instead saving money to buy bigger items is a form of opportunity cost.
34	C	V	Whenever you see the words critical thinking, look for the high-level Bloom's Taxonomy verb. In answer choices A, B, and D, students are simply identifying and categorizing. The activity in answer choice C is the only activity where students are evaluating information.

Number	Answer	Category	Explanation
35	B	V	Remembering Bloom's Taxonomy, analyze and evaluate are at the top of the pyramid. Any answer choice with "analyze and evaluate" will most likely be the correct answer because it indicates a higher level of critical thinking. A performance-based assignment where students conduct a real-world task is also a strong indicator that this answer choice is correct.
36	D	V	During the Industrial Revolution, conditions in factories became very problematic. Therefore, workers formed unions to ensure they were being treated humanely.
37	D	V	This lesson is about the cause-and-effect relationship of development in the South and the Everglades. Therefore, answer choice D is the best choice here.
38	D	IV	In a free market, the consumer decides what he or she wants, and the market responds accordingly.
39	B	II	The Preamble of the US Constitution outlines the purpose of the document, which is to establish justice, ensure safety, and secure liberty.
40	C	I	A primary source is an original source or evidence: artifact, document, diary, manuscript, autobiography, recording, etc. The US Constitution is an original document.
41	B	V	A dialogue journal helps students write what they cannot say aloud. This type of differentiation is a way to support all students.
42	D	II	The US Constitution is a primary resource. The Internet article and online forum are not reliable resources. A documentary is a secondary source. It includes interviews with people who were there, which is a primary source. However, the documentary itself is a secondary source. The interviews makes it the most reliable source in this situation.
43	B	II	The three branches of government counterbalance influences by any one branch. The President is no more powerful than the Supreme Court or Congress. The three-branch structure is supposed to prevent tyranny by the government.
44	C	II	The governor is the head of the executive branch at the state-level. This is an elected position determined by the popular vote in a state.
45	A	II	The US Constitution mandates that each state must operate as a republic where candidates are elected to office to represent constituents.

Number	Answer	Category	Explanation
46	B	II	The executive branch, along with the Electoral College, was established by Article II of the Constitution. Article I established the legislative branch. Article 3 established the judicial branch
47	D	II	There are 9 justices on the US Supreme Court. The body is made up of 8 Associate Justices and 1 Chief Justice.
48	C	II	US senators serve a six-year term. Senate elections are held every two years where about a third of the seats are up for election. Senators can serve an unlimited number of terms.
49	D	III	In this case, a globe would be the best resource because it includes all the features the teacher wants to show students in the lesson.
50	C	III	Maps often use a legend with symbols to indicate specific features. For example, a legend might include the following symbols: | △	Mountain
⬭	Lake
▭	Park	
51	B	II	The 4th Amendment protects people from unlawful search and seizure. That includes hotel rooms. Schools are district/state property, so officials can search lockers. Police can also search anything within reach in a car. Bags are subject to search in airports.
52	D	IV	Opportunity cost is the loss of potential gain when one option is chosen over another. The business owner loses income by shutting down for three months. However, the business owner is building a facility to expand operations and hopefully increase income. The opportunity cost is the revenue that was lost during the shutdown.
53	B	III	A region is a homogeneous area with physical and cultural characteristics distinct from those of neighboring areas. In this case, states grouped together based on population, location, and climate is a region.
54	C	IV	When the government controls manufacturing, they often set price ceilings on goods to keep prices down. This disincentivizes suppliers to produce goods and can cause economic shortages (think of the Soviet breadlines in the 1980s when people waited in lines for days for groceries because there were nationwide shortages).

Number	Answer	Category	Explanation
55	C	I	Most of the exploration, according to the timeline, happened in the 1500s. The period from 1500 to 1600 has the most entries in the timeline. The 1500s is the 16th century. Therefore, student 3 has interpreted the timeline correctly.
56	A	II	The judicial branch interprets the laws. Therefore, a dissenting opinion from a Supreme Court justice would be most appropriate for this activity.
57	B	IV	Investing in retirement is a type of opportunity cost. You choose to invest the money rather than spend it.
58	B	IV	A surplus describes the amount of an asset or resource that exceeds the portion that is actively needed or used.
59	C & D	II	A KWL chart is used before reading to determine what students already know about the topic. That is what the K stands for in KWL. This is background knowledge. Also, while the students are discussing what they already know, the teacher can determine if students have misconceptions or preconceptions about the topic. Analysis comes later when students have already read or engaged with the topic. Metacognition is thinking about thinking, which is usually done in a read aloud/think aloud or similar activity. Fluency is assessed while students are engaged in reading a passage.
60	A	II	The students are using their right to assemble and organize. This is part of the First Amendment of the US Constitution.

This page intentionally left blank.

Data Driven Decisions Using Assessments

This page intentionally left blank.

Data Driven Decisions Using Assessments

A pervasive theme on all teacher certification exams is the importance of using data to make decisions. While this section is not specifically outlined in the test specifications for this exam, it is very important that you understand these concepts to be successful on the test.

You will be required to understand different assessments and how to use them effectively in the classroom. Remember, assessments should always be used to make instructional decisions.

There are two main types of assessments used in K-12 education: formative assessments and summative assessments.

Formative Assessments

Formative assessments inform instruction and are referred to as informal checks or observations.

Examples of formative assessments:

- Observations
- Exit tickets
- Show of hands
- Student writing/journals
- Anecdotal notes

Test Tip

You may see the term *anecdotal notes* on the exam. Anecdotal notes are detailed summaries of student behavior. The teacher may write anecdotal notes as she observes students in cooperative groups. The notes provide valuable data the teacher can use to make decisions in the classroom.

Summative Assessments

Summative assessments measure outcomes of a particular program, strategy, or approach in the classroom. They are the end measure of mastery of the standards. They are sometimes used to measure teacher performance.

- Mid-term/final exam
- District benchmark tests
- State assessments
- Final performance-based assessments like a research paper or presentation
- Chapter tests

Data

K-12 teachers use a variety of data to make decisions in the classroom. The two types of data are qualitative and quantitative data. Both types of data are essential in making decisions.

Qualitative data. Qualitative data cannot be quantified in numbers. Instead, the data comes in the form of observations and written communication.

- Student surveys
- Observations
- Conferences
- Case studies
- Anecdotal notes

Quantitative data. Quantitative data can be quantified numerically. Quantitative data comes in the form of statistical data.

- State test scores
- Reading scores
- Words per minute

Quick Tip

You may see the terms ***evidence-based*** or ***research-based*** exam. These are education buzz words that have to do with using data to make decisions. The evidence is the trends and outcomes presented in the data you use to justify instructional decisions.

Research-based decision-making means you have looked over the academic research outlining a strategy or approach before deciding to use it in the classroom. This is still analyzing data because you are seeing if the strategy was effective based on the outcomes in the research.

The first thing you can do in preparing for this exam is to understand the different types of assessments. The following table outlines assessment types and how they are used to drive instructional decisions.

Types of Assessments

Assessment Type	Definition	Example
Diagnostic	A pre-assessment providing instructors with information about students' prior knowledge, preconceptions, and misconceptions before beginning a learning activity.	Before starting a reading unit on earth space science, a teacher gives a quick assessment to determine students' prior knowledge of concepts in the text. She uses this information to make instructional decisions moving forward.
Formative	A range of formal and informal assessments or checks conducted by the teacher before, during, and after the learning process in order to modify instruction.	A teacher walks around the room checking on students as they read. She might also write anecdotal notes to review later to help her design further instruction.
Summative	An assessment that focuses on the outcomes. It is frequently used to measure the effectiveness of a program, lesson, or strategy.	A reading teacher gives a mid-term exam at the end of the semester.
Performance-based	An assessment that measures students' ability to apply the skills and knowledge learned from a unit or units of study; the task challenges students to use their higher-order, critical thinking skills to create a product or complete a process (Chun, 2010).	After reading text about the Civil War, students develop stories about different historical figures in the war. Students then perform these stories in front of the class and answer questions.
Criterion-referenced	An assessment that measures student performance against a fixed set of predetermined criteria or learning standards.	At the end of the spring semester, students take the Florida Standards Assessment. The state uses the scores for accountability measures.

Assessment Type	Definition	Example
Norm-referenced (percentile)	An assessment or evaluation that yields an estimate of the position of the tested individual in a predefined population with respect to the trait being measured.	The NAEP is an exam given every few years for data purposes only to compare students' reading scores across the US.
Screening	An assessment used to place students in appropriate classrooms or grade level.	Students are typically screened throughout the year to determine at what level they are reading. Placement decisions are made based on the outcomes of the screening.

Authentic assessments

There are also other assessments called authentic assessments. These are different from multiple-choice tests in that students must apply their learning. These assessments come in all forms. The following are a few you will see referenced on the exam. These will be referred to as authentic assessments and alternative assessments.

Oral assessments. Assessments that are conducted, either wholly or in part, by word of mouth. Oral assessments include:

- Answering questions orally
- Performances
- Presentations
- Role-play

Written assessments. Assessments where students write to communicate their learning. Written assessments often yield more information than a multiple-choice test. Teachers should use rubrics to assess written assessments. Written assessments include:

- Essays
- Lab write-up
- Letters
- Journals

Performance-based. Assessments where students are required to solve problems demonstrating their knowledge and skills. Performance-based assessments require students to perform a task rather than simply fill in multiple choice bubbles. Performance-based assessments are considered **authentic assessments** and include:

- Participating in a lab or experiment
- Solving and showing work for math problems
- Engaging in role-play
- Conducting a presentation
- Building picture books

Portfolios. Assessments where the teacher uses a series of student-developed artifacts to determine student learning. Portfolios are considered a form of **authentic** assessment and **alternative** assessment. Portfolios offer an **alternative** or an addition to traditional methods of grading and high-stakes exams. Portfolios are tools to help students establish short-term and long-term goals.

Progress monitoring should be a component of student learning and assessment. Progress monitoring is when the teacher and the student track progress and modify instruction and behaviors to increase student learning. Students and teachers can progress monitor through a variety of ways including:

- Data folders
- Fluency checks
- Portfolios
- Student-led conferences

Quick Tip

Student-led conferences are a twist on the old-school parent-teacher conference. In a student-led conference, students oversee communicating their progress to parents. The teacher and parent(s) listen to the student as the student goes over assessment data, portfolios, and progress. This helps the student take ownership of the learning and shows the parents how involved students are in analyzing their own data.

Math and Science Skills Progression

Webb's Depth of Knowledge is a framework that is used to identify the cognitive complexity of a problem.

- **Low complexity**. Tasks that rely heavily on recall; tasks that require one step or a set procedure.

  Example: Count to 100 by 10s (skip counting)

- **Moderate complexity**. Tasks that require some sort of decision making by the student.

  Example: Rewriting 12 + 13 as 10 + 10 + 5 as another way to find the sum.

- **High complexity**. Tasks that require students to think more abstractly; tasks that require multiple decisions or steps.

  Example: Finding the square feet of carpet needed to carpet a room given in fractional measurements and knowing to round the answer to the nearest square foot.

Tiered ability grouping is a process used to structure activities for small and large groups of students.

- **Compacting.** Groups of students who can skip steps and move quickly because they have advanced math fluency.

- **Interest grouping.** Groups of students based on student interest.

- **Flexible grouping.** Groups change from day to day and even within a class period.

1. **Analyze learning progressions to show how students' mathematical knowledge, skills, and understanding develop over time.**

Student **learning progressions** are how a student moves from a simple understanding of a concept or skill to more complex, deeper understanding of the skill. For this subskill you will have to identify an appropriate learning progression for a given math skill.

Example:

The following terms are used to describe the progression of students learning to count.

- **Reciter.** A student in the reciter phase verbally counts, but not necessarily in order.

- **Counter.** A student in the counter phase can count a small group of objects accurately.

- **Producer.** A student in the producer phase can count out a small group of objects and understands that counting leads to how many.

2. Distinguish among the components of math fluency (i.e., accuracy, automaticity, rate, flexibility).

Students evolve as they learn math. Understanding math is just like understanding anything; you start with the concrete and move toward the abstract.

Think CRA!

C	R	A
⬇	⬇	⬇
Concrete tiling base ten blocks	**Representation** pictures, graphics and charts	**Abstract** Just knowing 2 x 5 is 10.

Fluency in elementary mathematics relates to the speed and accuracy of which a student can answer a basic math fact. Math fact fluency is a four-step process.

- **Accuracy.** Solving problems using a correct method and arriving at the correct answer. This step relates to a student's understanding, not speed or recall.
- **Automaticity.** Exploring efficient strategies for finding the correct answer. Students achieving automaticity can give a correct answer as an automatic response.
- **Rate.** Working toward quick recall of a math fact. Students who are fluent in math facts can respond to an answer at a quick rate.
- **Flexibility.** Choosing and explaining different strategies for arriving at a correct answer. This step relates to a student's deep understanding, not speed or recall.

This page intentionally left blank.

1. Which of the following is the most effective way to use a norm-referenced assessment?

    A. To display student progress on the bulletin board

    B. To make instructional decisions in the classroom

    C. To measure outcomes of reading programs

    D. To informally observe students during reading

2. Which of the following is a criterion-referenced exam?

    A. Pre-assessment

    B. Informal assessment

    C. Standards assessment

    D. Screening

3. A teacher is walking around the room and observing students as they read. This is considered a:

    A. Formative assessment

    B. Summative assessment

    C. Criterion-referenced assessment

    D. Diagnostic assessment

4. A teacher is using a new program in her classroom. She wants to measure the program's effectiveness by evaluating outcomes. Which of the following assessments would be most appropriate in this situation?

    A. Criterion-referenced

    B. Norm-referenced

    C. Formative

    D. Summative

5. Assessments used to measure standards mastery and expertise are:

    A. Labs, notebooks, running records, homework assignments

    B. Norm-referenced tests, homework assignments, quizzes

    C. Observations, checklists, surveys

    D. Research papers, presentations, formal debates

6. A teacher is having students engage in a writing project that will take some time over the course of the semester. Which of the following assessment tools will benefit students most so they understand expectations?

    A. Rubric

    B. Formative

    C. Summative

    D. Diagnostic

7. After reading a science leveled passage, a teacher asks a student questions; the student responds orally to follow-up questions, and the teacher assesses comprehension and recall. This process is used to measure progress in comprehension and other skills. This type of assessment is called a(n):

    A. Fluency read

    B. Informal reading inventory

    C. Summative assessment

    D. Norm-referenced assessment

8. How do criterion-referenced assessments differ from norm-referenced assessments?

    A. Criterion-referenced assessments measure the average score, while norm-referenced assessments are based on a curve.

    B. Norm-referenced assessments measure student performance against a fixed set of predetermined criteria, and criterion-referenced assessments are designed to compare and rank test-takers in relation to one another.

    C. Criterion-referenced assessments measure student performance against a fixed set of predetermined criteria, and norm-referenced assessments are designed to compare and rank test-takers in relation to one another.

    D. Criterion-referenced assessments occur throughout learning, while norm-referenced assessments occur at the end of learning.

9. A 4th grade teacher wants to determine her students' knowledge of cell parts and functions before moving to the lesson. Which of the following is the most effective assessment she can use?

    A. Norm-referenced test

    B. Criterion-referenced test

    C. Diagnostic test

    D. Portfolios

10. Which of the following is the most effective way to use formative assessments?

    A. To rank students

    B. To monitor progress

    C. To measure outcomes

    D. To grade on a curve

Number	Question	Explanation
1.	B	The most effective way to use any assessment is to inform instructional decisions. Remember, data-driven decision making will come in many different forms on this test. This question is an example of that.
2.	C	Criterion-referenced exams measure student performance on a set of learning criteria or standards. Pre-assessment and informal assessments are considered formative assessments. Screening is used to place students in certain classes or groups.
3.	A	Formative assessments are informal checks to monitor student progress. Observations are considered formative assessments.
4.	D	Summative assessments measure outcomes. Summative assessments come at the end of learning. To measure if a program worked, ideally, the teacher would administer a pre-assessment, use the program, and then administer a summative assessment. If there was growth from the pre-assessment to the summative, the program is working.
5.	D	When students have mastered the standards, they can apply their knowledge to higher-order thinking activities. Out of all the answer choices, the higher-order thinking activities listed are research papers, presentations, and formal debates. Also, never use homework to assess expertise or mastery; homework is for practice. This eliminates answers A and B. Finally, checklists and surveys in answer choice C do not measure expertise.
6.	A	A rubric is an evaluation tool or set of guidelines used to promote the consistent application of learning expectations, learning objectives, or learning standards in the classroom or to measure their attainment against a consistent set of criteria. None of the other answer choices convey expectations.
7.	B	An informal reading inventory (IRI) is an individually administered diagnostic assessment designed to evaluate a number of different aspects of students' reading performance. Typically, students read a text and then the teacher asks informal comprehension questions to measure progress.
8.	C	Criterion-referenced exams measure the standards, which is the criteria of the exam. Norm-referenced assessments use a percentile to compare students to other students.
9.	C	A diagnostic test can be used in the beginning of a lesson to determine preconceptions and misconceptions of a topic. Portfolios are collections of work over time. Norm-referenced and criterion-referenced are not appropriate assessments in this situation.
10.	B	Formative assessments are informal assessments used to monitor progress and make instructional decisions.

This page intentionally left blank.

Good Words List

If you've seen any of my YouTube videos, you know that my main methodology for identifying correct answers is to find *good words* in the answer choices. Good words are terms and phrases taken from the test specifications that highlight best practices. If you see these words or phrases in answer choices on the exam, slow down and have a closer look. There is a possibility these words are in the correct answer choice. Here is a list of good words to be on the lookout for and bad words to avoid.

Good Words and Phrases

Accommodations. Modifying instruction or using supports to help special education students achieve. Accommodations do NOT involve lowering the standard or delaying learning.

Action research. The process of evaluating data in the classroom to identify issues and implement effective and quick actions to solve problems.

Assessments. Using formative and summative data to monitor progress and measure outcomes.

Authentic instruction. Providing students with meaningful, relevant, and useful learning experiences and activities.

Balanced literacy. Reading and writing instruction that uses a variety of literary genres including literary and informational texts.

Bilingual instruction. Helping students use elements of their first language to support learning in English.

Celebrate culture. Finding materials and resources to celebrate the different cultures represented in your classroom.

Classroom management. A variety of skills and techniques that teachers use to keep students organized, orderly, focused, attentive, on task, and academically productive during class.

Close Reading. The process of reading and rereading a piece of text multipipe times for different purposes. This helps students with their comprehension.

Collaborative learning. These are strategies that are student-centered and self-directed rather than led by the teacher. Collaboration can also be working with colleagues or stakeholders to improve, create, or produce something.

Concept map. Visual representation of content. Especially useful for illustrating concepts like cause and effect, problem and solution, compare and contrast, etc.

Critical thinking. Higher-order thinking skills that involve evaluating, analyzing, creating, and applying knowledge.

Cultural responsiveness. Instruction as a pedagogy that empowers students intellectually, socially, and emotionally by celebrating and learning about other cultures. This includes recognizing the importance of including students' cultural references in all aspects of learning and designing a productive learning environment.

Data-driven decisions. Using scores, writing samples, observations, and other types of qualitative and quantitative data to make instructional decisions.

Developmentally appropriate instruction (DAP). Choosing text, tools, and activities that are appropriate for the students' grade level.

Differentiated instruction. Providing all learners in a diverse classroom with different methods to understand instruction.

Diversity as an asset. Seeing diversity in the classroom as an opportunity to learn new things through the perspectives of others.

Evidenced-based. Providing instruction using materials with the best scientific evidence available.

Flexible grouping. The heart of differentiated instruction. It provides opportunities for students to be part of many different groups based on their readiness, interest, or learning style.

High expectations for ALL learners. Holding all students to high academic standards regardless of the students' achievement level, ethnicity, language, or socioeconomic status.

Horizontal alignment. Organization and coordination of standards and learning goals across content areas in the same grade level.

Inclusive. Providing students with resources and experiences that represent their culture and ethnicity.

Interdisciplinary activities. Activities that connect two or more content areas; promotes relevance and critical thinking.

Interventions. Provides students with an opportunity to increase reading, writing, test-taking, and study skills at their instructional level.

Intrinsic motivation. Answers that promote autonomy, relatedness, and competence are ways to apply intrinsic motivation. Be on the lookout for these answer choices.

Mentor texts. Pieces of literature that both teacher and student can return to and reread for many different purposes. They are texts to be studied and imitated.

Metacognition. Analysis of your own thinking.

Modeling. Demonstrating the application of a skill or knowledge.

Modifications. Changes to the curriculum and learning environment in accordance with a student's IEP. Modifications change the expectations for learning and the level of assessment.

Outcomes. The results of a program, strategy, or resources implemented in the classroom.

Performance assessment. An activity assigned to students to assess their mastery of multiple learning goals aligned to standards.

Primary resource. These are materials and information in their original form like diaries, journals, songs, paintings, and autobiographies.

Prior knowledge. What students know about a topic from their previous experiences and learning.

Progress monitor. Keeping track of student or whole class learning in real-time. Quantifiable measures of progress, conferring, observing, exit tickets, and student self-assessment.

Recursive Teaching Methods. Using information or skills that is already known and acquired to learn new skills and knowledge.

Relevance, real-world, and relatable. Be sure to choose answers that promote real-world application and make learning relatable to students' lives.

Reliable. Consistent. Producing consistent results under similar conditions.

Remediation. Correcting or changing something to make it better.

Rigorous. A word used to describe curriculum that is challenging and requires students to use higher-order thinking skills.

Scaffolding. Using supports to help students achieve a standard that they would not achieve on their own.

Secondary resource. These are materials and information derived from the original like newspaper articles, history textbooks, and reviews.

Self-assessment. An assessment or evaluation of oneself or one's actions and attitudes, performance, and skills.

Specific and meaningful feedback. More than just a grade at the top of a paper, effective feedback includes positive aspects and how students can apply those positive aspects to improve. In addition, feedback should contain specific things the student should do to improve.

Standards-aligned. Ensuring that curriculum and instruction are aligned to the state-adopted standards.

Student-centered/learner-centered. A variety of educational programs, learning experiences, instructional approaches, and academic support strategies that address students' distinct learning needs, interests, or cultural backgrounds.

Validity. Accuracy. How accurately knowledge or skills are measured.

Vertical alignment. Organization of standards and learning goals across grade levels. Structure for which learning and understanding is built from grade level to grade level.

Vocabulary in context. Always teach vocabulary in context. It helps to relate the vocabulary to the real world.

Wait time. The time between a question and when a student is called on or a response to a student's reply.

Word Consciousness. Students are aware and interested in words and word meanings. Students who are word conscious also notice when and how new words are used. Word-conscious students are motivated to learn new words and to be able to use them skillfully.

Bad Words and Phrases

Bias. Inserting personal beliefs, stereotypes, and assumptions in the learning process. This can also include learning materials developed from the perspective of the dominant culture that exclude minority perspectives.

Extra homework. On this exam, students should be getting all of the instruction they need in class. In real life, we all assign homework. However, on this exam, extra homework is not the correct answer choice.

Extrinsic motivators. These are rewards of extrinsic value like pizza parties, recess time, etc. Students should be motivated by intrinsic motivators like self-confidence, sense of accomplishment, and feeling successful.

Homogenous grouping. Grouping by gender, English proficiency, or learning level is never a best practice on this exam or in your classroom. Homogenous groups should only be used in special circumstances and on a temporary basis.

Punitive solutions. Avoid answer choices that sound like punishments. For this exam, teachers are expected to be implementing positive behavior support methods, so avoid any answer choices that sounds punitive.

Silent independent reading. When this practice is attached to a struggling reader scenario, it is usually not the correct answer because if students are struggling, reading independently is not going to help the student get better.

Standardized test-taking strategies. While students need to be strategic and learn how to approach their state exams, this concept is usually not the correct answer on the exam.

Worksheets. Do we use worksheets? Yes, absolutely. However, on this exam, using worksheets is probably not the correct answer, so avoid these answer choices.

This page intentionally left blank.

Bibliography

1-WorldGlobes (n.d.). Frequently asked questions. Retrieved form https://www.1worldglobes.com/world-globe-FAQ/

Agosto, D. E. (2002). *Criteria for evaluating multicultural literature*. Retrieved from http://www.pages.drexel.edu/~dea22/multicultural.html

Amadeo, K. (2018). *Comparative advantage: Theory and examples*. Economic Theory-The Balance. Retrieved from https://www.thebalance.com/comparative-advantage-3305915

Amadeo, K. (2018). Labor, one of four factors of production. Retrieved from https://www.thebalance.com/labor-definition-types-and-how-it-affects-the-economy-3305859

Andrews, E. (n.d.). *11 innovations that changed history*. Retrieved from: https://www.history.com/news/11-innovations-that-changed-history

Asrar, Shakeeb (2017). *How India, Pakistan and Bangladesh were formed*. Retrieved from: https://www.aljazeera.com/indepth/interactive/2017/08/india-pakistan-bangladesh-formed-170807142655673.html

Bradley, B. A., & Stahl, S. A. (2001). Learning the alphabet. Presented at the National Reading Conference. http://www.ciera.org/library/presos/2001/2001nrc/01nrcstahl/01nrcsta.pdf

Bailey, R. G. (1996) *Ecosystem Geography*. New York: Springer-Verlag

Briney, A. (2019). *A brief history of the age of exploration*. ThoughtCo. Retrieved from https://www.thoughtco.com/age-of-exploration-1435006

Caldwell, Jennings, and Lerner. (2014). *Deleting Phonemes*. Retrieved from https://block3strategies.weebly.com/deleting-phonemes.html

Claval, P. (2015). Religions and ideologies. In S. Brunn (Ed.), *The changing world religion map* (349-362). Dordrecht: Springer.

Common Core State Standards (2019). English Language Arts Standards. Retrieved from http://www.corestandards.org/ELA-Literacy/introduction/students-who-are-college-and-career-ready-in-reading-writing-speaking-listening-language/

Darling, Charles Dr. (n.d.). Guide to Grammar & Writing. Considering Audience, Purpose, and Tone. Retrieved from http://plato.algonquincollege.com/applications/guideToGrammar/?page_id=3304

Ehri, L. (1999). Phases of development in learning to read words. In J. Oakhill & R. Beard (Eds.), Reading Development and the Teaching of Reading: A Psychological Perspective, 79-108. Oxford, UK: Blackwell Publishers.

Encyclopedia Britannica Editors. (n.d.). Assimilation. Encyclopedia Britannica. Retrieved from https://www.britannica.com/topic/assimilation-society

Encyclopedia Britannica Editors. (n.d.). Socialization. Encyclopedia Britannica. Retrieved from https://www.britannica.com/science/socialization

Educational Testing Services. (n.d.). *Elementary Education: Content Knowledge for Teaching (7811)*. Retrieved from https://www.ets.org/pdfs/praxis/7811.pdf

Gleckman, H. (2018). *What is a tariff and who pays it?* Tax Policy Center. Retrieved from https://www.taxpolicycenter.org/taxvox/what-tariff-and-who-pays-it

Glossary of Education Reform (2013). Rubrics. Retrieved from https://www.edglossary.org/rubric/

Heim, D. (2018). *The international dateline, explained*. LifeScience. Retrieved from https://www.livescience.com/44292-international-date-line-explained.html

History.com Editors. (n.d.). *Religion.* Retrieved from: http://history.com/topics/religion

History.com Editors. (2009). *Ford's assembly line starts rolling.* Retrieved from: https://www.history.com/this-day-in-history/fords-assembly-line-starts-rolling

History.com Editors. (2009). *Lewis and Clark.* Retrieved from: https://www.history.com/topics/westward-expansion/lewis-and-clark

History.com Editors. (2009) *Marshall plan.* Retrieved from: https://www.history.com/topics/ world-war-ii/ marshall-plan-1

History.com Editors. (2009) *Pyramids in Latin America.* Retrieved from: https://www.history.com/topics/ ancient-history/pyramids-in-latin-america

History.com Editors. (2017). *The Dust Bowl.* Retrieved from https://www.history.com/topics/great-depression/ dust-bowl

History.com Editors. (2017). *Mesopotamia.* Retrieved from https://www.history.com/topics/ancient-middle-east/mesopotamia

History.com Editors. (2018). *The 13 Colonies.* Retrieved from https://www.history.com/topics/colonial-america/thirteen-colonies

History.com Editors. (2018). *Townshend Acts.* Retrieved from https://www.history.com/topics/american-revolution/townshend-acts

History.com Editors. (2019). *Battle of Yorktown.* Retrieved from https://www.history.com/topics/ americanrevolution/siege-of-yorktown

History.com Editors. (2019). *Berlin Wall.* Retrieved from https://www.history.com/topics/cold-war/berlin-wall.

History.com Editors. (2019). *Great Depression history.* Retrieved from https://www.history.com/topics/great-depression/great-depression-history

History.com Editors. (2019). *Slavery in America.* Retrieved from: https://www.history.com/topics/black-history/slavery.

History.com Editors. (2019). *Westward expansion.* Retrieved from https://www.history.com/topics/westward-expansion

History.net. (2019). *Antebellum Period.* Retrieved from https://www.historynet.com/antebellum-period

Klein, C. (2018). 8 ways the Erie Canal changed America. History.com Retrieved from https://www.history.com/news/8-ways-the-erie-canal-changed-america

Landt, S. M. (2006). Multicultural literature and young adolescents: A kaleidoscope of opportunity. Journal of Adolescent & Adult Literacy, 49(8), 690-697.

Lapp, D., Moss, B., Grant, M., and Johnson, K. (2015). Close look at close reading: teaching students to analyze complex texts, grades K–5. Retrieved from http://www.ascd.org/publications/books/114008/chapters/Understanding-and-Evaluating-Text-Complexity.aspx

Lewis, T. (2015). *Transatlantic slave trade: Slavery.* Encyclopedia Britannica. Retrieved from https://www.britannica.com/topic/transatlantic-slave-trade

Lippert, M. (2019). *8 facts you didn't know about America's Everglades – And why we must resore this incredible place.* National Wildife Federation. Retrieved from: https://blog.nwf.org/2019/12/8-facts-you-didnt-know-about-americas-everglades-and-why-we-must-restore-this-incredible-place/

Lyon, G. R., & Moats, L. C. (1997). Critical Conceptual and Methodological Considerations in Reading Intervention Research. *Journal of Learning Disabilities*, 30(6), 578–588. https://doi.org/10.1177/002221949703000601

Mann, C. C. (2011). *The birth of religion.* National Geographic Magazine 219(6), 34-59. Retrieved from http://www2.nau.edu/~gaud/bio301/content/neolth.htm.

Mayer, K. (2007). Research in review: Emerging knowledge about emergent writing. Retrieved from http://resourcebinderecse.weebly.com/uploads/2/0/1/3/20133951/emerging_knowledge_about_emergent_writing-mayer-1.pdf

Merriam Webster (2019). Anthropology - Definition. Retrieved from https://www.merriam-webster.com/dictionary/anthropology

Merriam Webster (2019). Checks and Balances - Definition. Retrieved from https://www.merriam-webster.com/dictionary/checks%20and%20balancesy

Merriam Webster (2019). Community - Definition. Retrieved from https://www.merriam-webster.com/dictionary/community

Merriam Webster (2019). Country - Definition. Retrieved from https://www.merriam-webster.com/dictionary/country

Merriam Webster (2019). Cultural Anthropology - Definition. Retrieved from https://www.merriam-webster.com/dictionary/cultural%20anthropology

Merriam Webster (2019). Language - Definition. Retrieved from https://www.merriam-webster.com/dictionary/community

Merriam Webster (2019). Monarchy - Definition. Retrieved from https://www.merriam-webster.com/dictionary/monarchy

Merriam Webster (2019). Nation - Definition. Retrieved from https://www.merriam-webster.com/dictionary/nation

Merriam Webster (2019). Paraphrase - Definition. Retrieved from https://www.merriam-webster.com/dictionary/paraphrase

Merriam Webster (2019). Plaigarize - Definition. Retrieved from https://www.merriam-webster.com/dictionary/plaigarize

Merriam Webster (2019). Physical Anthropology - Definition. Retrieved from https://www.merriam-webster.com/dictionary/physical%20anthropology

Mesopotamia.co.uk. (n.d.). Ancient civilizations: Mesopotamia. Retrieved from http://www.mesopotamia.co.uk/

Mokyr, J. (2019). *Great famine.* Retrieved from: https://www.britannica.com/event/Great-Famine-Irish-history

NASA (n.d.). Earth. Solar System Exploration. Retrieved from https://solarsystem.nasa.gov/planets/earth/in-depth/

NASA (n.d.). Newton's Laws of Motion. Retrieved from https://www.grc.nasa.gov/www/k-12/airplane/newton.html

NASA (n.d.). Our Solar System. Retrieved from https://solarsystem.nasa.gov/solar-system/our-solar-system/overview/

National Geographic (n.d.). Continental Drift. Retrieved from https://www.nationalgeographic.org/encyclopedia/continental-drift/

National Geographic (n.d.). Ecological relationships. Retrieved from https://www.nationalgeographic.org/activity/ecological-relationships/

National Geographic (n.d.). *Geography.* National Geographic: Resource Library. Retrieved from https://www.nationalgeographic.org/encyclopedia/geography/

National Geographic (n.d.). *Hemisphere.* National Geographic: Resource Library. Retrieved from https://www.nationalgeographic.org/encyclopedia/hemisphere/

National Geographic (n.d.). Magnetism. Retrieved from https://www.nationalgeographic.org/encyclopedia/magnetism/

BIBLIOGRAPHY

National Geographic (n.d.). The atmosphere. Resource Library Retrieved from https://www.nationalgeographic.org/encyclopedia/atmosphere/

National Oceanic and Atmospheric Administration (NOAA) (2019). What is a Tsunami? Retrieved from https://oceanservice.noaa.gov/facts/tsunami.html

National Oceanic and Atmospheric Administration. (n.d.). Stratospheric Ozone. Retrieved from https://www.ozonelayer.noaa.gov/science/basics.htm

National Research Council (2012). *A framework for k-12 science education: Practices, crosscutting concepts, and core ideas.* Washington, DC: The National Academies Press. https://doi.org/10.17226/13165.

National Severe Storms Laboratory (NSSL) (2019). Lightning Basics. https://www.nssl.noaa.gov/education/svrwx101/lightning/

Native Languages of the America (2015). Native American tribes of Florida Retrieved from: http://www.native-languages.org/florida.htm

NC State University (n.d.). Prokaryotes: Single-celled Organisms. Retrieved from http://projects.ncsu.edu/project/bio183de/Black/prokaryote/prokaryote1.html

Nordquist, R. (2020). Definition and examples of context clues: How we infer meaning. *Thought Co.* Retrieved from https://www.thoughtco.com/context-clue-vocabulary-1689919

Office of the Historian (n.d.). The development of foreign policy. Retrieved from https://history.state.gov/departmenthistory/short-history/development

Osewalt, G. (2019). 14 phonics rules for reading and spelling. Retrieved from https://www.understood.org/en/learning-attention-issues/child-learning-disabilities/reading-issues/14-phonics-rules-for-reading-and-spelling

O'Sullivan, A., Sheffrin, S, M. (2003), Economics: Principles in Action, Upper Saddle River, New Jersey 07458: Pearson Prentice Hall, p. 57

Palmer, R. & Colton, J. (1978) *A History of the Modern World* (5th ed)

Penn State University (2019) College of Earth and Mineral Science: The structure of the Earth. Retrieved from https://www.e-education.psu.edu/marcellus/node/870

Philpott, D. (2003). Sovereignty. In *Stanford Encyclopedia of Philosophy.* Retrieved from https://plato.stanford.edu/entries/sovereignty/

Pidwirny, M. (2006). Organization of life: species, populations, communities, and ecosystems. *Fundamentals of Physical Geography, 2nd Edition.* Date Viewed. http://www.physicalgeography.net/fundamentals/9d.html

Plamper, J. (2012). *The Stalin Cult: A Study in the Alchemy of Power.* (The Yale-Hoover Series on Stalin, Stalinism, and the Cold War.) New Haven: Yale University Press.

Poole, W. & Wheelock, D. C. (2008). Stable prices, stable economy: Keeping inflation in check must be No. 1 goal of monetary policymakers. The Regional Economist. Retrieved from https://www.stlouisfed.org/publications/regional-economist/january-2008/stable-prices-stable-economy-keeping-inflation-in-check-must-be-no-1-goal-of-monetary-policymakers

Rampton, M. (n.d.). *Four Waves of Feminism.* Pacific University Oregon. Retrieved from: https://www.pacificu.edu/about/media/four-waves-feminism

Schaum's outline of theory and problems of physics for engineering and science (Series: Schaum's Outline Series). McGraw-Hill Companies. p. 58. ISBN 978-0-07-008498-8.

Siddiqui, A. S. (2011). Comprehensive Economics XII. Laxmi Publications Pvt Limited.

Smithsonian. (n.d.). Lighting a revolution: Consequences of Edison's lamp. Retrieved from: https://americanhistory.si.edu/lighting/19thcent/consq19.htm

Temming, M (2014). What is a star? *Sky and Telescope*. Retrieved from https://www.skyandtelescope.com/astronomy-resources/what-is-a-star/

The Florida Department of Education (2018). Assessments. Retrieved from http://www.fldoe.org/accountability/assessments/

The International Reading Association (n.d.). A critical analysis of eight informal reading inventories. Retrieved from https://www.readingrockets.org/article/critical-analysis-eight-informal-reading-inventories.

The White House (n.d.). State and local government. Retrieved from: https://www.whitehouse.gov/about-the-white-house/state-local-government/

Treiman, R., Kessler, B., & Pollo, T. C. (2006). Learning about the letter name subset of the vocabulary: Evidence from U.S. and Brazilian preschoolers. Applied Psycholinguistics, 27, 211–227.

University of Cambridge (n.d.). *The scramble for Africa*. Retrieved from: https://www.joh.cam.ac.uk/library/library_exhibitions/schoolresources/exploration/scramble_for_africa

U.S. Bureau of Economic Analysis. (2019). Gross domestic product. BEA. Retrieved from https://www.bea.gov/resources/learning-center/what-to-know-gdp

U.S. Census (2010). Population density. Data. Retrieved from https://www.census.gov/data/tables/2010/dec/density-data-text.html

U.S. National Library of Medicine (2019). How do Cells Divide? Retrieved from https://ghr.nlm.nih.gov/primer/howgeneswork/cellsdivide

U.S. National Library of Medicine (2019). What is DNA? Genetics Home Reference. Retrieved from https://ghr.nlm.nih.gov/primer/basics/dna

U.S. Senate (n.d.) *The Constitution: The Bill of Rights*. Retrieved from https://www.senate.gov/civics/constitution_item/constitution.htm

Violatti, C. (2018). Neolithic period. In *Ancient History Encyclopedia*. Retrieved from https://www.ancient.eu/Neolithic/

Whitehurst, G., & Lonigan, C. (1998). Child Development and Emergent Literacy. *Child Development, 69*(3), 848-872. doi:10.2307/1132208

Made in the USA
Las Vegas, NV
10 December 2024

13807224R00214